# girl in the mirror

# girl in the mirror

**Mothers and Daughters in the Years of Adolescence**

## NANCY L. SNYDERMAN, M.D.,
### AND PEG STREEP

HYPERION NEW YORK

Hyperion books are available for special promotions and premiums. For details contact
Hyperion Special Markets, 77 West 66th Street, 11th floor, New York, New York,
10023-6298, or call 212-456-0100.

Library of Congress Cataloging-in-Publication Data

Snyderman, Nancy L.
Girl in the mirror: mothers and daughters in the years of adolescence /
Nancy L. Snyderman and Peg Streep—1st ed.
p. cm.
Includes bibliographical references
ISBN 0-7868-6743-4
1. Parent and teenager. 2. Mothers and daughters. 3. Teenage girls.
4. Adolescence. 5. Parenting. I. Peg Streep
HQ799.15 .S59 2002
306.874/3 21
2001-051674

FIRST PAPERBACK EDITION
PAPERBACK ISBN: 0-7868-8641-2

10 9 8 7 6 5 4 3 2

For our daughters, the women of the future:
Kate Elizabeth Snyderman, Alexandra Emily Israel, and Rachel Bergen Snyderman
And the daughters of women everywhere

# Acknowledgments

While writing is a solitary activity, making a book like this one required the help and support of a great many people. And while the authors are solely responsible for any errors or omissions, *Girl in the Mirror* couldn't have been written without, first and foremost, the extraordinary amount of research done in the field of adolescence over the last few decades. We hope the selected bibliography covers every book we read and learned from—and we encourage mothers everywhere to read and learn from them too. We'd particularly like to thank the professionals and writers in the field who gave of their time and expertise by either agreeing to be interviewed, helping us find the salient research on each particular topic pertaining to adolescent girls, or sending us their work, among them: Terri Apter; Anne Becker, M.D., Ph.D.; Bill Beard at NCADI; Ilene Berson, Ph.D.; Stephanie Brandt, M.D.; Jeffrey Cappizano; Betsy Davis, Ph.D.; Lisa Diamond, Ph.D.; Mary B. Eberly, Ph.D.; Jaquelynne Eccles, Ph.D.; Claudia Edwards, Ph.D.; Sharon Frith, Ph.D.; Loren Eskenazi, M.D.; Arlene Gibson; Rachel Harris, Ph.D.; Joan Kelly, Ph.D.; Susan Silverberg Koerner, Ph.D.; Don McCabe, Ph.D.; Lisa Miller, Ph.D.; Peggy Orenstein; Annie G. Rogers, Ph.D.; Esther Rothblum, Ph.D.; Caitlin Ryan, MSW, ACSW; Ritch Savin-Williams, Ph.D; Peter C. Scales, Ph.D.; Pepper Schwartz, Ph.D.; Lisa Sheeber, Ph.D.; Nancy E. Sherwood, Ph.D.; Robin Tepper, Ph.D.; Diana Walsh, Ph.D.; Karen Zager, Ph.D.

A special thank-you to the Goddess of Research, who, we believe, can find anything, anywhere, on a moment's notice: Sarah Maire

Adler. And then, of course, there are the mothers and fathers—some of them friends, others strangers—who shared their thoughts and experiences with us, many of which are part of the text and some of which helped inform our opinions. Thank you all for your stories—especially those who asked that we disguise their identities in the text and omit them from these acknowledgments. Thanks, too, to all those who filled out questionnaires and who took the time to talk, among them Angela Bates, Connie Fails, Leslie Garisto, Rachel Harris, Donna Howell-Sickles, Peter Israel, Abigail Manheim, Mary Ellen O'Neill, Patti Pitcher, Margot Sage-El. Special thanks to our own daughters who agreed to let us write about them in these pages, and to Melee and Hy Agens, Henia Drucker, Jane Lahr, Erika Rosenfeld, and Claudia Karabaic Sargent for various and sundry good deeds.

Thanks, too, to the publishing team at Hyperion—our editor, Mary Ellen O'Neill and her assistant, Carrie Covert; president Bob Miller; and everyone else who helped make an idea into a book. Leslie Garisto—red pencil in hand—helped polish these pages, as did Donna Ellis and Lisa Stokes at Hyperion.

# Table of Contents

# Introduction

We do not grow absolutely, chronologically. We grow sometimes in one dimension, and not in another, unevenly. We grow partially. We are relative. We are mature in one realm, childish in another. The past, present, and future mingle and pull us backward, forward, or fix us in the present. We are made up of layers, cells, constellations.

—Anaïs Nin

THE IDEA FOR THIS BOOK came out of a series of conversations between two women who'd become friends—you know, those conversations that sound as if they're just a series of disconnected thoughts but, in the end, head off in an important direction. During the writing of *Necessary Journeys: Letting Ourselves Learn from Life*, Peg and I had spent hours and hours talking; even though the book was done, our talking wasn't. No matter where the conversation started, we'd end up talking about ourselves and the past, where we found ourselves now, our changing bodies (in your forties, perimenopause appears to be with you every waking moment), and, of course, our daughters. All three of the girls—I have two, Kate and Rachel, and Peg has one, Alexandra—seemed to be on the cusp of change. At the time, Kate was just starting seventh grade after a rather miserable, friendless year in sixth, and was starting to go through puberty. Alexandra had just started going to a large middle school for sixth grade, and Peg had her heart in her mouth. Rachel, my youngest, was suddenly acting up like crazy. We live on opposite coasts but the various "horror" stories we swapped, gleaned from friends and neighbors whose kids were already in the midst of adolescence, all had a basic theme: Adolescence was something we'd have to cope with, get through, somehow. It did not, by all accounts, sound like fun.

But, as we talked, we also began to wonder: What happens to the mother in all this? In truth, just as our girls approached adolescence, we found our own lives changing. The years that comprised our forties seemed, on reflection, less a time of settling in than moving forward and, in the wake of that forward motion, we each raised new questions about how we saw the rest of our lives rolling out. The inevitable winding down of our reproductive systems wasn't just a matter of my dealing with forgetting my keys everywhere and even my wallet once (at a bookstore signing!) or Peg's coping with her fibroids but, instead, reenvisioning ourselves. We both thought it hugely important—if rarely mentioned—that these stages in female life, adolescence and midlife, often coincide in the lives of mothers and daughters. We got to wondering out loud: How did the changes in her daughter affect a mother's sense of self? Conversely, how was a girl's experience of adolescence affected by where, in life, her mother found herself?

We'd also both gotten to a place where other women were more important than ever in our lives, and, in conversations with friends, the centrality of the mother-daughter relationship to the formation of self came up again and again. For our parts, while each of us was enormously influenced by the love and example of our fathers, there were important ways in which we each had been shaped by our mothers. Between us, though, there were monumental differences. My own relationship with my mother had always been marked by love, trust, and support; Peg's, on the other hand, was never close and had become, when she was an adolescent, deeply painful. She remained fully estranged from her mother during her adulthood. When I became a mother, I struggled to accept the ways in which I mothered differently than my mother had—and in my eyes she was a master at it. When Peg became a mother, she felt she had to invent motherhood from scratch. Our experiences were at the opposite ends of a spectrum but had something in common nonetheless: To mother, each of us had to try to emerge from our mother's shadow, whether it was beneficent or dark and looming. Most of the women with daughters we knew described relationships to their own mothers that fell somewhere in between our own but confirmed the importance of those relationships.

*Girl in the Mirror* is different from other books on parenting adolescents not just because it focuses almost exclusively on the mother-daughter dyad but because it is essentially optimistic in tone. We see the challenges of adolescence as an opportunity—for women to grow into greater consciousness even as their daughters go through the exercise of testing their wings by testing their mothers. Mothering is hard work, and there's no question that the work of mothering an adolescent is not exactly easy. But—and it is a big "but"—there is much to be learned from the experience. It may not, in the end, be entirely "coincidental" that two stages of female life—adolescence and midlife—so often coincide. Even those of you who are still some years away from midlife will experience it in a slightly different form when that stage coincides with your daughter's early adulthood.

Unlike many other books, *Girl in the Mirror* isn't based on individual case studies—I am a physician, not a psychologist. Instead we've had the privilege and opportunity to draw on the amazing amount of research done on adolescence in the last decade, little of which ever makes it into the popular press. We've been lucky, too, to have had the cooperation of specialists and researchers who've shared their work and their thoughts with us in telephone interviews and e-mail exchanges. Last but not least, we've had the help of other mothers across the country (and a few fathers too) who were willing to share their experiences with us. Our thank-yous to all who helped can be found on page vii.

Writing this book has itself been a journey. We've learned that much that passes for popular wisdom about adolescent girls isn't, and that some of our own ideas about adolescence needed radical adjustment. By looking at mothers and daughters, we've gained new understanding of the meaningful ways in which women are possessed of unique talents and perspectives on the world, different in kind from those possessed by men. Ultimately, though, this book is about growth. Apart from infancy, the growth during adolescence is unparalleled in the human life cycle; the changes in our daughters will be physical, cognitive, emotional, and social in scope. While decidedly different from the growth our daughters will experience, this same period offers the mothers of daughters a unique opportunity to grow and change as well. Some 150 years ago, the writer George Eliot wrote that "our consciousness rarely registers a growth within us anymore than without us; there have been many circulations of the sap before we detect the smallest sign of a bud." We wrote this book so that each of us can become not simply better caretakers of our daughters' flowering but better gardeners of our own inner selves.

**A Postscript:** On September 11, 2001, the day of the terrorist attacks, this book was already in production. Because the world in which our daughters are coming of age had changed radically and violently, we felt the effects of September 11 and the events that followed needed to be addressed. A new chapter now ends the book.

## CHAPTER ONE

# Sea Changes

> Our mothers are our most direct connection to our history and our gender.
>
> —Hope Edelman

I AM STANDING IN MY KITCHEN, stirring the pasta sauce and waiting for the water to boil, half-listening to the evening news, when my eldest daughter comes in, flings her backpack onto the table, and takes out a crumpled piece of paper. She hands it to me without saying a word. It is a note from one of her teachers, dated well over a week ago, reporting that she has not completed most of her homework assignments. I take a deep breath. This is not the first time this has happened, nor will the conversation we are about to have be the first on the subject.

Every night, I ask her whether she has finished her homework or whether she needs some help, and each time she answers "yes" to the first and "no" to the second. Her teachers have stressed that being independent is important, so going through her backpack to make sure she's telling the truth isn't an option.

I resolve not to lose my temper, and turn to face her. I can see that she is already armored, ready to retort to anything I say or to deflect the importance of any punishment—grounding, no television, no movies—I might be ready to hand her. We are almost the same height—she is about to turn fourteen—and when I sit down at the table, she remains standing . . .

The moment or two I've taken to collect myself helps us both. I get up to adjust the heat under the sauce, giving Kate some room to maneuver, literally and psychologically.

She takes a deep breath as she sits down.

I reach for her hand across the table and, as I sit down, slowly and deliberately say, "*So*, what's going on here? . . ."

The scene in my kitchen is, I realize, a fairly predictable adolescent crisis. Lost homework and sweaters, last-minute studying, and forgotten orthodontist appointments all seem pretty much par for the course, as are the inevitable arguments about the state of her room, the time spent online, the way in which she talks to her sister who, at almost twelve, is going through an adolescence of her own. Looking at her tonight, it seems as though her babyhood—when she was a swaddled bundle in my arms—was a very long time ago. Despite the tension in the air, I find myself smiling at the memory of Kate, my dark-haired, compliant beauty.

There is nothing compliant about Kate at this moment.

But I, too, have changed. I am no longer the tentative young woman I was at thirty-four, the year I adopted Kate, or the same person who gave birth to Rachel two years later. My fiftieth birthday is no longer in the distant future. My childbearing years are over; there's a new stage of my life ahead, and I'm looking forward to it. The young woman who cradled Kate in her arms was still a person in search of herself; the woman who sits across from the teenager knows who she is and must appear to be a formidable opponent.

Sitting here reminds me of my own adolescence when, at another table in a kitchen a thousand miles away, I sat across from my own mother. She was, I realize with a tiny shock, only thirty-eight when I was fourteen, a full ten years younger than I am today. I remember my mother as confident, competent, and adult—a stay-at-home mom who handled the demands and pressures of a household with four children with perfect aplomb. If it were my own thirty-eight-year-old self facing my unsmiling daughter, the evening would have gone very differently and not very well. So much depends, I realize, on where we as mothers find ourselves as our daughters enter these years of growth.

I try to recall what I was like when I sat across from my mother, long before years of experience and a certain amount of success in the world gave me the confident voice I have now. Did I become defiant, as Kate does, when I was found out? Better put: Was I really as obedient, as compliant, as I remember myself? Would I have dared *not* to do my homework? Did I try, ever, to face my mother down?

I can't, for the life of me, imagine myself sitting in my parents' kitchen in Fort Wayne all those years ago (it was 1966 when I was Kate's age), looking defiant. The world I grew up in was distinctly undemocratic: My parents set the rules and I followed them. I never really did find out what would happen to me if I didn't obey them because, frankly, I didn't have the guts or inclination. My job was to go to school and do the work, and it never occurred to me to do anything else. My only rebellion, if it was one, was to marry at the age of twenty-four despite my father's opposition.

Kate's attitude leaves me more than slightly bewildered. It's not as though the homework is beyond her grasp. Is she being rebellious, or is she simply unmotivated? Is she trying to get my attention? Is she testing me because, of my three children, she alone is adopted? Or, in the alternative, is this a way of distinguishing herself from her straight-A younger sister? Her explanations—why there's no point in writing a book report when you've already read the book ("It's a waste of time," she says, "time you could use reading another book."), why she hasn't done her Spanish homework ("Why bother? I speak Spanish really well, and participate all the time in class.")—have the kind of upside-down logic adolescents sometimes seem to specialize in. My arguments don't appear to make a dent, and are greeted with a sigh of exasperation.

If I could draw well enough to capture the scene in a cartoon, the thought bubble above Kate's head would contain a single word: "Whatever . . ." We are clearly getting nowhere, and it's time to stop.

She leaves the room and I do the only truly useful thing I can: I go back to stirring the spaghetti sauce and try to figure out a way to talk to her so that, next time, she can begin to hear me.

~ ~ ~

By the time I was thirteen, I was dismissive of my mother. I thought she was old (she was forty-three) and didn't do anything *real*—she was a stay-at-home mom. I didn't think she knew anything either— I guess because I thought I knew *everything*.

"Katie," now forty-four herself, and the mother of a thirteen-year-old

When I describe the scene in my kitchen to a friend, her response is telling: "Oh, she's just being a teenager." In American culture, the word "teenager" is a loaded one, summoning up not just its narrowest definition (someone between the ages of thirteen and nineteen) but a host of images and adjectives. To me, "teenager" connotes "vulnerable", but other adjectives—"adventurous," "self-centered," "blossoming," "fragile," "confused," "rebellious," or "ornery"—would do just as well. In recent times, the word "teenager" has conjured up more frightening associations and images: risky sexual behavior, eating disorders, loss of self-esteem, drug use, violence. (As a doctor, I despair at the number of girls smoking. As a mother, I find it hard not to free-associate blood-stained school hallways and dead babies in trash cans.) It comes as a surprise to me, reading Thomas Hine's *The Rise and Fall of the American Teenager*, that the word wasn't coined until 1921, to describe what, in the new world of marketing, was a specific, demographic population—a descriptive group for the first time.[1] In our culture, teenagers are still an enormous target audience and American business spends a lot of time and money getting them to buy its products. (It's apparently a good investment: According to Teenage

Research Unlimited, a firm that specializes in teen market research, teenagers spent 153 billion dollars in 1999![2]) The word "teenager" is so freighted and has so many different behaviors associated with it—the supposedly "inevitable" rebellion, the "necessary" emotional upheaval, the "raging" hormones—that it's used as a short-hand excuse or explanation by parents and children alike.

But the word "teenager," while good for selling all manner of products, isn't really useful when it comes to raising our daughters. For one thing, the word is misleading: The physical, emotional, and intellectual changes that become manifest when our daughters reach roughly thirteen have, in fact, been going on for years, and the foundations for some of the issues that adolescence brings to the fore have already been laid. Recent studies have shown that body image is formed in girls by the age of eight and perhaps as early as seven; according to the Harvard Eating Disorders Center, a study of eight-to-ten-year-olds revealed that roughly half of the girls were already dissatisfied with their size, and longed to be thinner.[3] By the time they actually reach the "teen" years, girls are acting on what they have been feeling for years: The Office on Women's Health of the U.S. Department of Health and Human Services reports that nearly half of all girls skip a meal to control their weight, one-third of all girls in grades nine through twelve see themselves as over-weight, and 60 percent of them are on diets.[4] At the end of the continuum is the sobering fact that eating disorders affect 5–10 per-cent of post-pubescent females.[5] Visualizing the statistic is helpful: Imagine a classroom with twenty girls in it, and focus on the fact that at least one and perhaps two of them will suffer from anorexia, bulimia, or binge eating.

There's another reason to let go of the word "teenager": Our daughters are reaching physical maturity earlier than we did. Our girls are getting their periods earlier and experiencing the other physical changes that presage menarche sooner (growth of pubic hair, breast development, increase in body fat), some as early as nine, with ten and eleven now considered normative. (The average age of menarche is now 12.5 years. In the last 150 years, the onset of menarche has advanced, on average, three years, largely because of good nutrition.) For some of our girls, early menarche may mean changes in themselves and in how their peers perceive them that they are not emotionally ready to handle. These changes may feel like an unwanted, premature end to childhood and, as mothers, we need to attend to them.

Taking all the factors into account, in its landmark 1995 study *Great Transitions*, the Carnegie Council on Adolescent Development recommended that the age of ten mark the beginning of adolescence for, in their words, the ages between ten and fourteen are "a crucial turning point in life's trajectory." The study, overall, encourages us to get rid of the stereotypes marketing people are so fond of because "although young adolescents are often stereotyped as moody, rebellious, self-indulgent, and incapable of learning anything serious, research indicates that this portrait is greatly overdrawn. Young adolescents are also, at this time, full of curiosity, imagination, and emerging idealism."[6]

The implications are profound. First, it means that we cannot wait until our daughters are "teenagers" to talk, mentor, and guide them as they move toward womanhood and selfhood. It means that, as mothers, we need to reexamine the boundaries of childhood and adolescence and locate our own daughters within them. A study conducted by the Kaiser Family Foundation and Children Now in 1999 revealed interesting, if sobering, information about successful communication between parents and children and when it needs to start on such issues as sex, violence, AIDS, drugs, and alcohol. At the ages of ten to twelve, the children surveyed ranked television and movies as *equally* valuable sources of information as their mothers, each getting 38 percent. (Teachers and friends were listed, too, and got almost the same ranking.) By ages thirteen to fifteen, though, the sphere of influence had shifted importantly: 64 percent report that their friends are their most important source of information, followed closely by television (61 percent). Teachers and the Internet follow, with mothers trailing last at 38 percent.[7] The competition for our daughters' attention is fierce and if we don't begin talking to them about the important issues early, the people who write the scripts and dialogue for movies and television shows will. Another study at Columbia University suggests that children make up their minds about important issues such as drugs between the ages of twelve and thirteen and are, at that time, most open to parental influence.[8] Once again, the word "teenager" could lead us to miss the important window of opportunity we have to guide our daughters when they are most ready to listen.

There is another important consequence of redefining when these years of transition begin: Adolescence will occupy roughly a decade of a mother's and daughter's lives. *Ten years*: As you read this, just imagine yourself ten years ago and take a moment to reflect on the incredible changes in you over that period of time—and those changes took place *without* adolescence. Those changes didn't happen all at once, of course; the changes that take place over a decade in both our lives and our daughters' lives are more akin to how the ocean's shoreline changes in the same period of time. While the cataclysmic events of nature—the storm or hurricane—create the changes most easily perceived, what actually alters the landscape over time is far more subtle and less dramatic: the slow erosion of the sand, grain by grain, accomplished by the everyday processes of weather and tides. So, too, in women's lives: While the storms are easiest to mark and remember—the catastrophes of death, divorce, or loss—these events alone do not create the changes within us. It is how they combine with our everyday lives—the small sea changes made up of daily interactions and relationships—that will change us over time. What goes on in my kitchen and yours matters in the truest sense: Mother and daughter alike will emerge from the period we call adolescence different people than they were at its beginning.

And that is why this book is called *Girl in the Mirror*. Just as we once peered over the crib rails to search our newborn daughters' faces for signs of personality or family resemblances, so, too, during the years of adolescence, mother and daughter alike peer into the mirror of each other's face, looking for hints of their past and future selves, of resemblance and connection or—when the relationship is fractious or difficult—evidence of difference and separateness.

As Hope Edelman puts it so well in her book *Motherless Daughters* (the words quoted at the beginning of this chapter): "Our mothers are our most direct connection to our history and our gender." By their presence or absence, the example they set or the lack of it, their positive influence or their negative one, by what they gave us and what they couldn't, for every girl who makes the journey from child to woman, the first mirror in which she looks is the mirror of her mother's face.

What we do and don't see there is a part of us forever.

When we talk to our adolescent daughters—whether it is a quiet evening heart-to-heart or a heated confrontation—we are never really alone with them. This is the one simple truth about mothers and daughters and the years of adolescence. And it is universal.

In the room with us are our past selves, the adolescent girls we once were. Our own mothers' words echo when we talk, and sometimes those of our grandmothers. There are the voices of old friends and their mothers. Our younger selves—the women we were before we became mothers—keep us company too. The room in which we find ourselves, seemingly alone with our daughters, can be a crowded place.

Past, present, and future collide when we look into our daughters' faces. All of our dreams—those we've realized and those we think beyond our grasp—are in the room with us. Not a small number of these dreams are those we dream for our children.

Our daughters, too, are not alone. All of their girlfriends, to whom they look for self-definition, keep them company. The mothers of their friends are there as well and play a role in how they see us by comparison. The outside world crowds in too: all the images of woman, girl, mother, and daughter gleaned from books and magazines, television and movies. These images influence our daughters as they begin to carve out their own definitions of self, just as they continue to influence us as grown women.

Negotiating the waters of these years of transition takes work, effort, skill, and a fair amount of resilience on the part of mother and daughter alike. Change is everywhere: in our daughters' bodies, minds, emotions, and even the microcosm in which they live. They leave the cozy world of elementary school—birthday parties with cupcakes, each child carefully accounted for every minute of the day—for the sudden autonomy of middle school or junior high school at eleven or twelve, complete with too-heavy backpacks, schedules, unforgiving combination locks, and a raft of teachers. They find themselves confronting a new set of societal expectations and, from where they sit, it must feel as though the whole world is screaming, "Grow up, grow up, grow up!" In July 2000, on its front pages, *The New York Times* concluded—after conducting roundtable discussions with over two hundred sixth-graders in eleven states and the District of Columbia—that the pressure on sixth-graders to succeed both academically and at standardized testing is enormous and different in kind from the pressures their parents faced.[9] It is hard to believe that the children they interviewed were actually worrying about college.

For mothers, too, it is a time of change: Suddenly it seems as though the very ways in which we've nurtured our children over the years are outmoded and out of sync. Some of us will feel that we've been undone by the rapidity of the changes: We may go from dry-ing our little girls' tears to snuffling into Kleenexes ourselves because our daughters have, in anger, wounded us to the core. The child who loved cuddling suddenly doesn't want to be touched. The child we used to read to becomes a girl who goes back online to chat with strangers, long after the house lights are out for the night. The shy child blossoms into an orator; the supremely confident little girl disappears into a round-shouldered and sullen fourteen-year-old. Our daughters' telephone calls are suddenly hushed, whispered events, out of earshot. Some of us will find ourselves searching our daughters' faces for the children whose shoelaces we once tied, who ran to us for comfort. One exasperated but witty mother described living with her sixteen-year-old as "right out of *Alice in Wonderland*—you never know, from day to day, whether it's the Red Queen or Alice herself who's coming down to breakfast." Peg's daughter, Alexandra, went to middle school after seven years at a small public elementary school and, for mother and daughter alike, it was a time of letting go:

On the first day, she got out of the car by herself and I sat there, watching her go up the steps to the big red door. She still looked so little, her petite frame dwarfed by an enormous backpack, in contrast to the fast-moving stream of seventh and eight graders, all of whom looked about seven feet tall. She walked steadily, holding her own in the flow, and then, at the very last minute, turned to see if I was watching. My routine didn't change all year—I still sat in the car, waiting to see that she got inside safely—but about a few months into the school year, she stopped turning around. Now she's got her own rules about being dropped off and picked up. I can't kiss her in public. I can't wear my "dorky" orange clogs. I should park across the street, not in front of the school. These are small details but they are powerful reminders that her universe is expanding beyond what it was in childhood—when Mommy was at its very center.

But despite our daughters' hunger for independence, the peer pressure to be grown-up, and the emphasis middle schools place on responsibility and autonomy, study after study confirms that our daughters need us more than ever, if in different ways than they did when they were five, eight, or even just a year ago. What they need will continue to change, from one year to the next, as they move from the early part of adolescence to the middle stage and, then, to late adolescence. For many of us, switching gears as mothers is as difficult as the transition out of childhood is for our daughters.

Mothering—for humans, at least—is learned, not instinctual, and, at certain times, the challenge of being the mothers our daughters need seems impossible. (Being the mothers they think they want is another matter entirely, and one that no sane woman should even speculate about.) The child who stands before us is changeable, contradictory, as she crosses the boundary between childhood and adulthood: Eager to be perceived as independent, she begs us to please do her laundry the way we used to; desperate to grow up, she demands to know why we have packed up her dolls; the fiercely independent fifteen-year-old suddenly becomes clingy, jealous of the attention her younger siblings get. Sometimes, too, the tasks we face as the mothers of adolescents seem utterly contradictory. How can we protect our daughters from danger while, at the same time, giving them the freedom they need? How can we stay connected when they're pushing us away with both hands? How can we talk to them when they are determined not to listen? What can we do when we simply don't understand them— when we haven't experienced what they are experiencing and we don't have an emotional analogy to draw on? How can we set an example without insisting that it is the only example for them to follow?

This book was written so that we can learn how.

~ ~ ~

My mother was a strong influence on me yet, at the same time, she didn't know how to be supportive enough. She was very accepting and gave me almost complete freedom. My friends used to like chatting with her at the kitchen table over coffee and cigarettes whether I was home or not. On the other hand, she didn't give me the support I needed psychologically to deal with my parents' divorce and my relationship with my father.

My daughter's father and I separated when she was in sixth grade and we were divorced when she was in eighth. She's been in therapy since seventh grade, and I've made sure she's okay in ways I wasn't.

Rachel, fifty-three, a psychologist and divorced mother of a daughter, now eighteen

I came of age in a world very different from the one my daughters, their friends, and their peers all over American experience. While the larger world may have seemed dangerous and unsettled (I was eleven when President Kennedy was shot, and I remember huddling under my desk, along with all of my classmates, in drills designed to help us survive a Russian nuclear attack), my little world was safe and sound. My own parents were and still are married and loving. I knew no one whose parents were divorced. What has happened to the American family in the intervening years—some thirty-five—since I was an adolescent is reflected in the adult lives of my parents' four children. Despite his tumultuous adolescence (which I've promised to keep a family secret), only one brother has been married to the same woman for over twenty years, with whom he's had two children—a genuine nuclear family. My sister, who has no biological children, is a loving and involved stepmother. My other brother is now divorced and his children live with their mother; he sees them on a schedule familiar to children all over America. I have been married three times and while my husband is the biological father of my son and the adoptive father of my two daughters who call him Dad, it's still not exactly "Ozzie and Harriet."

So, too, all across America, girls will experience adolescence in families that are differently configured than most of the families their mothers grew up in. When the mothers of today's adolescents were born—1950 to 1965—the percentage of children under the age of eighteen living in single-parent households went from a low of 7.1 percent to a high of 11.3 percent in 1970.[10] Fewer than one in ten of today's mothers grew up in single-parent households. In contrast, by 1999, just under 26 percent of all children under the age of seventeen in the United States were living in single-parent households and an additional 3.7 percent lived with other relatives or nonrelatives. By the ages of fifteen to seventeen, just under 28 percent live in single-parent families.[11] Of the 19.8 million children who live in a single-parent household, 88 percent of them live with their mothers, either alone or with the mother's partner.[12] But the remaining 71 percent who are living in two-parent families may not be living in an "Ozzie and Harriet"–type scenario either, since the data doesn't distinguish between biological or adopted children and stepchildren. It's been estimated that 12–13 percent of children under the age of eighteen live with a stepparent as part of the "two-parent" family.[13] At some point before they turn sixteen, approximately 70 percent of kids will find themselves living in a single-parent family. It is estimated, too, that 10 percent of all children who experience divorce will—before age sixteen—reexperience it as their mothers and fathers find new partners, remarry, and then divorce again.[14]

Not surprisingly, the ramifications for our daughters are enormous. For many adolescents, the "family" as their mothers experienced it simply doesn't exist. Many of them will find themselves in more complicated, often more stressful environments during the years of adolescence. They may find themselves, during these years of change, having to puzzle their way through new relationships with stepfathers, stepmothers, stepbrothers and -sisters.

They may find themselves having to cope with more temporary connections to lovers of either or both parents. They may find their relationship to their fathers utterly changed or nonexistent. As the children of divorce, they are likely to encounter radically changed economic circumstances since, from a statistical point of view, the mother—usually the custodial parent—is likely to find herself considerably poorer than she was when the marriage was intact.[15]

But divorce is not the only factor that has redefined the "family" for our daughters. Even if they are living in a two-parent family— even with their own biological parents—they are as likely as not to find themselves spending more time alone than their mothers ever did because most adolescent girls have a mother who works. Despite how our society mythologizes the stay-at-home mom, roughly 75 percent of all married women with children ages six to seventeen living in two-parent families work; in women-maintained households, the percentage rises to 79.1 percent.[16] In most families, this means that adolescents will spend more time with their peers, alone, or, for the well-to-do, with a hired caretaker than they do with their parents. The emphasis put on "independence" once our children reach middle-school age has, perhaps, made parents more comfortable with this situation than they ought to be. (That seeing our kids less as they get older—and being less involved in their lives—is normative is proved out by one telling statistic: Parental involvement in schools and school activities drops precipitously after the age of ten.[17])

The redesigned American family not only changes day-to-day life for the adolescent girl and her mother—the "sea change" part of interacting—but affects them in ways that are both direct and subtle. Working mothers may discover that their daughters' adolescence coincides with their own "job burnout" or, alternatively, a career moment that demands more, rather than less, commitment to work. Generally, expectations of a woman's commitment to her job—once her children are perceived as "grown"—will increase; the empathy and leeway awarded to mothers of small children will often, in the workplace, fade over time. Then, there are the more subtle, harder to define effects of the choices parents make in their lives. The conclusions our daughters draw from the life experiences of the adults in their homes and communities—the "life lessons" on issues as various as priorities, obligations, commitments, marriage and relationships, and more—will be very different in kind from those their mothers drew from their surroundings at the same age. It's not surprising that the "flux" Peggy Orenstein has described in her book of the same name—the reconciliation of the postfeminist "I-can-have-it-all dreams" with their costs in real life—affects our daughters as well.[18]

As mothers, we all need to be aware that our daughters will learn not only from what we say but from what we do.

~ ~ ~

During a discussion about all the physical changes coming up in the next few years, Al suddenly looked up at me and said, "I'm sad, Mommy, that we'll never cycle together." Like many women of my generation, I've made a big deal about her getting her period, trying all the while not to romanticize it. She's right, of course—at my age, perimenopause is going to give over to menopause soon, maybe even before she starts her period. I don't feel conflicted about menopause but many of the women I know are. They complain about the finality of it; they hate how it forces them to acknowledge how they are aging. "Too many hormones in one house," says one woman talking about her own mood swings and those of her fourteen-year-old. Another woman, unhappy with the changes in her body, expresses a certain amount of jealousy about how her daughter's skin is poreless, her body taut. I don't share those feelings. I'm not saying that I wouldn't rather look forty than fifty-one but, at the same time, while nothing is perfect in my life, I rather like where I find myself.

Peg, fifty-one, my coauthor and the mother of Alexandra, age twelve

In addition to employment and divorce, there are life choices that directly affect the mother-daughter relationship in the adolescent years. Women are not only marrying later but having their children later, with the average age at thirty-one (as opposed to twenty-two only a generation ago). With our daughters reaching puberty earlier, what this means is simple: Two important landmarks in female life—menarche and perimenopause/menopause, events that in previous generations were separated in time, will, in daughter and mother, likely overlap. There's no generalizing about what this means to the mother-daughter relationship since there are few intelligent generalizations anyone can make about perimenopause and menopause. Not even medical statistics are useful: Some women will pass through this transition seamlessly while others will experience a range of emotional and physical symptoms. Dr. Claudia Edwards, a psychologist in private practice who deals with mother-daughter relationships, points to exhaustion, concentration problems, and emotionality as symptoms of perimenopause that can complicate and change daily life. She goes on to say that for women who have issues with getting older, this may be a particularly stressful time. In a culture fixated on youthfulness, where menopause has only recently come out of the closet, it's not surprising that, for some of us, this transition will create conflict not only within ourselves but with our daughters.[19]

The coincidence of these two stages in the female life cycle needs to be brought out into the open and discussed—among ourselves and with our daughters. We need to be able to sit down with our friends and talk about what being a woman entails—at every stage of life. Then—and only then—will we be able to guide our daughters through their own years of transition. There is little use bemoaning the anorexic models paraded on the pages of magazines or the culture of beauty that tells our daughters that how they look is who they are if, every time we step in front of a mirror, we complain about how fat we are, how our waists are thickening, or how our skin looks. If you need convincing about how important this is, keep in mind that a study published in October 2000 in *The Journal of the American Dietetic Association*, corroborating earlier research that mothers "play a central role in transmitting cultural values regarding weight, shape, and appearance to daughters," discovered that girls as young as the age of *five* form ideas about dieting—and the need for it—from their mothers' behavior![20] Forcing ourselves to become aware of the messages we send our daughters—about our womanhood, our looks, our bodies, and what we find meaningful and important in life—is the first step toward helping our daughters become healthy adolescents who will grow into fulfilled and secure women.

We owe it to ourselves and to them.

~ ~ ~

My major influence on both of my daughters derives from my own integrity and willingness to live by my values, to make hard choices and to stick by them. In other words, I believe I must model how I want my children to behave. If I want my girls to grow to be empowered, capable, creative, honest, responsible, and compassionate people, I must embody these traits myself. With my younger daughter, I see that I am most influential when I let her have enough space to be herself. We are similar in many ways, and I like to give her the room to discover who she is without my being in there with her. My older daughter honestly respects me and often asks for my opinion. Rather than just giving it to her, I often turn her questions back to her and let her work things out for herself with some emotional support. She seems to make generally wise decisions this way.

Patti, age forty-two, creative and merchandising director for two mail-order catalogues, and mother to four children, two of whom are fifteen and eighteen

Because the world in which our daughters are coming of age is so different from the one we experienced as children and adolescents, we may sometimes find ourselves bewildered or caught short by the variety of responses demanded of us as mothers and role models. It is sometimes hard to figure out precisely what we need to do and when.

My daughter Kate listens to a different drummer. Unlike most of her peers in the public school she attends in the well-heeled Northern California suburb where we live, she's not into clothes or doing her hair. In seventh grade, belonging to a group wasn't important to her, as it seemed to be for most of the girls and boys who attend the school, including her sister. She reads voraciously and shows considerable artistic talent; she is content to spend time alone. She is a still pond, whose surface belies the depths beneath. She has set herself apart for a variety of reasons, some conscious and others not.

About a year ago, the ways in which she is different made her an easy target for three boys who began with the teasing and cruel laughter that anyone who has been young or different would quickly recognize. They made fun of her in the classroom and on the playground. I moved on this slowly, discussing it with her teachers and school counselors, and talking about it at home. The teachers were on the lookout for trouble and Kate promised to tell them if any new incidents took place. I was loath to intercede; Kate needed, I thought, to learn how to avoid unnecessary confrontations, to fight her own battles. I thought any active parental intervention would make her less resilient—and if I had learned anything from life, it was the importance of resilience.

It seemed a wise course until, last winter, things suddenly escalated: The boys called her a "bitch" and pushed her into some lockers. She was reduced to tears and refused to go to school. I took immediate action, and decided to write the school a letter, charging the boys with sexual, verbal, and physical harassment. I reminded Kate that each and every accusation needed to be accurate. I reassured her that I would protect her and that she had every right to go to school without feeling frightened or unhappy. I sent a copy of the letter to each of the boys' parents since the letter demanded that the school take action. The superintendent of schools took charge: One boy was suspended for two weeks and the other two were put on probation. The reaction from the boys' parents was less straightforward: One mother apologized by mail, one never responded, and the third put the blame squarely on my daughter and on me for overreacting.

I don't doubt for a minute that I did the right thing. According to the American Association of University Women, harassment in schools is a very real problem in America, especially for girls.[21] And what most of us remember about the exclusionary power of high school cliques when we were growing up has, in the sped-up world our girls live in, been noted by researchers to take place as early as late elementary school. (According to a study conducted in 1998 by Nicki Crick, Ph.D., and Maureen Bigbee, M.S., M.S.W., while boys were likely to be overtly victimized [threatened by physical violence], girls were subject to "relational victimization" by purposeful exclusion from a group and bad-mouthing among peers. This study was conducted among fifth-graders.[22]) My story illustrates how it is sometimes difficult to know which course of action is best for our daughters. In retrospect, it is clear that Kate could not have won this battle on her own; not surprisingly, she didn't report the boys to her teachers on her own, in part because she was afraid of the social consequences. If I hadn't interceded, she would have learned more about helplessness than about resilience.

We have interviewed women from all over the country for this book, in the hopes of both finding the common threads of the changing mother-daughter relationship and discovering those meaningful differences that can help each of us learn from the other's example. We found many shared concerns, despite clear differences in our backgrounds, marital status, geographic location, and economic status. Prominent among them was worry about the seemingly premature end to our daughters' childhood and the increased sexualization of our culture and, by extension, the social

*helplessness vs. resiliency*

worlds in which our daughters find themselves. Just as some of our daughters are being pushed out of childhood too quickly and too traumatically by accelerated physical development, others are likely to find themselves, as early as the age of thirteen, in social situations for which they are emotionally unprepared. A joint survey by the Kaiser Family Foundation and *YM* magazine in 1998 (*YM* is read by 2 million girls, ages twelve to nineteen, each month) found that 55 percent of the girls interviewed (between the ages of thirteen and eighteen) found themselves in sexual situations that were uncomfortable. (According to this survey, teen girls are twice as likely as teen boys to find themselves in these situations.[23]) Even mothers who came of age in the "sexually liberated" late 1960s and 1970s expressed real worry about the sexual practices of today's adolescents and the dangers sexually transmitted diseases pose to our daughters' physical and emotional health. We found a commonality in our concerns about drugs and violence in our society and, most generally, the complexity of the choices set before our children. We wondered aloud whether the enormous progress made by women in the last thirty years will continue, and whether our daughters will find it easier to live a balanced and fulfilled life than we did.

Most important, we found in our own stories and those of other women an acknowledgment that being a good and responsive mother during the years of adolescence is challenging, even under the best of circumstances, and that sometimes, even with the best of intentions, we are our own worst enemies. These stories helped us understand how the dyad—the twosome—of mother and daughter constantly changes during these years, and how, in turn, our own parenting skills must continuously evolve. We spoke to women who had found ways of allowing their daughters to learn on their own without setting them adrift. We listened as women talked about reliving their own adolescence through their daughters and who, unwittingly, had tried to impose their own unfulfilled dreams on their children. We found women who had grown by seeing themselves through their daughters' eyes. And, then, there were the stories of struggle, of conflict, and of pain.

We have included many of these stories in *Girl in the Mirror* because we feel that sharing our stories is one way of learning. The time we have spent talking, researching, and writing *Girl in the Mirror* has reinforced our understanding that there are no simple step-by-step solutions to the many challenges adolescence poses for mother and daughter alike. In the next chapter of this book, we will describe what we have called the "I-Thou" of parenting—borrowing a phrase from the esteemed theologian Martin Buber—which we hope will be a useful tool for all of us. At the heart of this book is the understanding that the process of self-definition is an arduous and ongoing one that begins in adolescence and continues through adulthood. To help our daughters find their true selves, we must first be sure that we know who we are.

~ ~ ~

For me, the moment at which I felt the lack of a mother most acutely was when my daughter was born; it was a stressful time. I missed the support my mother might have given me, the guidance she might have offered about all the things I didn't know about babies. I remember being reduced to tears with envy when my cousin's daughter was born just a month after mine, and her mother stayed with her for six months. Things since then have been fine but I think Lily's years of adolescence will be another moment in time when my own motherlessness becomes an issue. My mother died when I was twelve—before I felt any resentment or rebellion—and if and when Lily chooses to rebel, I won't have any personal frame of reference. My memories of my mother are so positive, so idealized, so imagined, and our relationship so eternally perfect, that it's hard to see how I will cope with my own relationship with Lily changing. She's nine and, for now at least, she adores me.

My friends tell me that when they look in the mirror, they see their mothers. I never saw my mother age: When I look in the mirror, it's my grandmother I see.

Leslie, age forty-eight, freelance writer and editor, mother of Lily, age nine

Of all my children—I also have a son, now six—my middle daughter, Rachel, is most like me. As I write this, she is almost twelve. If my eldest is a still pond with hidden depths, then Rachel is a pool of clear blue water, sparkling with reflected sunlight. Things come easily to her: She is good at school and athletics, and has lots of friends. She is fiercely independent, driven to excel, and has the intellect to achieve her goals. On the surface, of my three children, she would seem to need my attentions least.

But in different ways, the years of adolescence may pose a greater risk to Rachel than they do to her sister. Rachel doesn't know how to pace herself: If a project is due in two weeks, she feels compelled to get it done the very first night it is assigned. The counterpoint to her need to succeed is the approbation she gets from others: She worries about what people think of her and, if a teacher is disappointed in her performance, she is crushed. For Rachel, the hardest life lesson will be learning that she cannot be all things to all people.

This lesson is one I have learned and relearned dozens and dozens of times in my own life; learning it once was never enough. (Why is it so hard to learn? I think high achievers are always partly motivated by the reflections of themselves they see in the faces of others. Pleasing people matters to them.) As her mother, I will have to teach Rachel that tolerating and accepting failure are necessary parts of success and true components of healthy self-esteem. Ironically, the character traits that may prove to be Rachel's greatest assets in adulthood put her at specific risk during adolescence. The loss of self-esteem experienced by girls as they pass into the years of adolescence in America has been well chronicled, and is deserving of every mother's attention; in the pages of this book, we will turn to it again and again.

If the ways in which Rachel and I are alike make it easy for me to understand her feelings (I remember those feelings well), I also need to pay attention to how we are different. This will take some effort on my part; I am more comfortable operating from the famil-

iar, proposing the solutions to the problems of pleasing and achiev-
ing that have worked for me. But family jokes about "my clone"
aside, Rachel and I are not the same person. I can teach her about
the paths available to her but, in the end, she will have to choose
and travel one herself.

There are other issues, too, some of them new to this generation
of mothers and daughters. Precisely because we are alike, I wonder
how having me as her mother will affect Rachel as she grows into
her own. Women of my generation—mostly raised by stay-at-home
mothers—often talk about the burdens of self-invention we experienced as we moved into jobs and professions traditionally domi-
nated by men. While it was true that there was a cost in being
"first," there was also a certain amount of freedom. We were free to
invent ourselves as we saw fit precisely because there were no role
models on whom to pattern ourselves. Our daughters, though, have
a different burden. Will my own accomplishments inspire Rachel or
will she come to perceive them as a source of pressure, a standard
she has to surpass? Will she feel that, to be herself, she has to first
emerge from my shadow, the way the sons of successful men did in
previous generations? How will she come to view the choices I've
made and how will my choices, in turn, affect the choices she feels
she needs to make?

These questions, too, are part of the sea changes that affect the
relationships between mothers and daughters in this new century.
Throughout this book, with the help of many different women, we
will begin to look for answers.

~ ~ ~

We do not grow absolutely, chronologically. We grow sometimes in
one dimension, and not in another, unevenly. We grow partially. We
are relative. We are mature in one realm, childish in another. The
past, present, and future mingle and pull us backward, forward, or
fix us in the present. We are made up of layers, cells, constellations.

Anaïs Nin

Even without full-fledged rebellion, redefining their relationship to their mothers is a necessary part of our daughters' development. For some girls, adolescence will require a new degree of separation. Growing up entails what Judith Viorst has called a "necessary loss," and it is a loss experienced by mother and daughter alike.[24] We may find ourselves mourning how our daughters used to need us. We may, at this moment, discover the parts of ourselves that are still rebelling against our own mothers. We may find ourselves drawn into confrontations based on our own immaturity that have little or nothing to do with the daughters standing before us. We may see in our daughters' growth the painful but incontrovertible truth of our own aging. We may become authoritarian simply because we hate the way our children seem to be spinning out of our orbit. We may discover flaws and faults we never knew we possessed.

Or we may find, in this "necessary loss"—this sea change of life—new meaning, new maturity, and a true voice to which our daughters can listen. We may emerge from this sea change stronger women, possessed of new self-knowledge, in the company of daughters who do us proud.

## CHAPTER TWO

# The "I-Thou" of Parenting

When the children were small, my wife was a perfect mother who doted on them and tended to their every need. She was terrifically good at it, and knowing that she was good at it made her even better at it. Then, as they got older, different things were required of her: setting rules and boundaries, finding ways of communicating, dealing with each of them as separate people with personalities. These were skills that were, for her, harder to acquire. She still looked to manage the kids' lives the way she did when they were little, to "fix" things for them. She couldn't master the art of listening. My daughter rebelled against the control and, by the time she was ready to go off to college, the positive aspects of their relationship were practically nonexistent.

"George," age fifty-three, an investment advisor, and the father of a daughter, now nineteen, and a son, twenty-one

MOTHERING, AT THE BEGINNING at least, is about stamina and attentiveness; desperately tired, wondering whether we will ever sleep again, we all begin as new mothers, learning on the job by listening to cues. We stock up on baby books, solicit advice from other women, and trade experiences with just about anyone who will listen. We judge our performance by how well we take care of our babies, how good we are at decoding the cries, smiles, and coos that are our daughters' only way of communicating. Although this part of motherhood certainly feels hard when we are in the thick of it and can elicit maternal emotions ranging from pure elation to borderline murderousness, its goals are straightforward: to make sure our children are stimulated, happy, healthy, and fed.

As our daughters grow out of babyhood, what is required of us as mothers begins, subtly, to shift. And for all that our culture has pronounced, if unrealistic, visions of what a "good mother" is—she's the understanding one who gives birthday parties at home, serves cookies baked from scratch, and finds the time to sew Halloween costumes, all the while ferrying little Susie between ballet classes and soccer games and talking to the office on her cell phone—there is little dialogue about how the job of mothering evolves. Or how our own personalities and experiences make us, at different times, better at the job than at others. Or how the dynamic between mother and daughter continually redefines itself. The "sea changes" in us begin as soon as our girls take their first leave of the small realm of early childhood and venture out into the world. Just listen to Mary Ellen, a full-time publishing professional, talk about her daughter, now six:

In Mary Kate's first year, her prematurity affected the way I cared for her. Not only was I wracked with a feeling of failure but I felt I had to make a Herculean effort to make her healthy and that it was entirely and solely up to me, even though my husband was support-ive. Caring for an infant is very much a "you and me against the world" kind of feeling, and I loved it.

Now, it's all changing. I'm obviously different with a six-year-old than I was with an infant or a two-year-old. I'm already into the self-esteem issues: She's into the age of perfectionism and is frustrated when her efforts aren't perfect. I spend a lot of time reassuring and guiding and, of course, worrying that she worries too much about being perfect and tries too hard to please. I'm already saying things like, "Do things to make yourself proud, rather than always thinking of making us proud." Of course, I waffle on this too.

She's still baby enough for me to lie next to her in bed, tell her stories, and watch her run around the house naked. But I miss the fact that I can't make all things better with a hug and kiss, and sur-prised that she's already dealing with feelings that confuse her.

It isn't just the child who is changing: Each stage of our daughters' lives requires us to take on new skills and to let go of old ways of interacting.

But the American cultural mythology of the Good Mother is oddly static, based on an ideal from the 1950s that, as it happens, itself was a historical aberration. Like other cultural stereotypes, the Good Mother isn't tethered to real life as we know it. It's important to remember that while roughly half of Americans still think the mom who stays at home is the ideal, only a quarter of American women with children over the age of six actually do. So only one out of four of us actually is baking those cookies and sewing those costumes. Amazingly enough, that doesn't seem to stop the other three mothers from feeling guilty and inadequate all the same. Cultural stereotypes are *very* powerful. The myth of the Good Mother is static in another important sense: It doesn't acknowledge that the job description filed under "Good Mother" continually changes, particularly during the years of adolescence.

An important corollary to the myth of the Good Mother is the cultural stereotype of the adolescent girl. "Enjoy her while you can," says the mother of a sixteen-year-old girl to the mother of an eight-year-old. "It's all going to change soon enough." "Get into survival mode," advises another whose daughter is, in her words, "finally" going off to college. Our culture teaches us to gird our loins and get ready for the inevitable: An eye-rolling hurricane of hormones and hostility, ready to turn our lives into chaos at a moment's notice.

Even the titles of popular books—such as *"I'm Not Mad, I Just Hate You!": A New Understanding of Mother-Daughter Conflict; Get Out of My Life, but First Could You Drive Me and Cheryl to the Mall?; Surviving Ophelia: Mothers Share Their Wisdom in Navigating the Tumultuous Teenage Years*—encourage us to see girls as necessarily either troublesome or troubled. It's a small wonder that few women look forward to these years with any kind of positive anticipation. Solutions to the problem of this supposedly inevitable hostility include this one, adapted from a book but distributed on various sites on the Internet: "Treat your teenager as an adult friend. By the time your child is twelve years old, start working on developing the kind of relationship you would like to have with her when she is grown up . . ."[1]

Read this and ask yourself: Do our twelve-year-olds really need or want another, if older and taller, buddy to hang out with? This kind of advice—based on the stereotype of rebellion, not necessarily the girl in front of you—has all sorts of implicit dangers, not the least of which is the blurring of who the adult is in the relationship. (No, it's not the twelve-year-old.) It also tacitly assumes that since their peer groups will be the most important part of our daughters' lives, the best way for mothers to stay in touch is to become a peer.

Our media-saturated daughters are exposed to precisely the same stereotypes, this time viewed through another prism. Take a look at the magazines aimed at girls in the adolescent years (ours is admittedly a random sample, culled from the piles in Peg's daughter's room), and you'll find, among the literally dozens of standard editorial features devoted to lipstick, hair, boys, nail polish, clothes, celebrities, and embarrassing moments, a virtually mother-free world. The sole exceptions are articles such as these (and, yes, these are all real articles), which cover the general topic of "dealing with Mom." *Cosmo Girl!* offers the following advice on shopping with Mom: "You know the drill—you like one thing and your mom likes something totally different. Well, there *is* a way to get what you want—without crying, arguing or begging (well, maybe a *little* begging!). And you don't even have to feel *guilty* about it! Here's our five-step plan for getting your mom to cave."[2] The assumption here? Her world and your world are totally separate. But you've got the money and she has to learn to manipulate you into getting what she wants. (And, with luck, you won't notice.) Then, too, there's advice on the predictable crisis about how old a girl needs to be to date. The message boards of various websites aimed at "teens" make it clear that this remains a hot topic. In answer to a fourteen-year-old whose parents won't let her date until she's sixteen, which means she can't "be with" the guy she likes, the "It's not fair" column of *YM* magazine offers the following advice: "Ah, parents. Can't live with 'em, and can't, um . . . live with 'em. When they treat you like a prisoner, it's hard not to feel like a prisoner. Yep, some folks are superstrict about letting their little girl date (and no matter how old you get, they will always look at you as if you're still frolicking on a swingset in frilly pink panties and pigtails). They worry that you will k-i-s-s someone! They worry that slimy studs will take advantage of you! They worry that you are growing up—and they may not be ready for that."[3] The subtext? It's the parents' problem: They're the ones invested in keeping their daughter a little girl. The coy editorial "teen talk" voice reinforces the notion that the parents are wrong and that you, the adolescent reader, are right— and that the battle will be ongoing ("They will always look at you as if you're still frolicking on a swingset . . ."). Even when an article delivers a fairly reasonable strategy for dealing with mother-daughter disagreements, there's usually a reinforcement of stereotypes first. The following is taken from "Is Your Mom Ready to Let You Grow Up?" from "Big Mother Is Watching" in *Girls' Life*. "Since your age has hit double digits, you're probably aching for awesome new experiences and a taste of freedom. After all, you're not a little girl anymore! Although it is crystal clear to you and your buds, your mother's not exactly seeing the light. She's treating you like a baby! Maybe she tries to make all your decisions, buy you ridiculous clothes, or butt into your business?"[4]

The lesson here? You and Mom live on different planets and she's trying to keep you from growing up; Mom and the peer group are opposed forces; you, the reader, are old enough to make your own decisions.

The same cultural message is delivered to the bedside tables of mother and daughter alike.

But are the cultural stereotypes of the adolescent girl any truer or, more important, *useful* than that of the Good Mother or, for that matter, all the other stereotypes pertaining to women? As mothers, we already know how powerfully the phantom of the Good Mother—the perfect and always understanding cookie-baker in the sky, a cross between Mother Teresa and Martha Stewart—can negatively shape our behavior and subtly influence our attitudes not only toward ourselves but toward other women as well. How much of what goes on between mothers and daughters in the adolescent years is fed or even created by cultural assumptions? Are we working with models for behavior—ours and our daughters'—that will enrich our daughters' experiences during these years, or make us better mentors and guides?

In her book *A Tribe Apart*, which describes her involvement with a small group of adolescent girls and boys, Patricia Hersch traces some of the current cultural assumptions about adolescence back to the 1960s:

> The sixties kids wanted freedom and space. Parents didn't think it was such a good idea. The parents in the 1960s, to their children's disgust, wanted rules and controls. So today's parents think the adolescent desire for space is part of the natural order of growing up. They extend to their own children the privilege of being alone. The sixties cemented in the public imagination that treating teens as a tribe apart is right and proper.[5]

 Research confirms that, as parents, we are making decisions based on these adolescent stereotypes. For example, a September 2000 study of the child-care patterns of employed mothers revealed that 24 percent of children ages ten to twelve are in "self care" when they are not in school and their mothers are working. "Self care"—

a phrase deliberately chosen by the authors of the report to be as neutral as possible—describes a child left alone and unsupervised by an adult for a regular amount of time with a sibling under the age of thirteen. Let the statistic sink in: The parents of nearly one quarter of early adolescent children in the United States use "self care" as the *primary* form of child care. The percentage, not surprisingly, rises when a single-parent household is involved. But 35 percent of all ten- to twelve-year-olds spend at least some time during the week in "self care" and, importantly, as the child gets older, the parental level of comfort appears to increase since, by age twelve, 44 percent spend at least some time alone at home. More than half of those children spend one to four hours a week alone; 15 percent care for themselves ten hours a week. Interestingly, the incidence of "self care" rises with higher income families; although it was not the intention of the study to discuss the factors that went into the parental choice of child care, it does venture that, perhaps, higher income families, living in better neighborhoods, perceive their children as being safe alone at home. The study also showed a significant disparity among the racial and ethnic groups concerning child-care arrangements: White parents are twice as likely as Hispanic parents and three times as likely as black parents to use self care as the primary form of child care (30 percent for whites, as opposed to 15 percent of Hispanics and 11 percent of blacks). It's worth noting that the authors of the study assume that all the statistics concerning self care are probably on the low side since some parents are unwilling to acknowledge, publicly at least, that they rely on self care at all.[6]

There's more evidence that, as our children move from early adolescence into the middle and late stages, we are willing to let them become "a tribe apart." According to the National Academy of Sciences, the amount of time parents spend with their children every week has dropped eleven hours since 1960.[7] *Teens and Their Parents in the 21st Century*, a report issued by the Council of Economic Advisors, confirmed that as our children head deeper into the years of adolescence, we are more and more inclined to let them live in a separate world, just as the books and magazines tell us to. Since the study found that parental involvement in an adolescent's life was predictive not only of academic success but of avoidance of harmful or self-destructive behavior, the researchers used simple measures of parental involvement: the dinner habits of a family and the adolescent's perception of how close he or she was to his or her parents. About 74 percent of children between the ages of twelve and fourteen reported that, in the previous week, they had eaten dinner with a parent at least five times. At ages fifteen to sixteen, though, only 61 percent reported eating with their parents the same number of times. By the time the adolescents reached seventeen to nineteen, those who ate dinner with their parents on any regular basis were in the minority: 42 percent. Yet as this and other studies show, adolescents who spent time eating with their parents and who perceived themselves as close to their parents were far less likely to smoke, drink, use illegal drugs, and initiate sexual activity and, conversely, far more likely to do well in school and to attend college.[8]

Where precisely does all of this leave our girls? Listening to the messages of our culture, have we unwittingly absented ourselves from our daughters' lives, leaving them to look to their peers to discover the women they want to become? And where does this leave us as mothers—somewhere between choosing to be our daughter's "best bud" and the Person Who's Holding Her Back? Has our culture taught our daughters to see fighting with their mothers as the necessary proof that they, like the girls in the magazines and perhaps some of their peers, are *not* babies, but grown-ups? And have we, as mothers, colluded by buying into precisely the same cultural assumptions?

Are there better models for us to adopt? We wondered out loud, and decided to take a closer look.

~ ~ ~

The other day, after a fruitless shopping expedition, my daughter started opening up about her fears about her body. Strange: I always had friends who were smaller than me, and now she does too. My daughter is not big or fat but has the developmental hip and tummy thing. She hates it. "All I want to be is skin, bone, and muscle," she says. Many of her pals are just that. I spoke to her honestly, and told her I had been bulimic at one time. (Her response: "How come it didn't work, Mom?") I told her she couldn't have found a better dieting expert—after all, the first time I joined Weight Watchers, the year was 1968! We talked about anorexia, and the societal pressure to be thin. It was an incredibly honest discussion and, by the end of it, she had cheered up considerably.

My daughter is entering eighth grade, and the most important thing in the world to her is her connection to her friends. I will continue my laid-back policy: Trust her until she gives me a reason not to. We even talked about sex, and my fear that some fifteen-year-old boy will sweet-talk her into something she's not ready for.

For the first time in a while, I feel like our relationship is meaningful to her. I hope this continues into this last important year of middle school. It means a lot to me that she can come and talk to me about the things that are troubling her.

"Martha," fifty-two, artist and PTA activist, whose adopted daughter is fourteen

In her best-selling and highly influential book *Reviving Ophelia*, Mary Pipher looks at what she calls our culture's "mixed messages" to mothers and daughters and concludes that "conflict between mothers and daughters is inevitable." She points out that, unlike fathers, who are "praised for their involvement with children," mothers are required to involve themselves in "precisely the right amount." (In her words: "Distant mothers are scorned, but mothers who are too close are accused of smothering and overprotecting.") Adolescence presents mothers with a variation on the theme that is impossible to satisfy, Pipher says: "They are to be devoted to their daughters and yet encourage them to leave. Mothers are asked to love completely and yet know exactly when to distance emotionally and physically." In Pipher's view, our daughters are presented with equally confusing cultural expectations:

> Girls are encouraged to separate from their mothers and to devalue their relationships to them. They are expected to respect their mothers but not to be like them. In our culture, loving one's mother is linked with dependency, passivity, and regression, while rejecting one's mother implies individuation, activity, and independence. Distancing from one's mother is viewed as a necessary step towards adult development.[9]

Reading these words as the mother of two adolescent girls leaves me dispirited for a moment. But surely, I think to myself, devaluing perhaps the most central relationship in a young girl's life—*just because the culture asks her to*—isn't good for her, or for her mother. Hope Edelman's book *Motherless Daughters* immediately springs to mind because of the picture it paints of what happens to women who are deprived of their mothers through death or other loss: "like a loud sound in an empty house, it echoes on and on."[10]

How did we get to this place? And what can we, as mothers, do about the cultural mythology that poisons the mother-daughter well? I'm still thinking about it when I tuck my girls into bed—a childhood ritual none of us is ready to let go of. For me, bedtime is a moment at which, in a household with three children and telephones constantly ringing, I can connect with each of my children, quietly and wholly, without the usual sibling competition for my attention. With the lights dimmed, I sit and talk to each of my girls in turn, and when I go back into Kate's room, to make sure she's actually going to sleep and not reading a book, I suddenly feel a sense of urgency about finding some answers.

As it happens, the answer to how we got here isn't hard to find: It's right on the cover of Peg's old college copy (vintage 1968) of Erik

Erikson's *Identity: Youth and Crisis*. Pictured on it is Michelangelo's statue of David: young, powerful, serene, heroic, and, most important, *male*. As a physician and a news correspondent who has devoted a lot of personal and air time to women's health, I suddenly feel that I'm in familiar territory: Medicine, after all, has only comparatively recently—the last twenty-five years or so—recognized "women's health" as an area of its own. Despite the obvious differences between male and female anatomy, when I went to medical school the body we studied as a model was male. We are still playing catch-up all these years later since there are many health issues pertaining to women that need and deserve study and research.

Michelangelo's David has all the cockiness of an adolescent male who is coming into his own; it's an odd word to use of a masterpiece but if you look at it carefully, he is *macho* in every sense of the word. The picture makes me think of those refrigerator magnets you can buy—the ones with the complete outfit to dress David in—and I mentally put a black leather jacket on him: instant rebellious adolescent, vintage 1965 or so. Today he'd have dyed his brown hair blond and he'd be wearing baggy pants, playing rap music; he would be an accomplished hacker. Now, in my imagination, I've got David on the soccer field or swatting a baseball. He is, without question, the captain of every team he's ever played on. He is, after all, a powerful archetype of maleness—solitary in his conquests, a slayer of fierce beasts and giants. And as William Pollack points out in his book *Real Boys*, part of the code of masculinity our society imposes on boys is that they must separate from their mothers, first when they go to school at around the age of six and then again as they approach manhood during adolescence.[11] From a cultural point of view, when boys individuate—to use the fancy psychological term for developing one's own identity—separating from mother is one of the first steps. The first step to becoming a man is getting rid of Mother's apron strings. (It's worth pointing out that *Real Boys* details precisely how destructive this assumption has been to boys in our society.)

The cultural stereotypes pertaining to girls in adolescence have their roots in psychological theory that was developed by looking at male models. If separation from Mom is necessary for development of the masculine self, then, too, separation from Mother must be necessary for girls as well. (Negative images of controlling mothers—reinforced in fiction and movies—probably contribute to the level of comfort we feel about this adolescent stereotype.) What's important to remember about cultural stereotypes is that they have an incredibly long shelf life; they persist in influencing how individuals in a culture see things long after scientific research has proved them spurious.

Close to twenty years ago, Carol Gilligan proposed, in her groundbreaking book *In a Different Voice*, that the psychology of girls and women was, in important respects, different from those of boys and men. Girls, she set forth, were relational thinkers and defined themselves not by separation but in the context of relationship.[12] The pressure on them to separate—following the male model of "cutting the apron strings"—put adolescent girls in a difficult, perhaps untenable, position:

> The pressure on boys to disassociate themselves from women early in childhood is analogous to the pressure girls feel to take themselves out of relationship with themselves and with women as they reach adolescence. For a girl to disconnect herself from women means to disassociate herself not only from her mother but also from herself . . . [13]

Amazingly, the implications of her work appear not to have made a dent on the popular vision of the necessary disassociation or alienation of girls from their mothers. But as Peggy Orenstein points out, the work of Gilligan and others did give rise to another popular stereotype and misconception: that women are born, by dint of their chromosomes, more "caring" than men.[14] Again, some cultural level of comfort or familiarity may have made this supposedly "feminist" stereotype stick: Think Marmee in *Little Women* and the Virgin Mary.

The mythology about girls needing to separate from Mother also survived the publication of Terri Apter's brilliant book, *Altered Loves*, a decade ago. In this well-written and nuanced book, which ought to be on the bookshelves of every mother in America, Apter elaborates on how we have to revise our notion of "separation" and "individuation" for girls, extrapolating from how relationship figures in female psychological development:

> The interesting story is how a girl develops within her family. Having, in general, less distinct self-boundaries than a boy, she negotiates her individuation differently. To emerge as a self, distinct from other family members (particularly her mother), she does not cut herself off from them. Her individuality matures with a constant reference to them.[15]

In addition, Apter points out that adolescent girls do not have relationships with "parents" but instead distinct relationships with their mothers and their fathers; what they seek from each parent yields not only a different dynamic but different behavior. Not surprisingly, working with mother-daughter pairs in England and the United States, Apter found that when the relationship between mother and daughter stayed close and relatively free of real discord, the mothers on both English-speaking sides of the ocean were quick to describe themselves as "lucky." Amazingly, as Apter points out, not even personal experience changed mothers' expectations that "an adolescent would be difficult, unruly, and surly."

Another researcher, Dr. Mary Eberly of Oakland University, had a similar experience, working on a study that examined how often adolescents helped their parents and how often they showed affection. The parents in the study developed a list of 121 behaviors that were helpful or considerate; they then reported on how many of those behaviors their children exhibited in the previous twenty-four-hour period. Parents frequently asked for copies of the checklist, Eberly notes, because they were surprised by the number of helpful behaviors; our cultural vision of adolescence as problematic had the parents geared to expect annoying or unhelpful behavior, not the positive attributes of adolescence behavior.[16]

Think for a moment about what you expect to happen to you and your daughter during the years of adolescence. After all, expectations govern a great deal of our adult behavior, and an analogy may help you understand how important a role both your and your daughter's expectations will play in your relationship. Imagine that your next-door neighbor is having work done on her house. You get home to find all manner of construction debris lying on your property, and several of your trees and bushes damaged. You (a) assume that she knows perfectly well that this junk is on your lawn and you storm over to her house, gunning for bear and ready to call your lawyer or (b) even though you are hugely annoyed, think it's likely the construction people left the mess and that the owner has every intention of removing the debris and compensating you for the careless damage done to your trees and bushes. While your expectations don't completely determine the outcome, they will affect both possibilities open to you and your neighbor in resolving the conflict and the tenor of your discussion. In the same way, both our styles of parenting and our expectations about adolescence will affect the dynamics of our relationships to our daughters.

Since all of us are, inevitably, influenced by cultural stereotypes, it's worth looking at some of the most common (mis)conceptions about girls in adolescence—in addition to the "necessary" separation of daughters from their mothers—and to see what science and research have to say about them:

### Adolescents have to learn to be autonomous.

This is a cultural message imparted to mothers and daughters alike: Just as I am told to stop going through my daughter's backpack the year she enters middle school, she is told that "it's time to be independent." But, as Dr. Joseph Allen of the Virginia Adolescence Research Group writes, autonomy is "not unfettered freedom for the adolescent nor emotional distance from the parent." The real problem is that, in our culture, "autonomy" is often confused with either "unfettered freedom" or "emotional distance" from both the parents' and child's point of view. Instead, Dr. Allen offers an important distinction for all mothers of adolescents: Children develop true "autonomy" by engaging in reasoned discussions with parents about areas of disagreements *as long as parents are ultimately in charge of behavioral outcomes.*[17] This means, as mothers, that we not only have to listen to our children openly but to pay attention to the reasoning and confidence level of their arguments and give them the freedom to express their differences of opinion without ceding our parental authority.

In fact, as Dr. Robin Tepper summarizes it, "Effective parenting has been shown to involve three components: 1) connection—establishing consistent, positive emotional bonds with children; 2) regulation—placing fair and consistent limits on adolescent behavior; and 3) support for psychological autonomy—allowing children to experience, value, and express their own thoughts and emotions.[18]

Adolescent "autonomy," then, cannot flourish on its own but only with the help of an involved parent or parents.

### Peer influences are nearly always bad.

Actually, research suggests that adolescents, like their adult counterparts, choose their friends on the basis of shared interests, and it is comparatively unusual for an adolescent who doesn't smoke or drink to choose a close friend who does. In the words of the National Academy of Sciences, "the popular notion of the reluctant teenager being pressured into trying a risky behavior by friends may be overly simplistic."[19]

While it *is* true that adolescents spend twice as much time with their peers as they do with parents or other adults, research has also shown that negative peer influence can be counterbalanced by parental involvement.

What can parents do? For one thing, we can work at debunking some of the myths pertaining to adolescent behavior, such as the notion that experimentation with drinking, smoking, illicit drugs, and sex is necessary or part of the adolescent rite of passage. The complexity of how cultural stereotypes actually influence behavior is demonstrated in a recent finding, reported by *The New York Times* (October 3, 2000). For years, in an effort to reduce drinking on college campuses, officials used "scare tactics"—images of wrecked cars and the like—to convince students of the dangers of binge drinking. But in fact, the campaign only served to reinforce the stereotype of drinking as a "necessary" and inevitable part of the college experience, which actually ended up encouraging students to drink "because everyone does." An entirely opposite tack—campaigns that focus on statistics that show that most students actually drink in moderation—has actually begun to show results for the first time in a decade. As one student quoted in the article put it, "I want to socialize but is everyone going to look at me if I don't drink? This helps you realize you don't have to stand there with a drink in your hand."[20] Similar peer myths, as studies have shown, also influence our daughters in adolescence; a recent longitudinal study conducted by Rick S. Zimmerman, Ph.D., and Katherine A. Atwood, M.Sc.D., showed that, along with excessive alcohol use, perceiving that many peers had sex was strongly associated with early initiation of sex.[21] The best way to deal with these peer myths is to separate fact from fiction.

On the other hand, the myths concerning peer influence also encourage us as mothers to overlook the important role of friendship in our daughters' lives, particularly same-sex friendship. Dr. Lisa Diamond, Assistant Professor of Psychology and Women's Studies at the University of Utah, points out that many of the alarmist presentations of peer influence are based on what we know happens when groups of boys are left without adult supervision. The pattern of girls' friendship differs in kind from that of boys; from elementary school forward, girls' friendships are formed in smaller groups, usually dyads or triads. ("You don't," she says wryly, "see bands of marauding girls in this or any other culture.") From the time they are seven or eight, girls tend to spend their time together talking, which means that, by early and middle adolescence, their friendships tend to be more socially nuanced than those of boys and reinforce normative social behavior. She is quick to point out this is not to say that all girls are, in her words, "sweetness and light," or that sometimes the female peer group doesn't reinforce negative behavior, but that, in general, girls' friendships provide great benefits, not the least of which is social support. Girls' friendships are different in kind from those of boys; for one thing, particularly during early and middle adolescence, girls' friendships have a physical component—girls cuddle, touch one another, braid one another's hair, and may, on a sleepover, share a sleeping bag or a bed—behaviors that carry no social stigma and that teach our girls the psychological benefits of physical intimacy. (These same behaviors are culturally unacceptable when they are associated with males.) The physical component of girls' friendships may be even more important because Americans tend to cuddle and touch their adolescent daughters less than they did when they were smaller children. Girls' friendships are a step toward learning how to have a mutual relationship—mutually supportive and confiding—and those lessons can, in Dr. Diamond's view, be extrapolated and transferred to other relationships later in life, including those with a partner or husband. Yet not only do we as a culture see peer influence as negative but, in Dr. Diamond's view, as parents, we tend not to honor the close relationships our daughters form. When a conflict arises between a commitment our daughter has made to a friend and family scheduling, parents tend, overall, to answer by saying the commitment to a friend is not "important."[22]

As mothers, we need to bring greater understanding to the importance of our daughter's friendships and the template they provide for healthy emotional connections later in life.

### "Raging" hormones explain adolescent behavior and turmoil.

The idea that adolescence is a time of turmoil (and an unpleasant time for unlucky parents) has been around since 1904, when G. Stanley Hall popularized it. For the last hundred years, "raging hormones" have been the popular explanation for just about anything an adolescent does. Recent research has shown, though, that biology is just one part of adolescent development, and scientific evidence does not support the idea that conflict between adolescents and their parents is either necessary or unavoidable.

And despite the culture's portrayal of adolescents as out of control and in trouble and adolescence as a time of storm and stress, roughly 80 percent of adolescents negotiate the transition between childhood and adulthood without experiencing any significant problems. Dr. Peter C. Scales, a development psychologist and senior researcher at Search Institute, remarks that the percentage holds true for adults and the negotiation of other stages of life; like their adolescent counterparts, roughly 20 percent of all adults will experience some mental health problems. He is quick to say that this does not mean that we should discount the 20 percent of adolescents who do have serious difficulties; if anything, the cultural mythology of adolescence inclines parents to be more accepting of behavior that really might signal a problem—such as misidentifying early signals of depression with the supposedly normal "mood swings" associated with the "normal" turmoil of adolescence, or ignoring the early signs of an eating disorder because "all teenage girls obsess about their bodies." The adolescent who is really in serious turmoil is not likely "to grow out of it." Then, too, our expectations about our daughters' being difficult or fractious may lead us as parents to focus on the negative, rather than the positive, aspects of their behavior, or to overreact to any responses that seem "rebellious" in nature.[23]

What the most recent scientific research *does* support is that, contrary to previously held beliefs, the adolescent brain is a work in progress and functions differently than the adult brain. Research conducted by Deborah Turgelun-Todd, Ph.D., using MRI imaging, showed that when young adolescents process emotion, the part of the brain that is most active is the amygdala—the area that guides instinctual, or "gut," reactions. In an adult, the part of the brain activated will be the frontal lobe—the area that governs reasoning. In later adolescence, the seat of activity will gradually shift from the amygdala to the frontal lobe.[24]

What this means for us as mothers is this: Even though the girl in front of us may look fully physically developed, she is still growing psychologically and learning how to think—in the most literal sense—as an adult. The continuing development of the adolescent brain—not "necessary separation" or "raging hormones" or "age-appropriate rebellion"—may well be the cause of the crossed signals and contradictory emotions that sometimes characterize the mother-daughter dialogue in the years of adolescence. In the pages that follow, we'll be looking at the implications of this and other research being done around the country, and see how what researchers have learned can help us all improve the mother-daughter dialogue.

### Adolescents take unreasonable risks because they think they are invulnerable.

This particular myth has been around for decades, familiar to most mothers from their own adolescence in the anecdotal version of why adolescent girls get pregnant ("She didn't think it would happen to her"). In fact, adolescents are no more inclined than adults to think themselves "invulnerable." Our culture's attitude toward adolescent risk-taking is oddly contradictory. On the one hand, as a society we assume that all adolescents will participate in at least some risky behavior and experimentation as part of proving that they are "adult" (putting risk-taking in the "normal" category). On the other, because the consequences of risk-taking (experimentation with drugs, alcohol, and sex) can be potentially disastrous, we tend to see all adolescent risk-taking as negative in nature and conceive of our parental role as either minimizing or completely cutting out risks entirely.

The facts belie the first common belief about risk-taking. According to the Urban Institute, overall risk-taking among high school students declined in the 1990s. In addition, most risks are taken by multiple-risk adolescents; that is, more than 85 percent of the adolescents who smoke take other risks as well.[25] This is not to say that, as mothers, we shouldn't be concerned about risks; it simply means we need to stop generalizing about them.

In addition, as mothers, we have to put the mythology in context by acknowledging that both learning to take risks *and* to assess them is a necessary preparation for adulthood. As adults, we take risks all the time—when we enter into a new relationship, start a new job, move our families, or even have a child. Every adult choice carries some element of risk. Yet as Dr. Peter C. Scales explains, even our educational system ignores the fact that risk-taking is part and parcel of learning how to regulate ourselves. Girls mature earlier than boys do, and, ironically, at the developmental point when girls need more opportunities to begin to act like adults—the higher grades of middle school and early high school—teachers and schools tend to exert more behavioral control, treating them less like adults. A parallel experience tends to happen in the home: As girls mature sexually, parents begin to worry and become even more strict in their supervision. (About this, Dr. Scales remarks, "girls tend to be over-supervised, boys get under-supervised.") But if our role as mothers is to guide our adolescent daughters into learning how to regulate themselves and assess risks, we must also permit our daughters to take on larger roles in decision-making as they mature. As Dr. Scales notes, this kind of parenting is not without risk—our daughters could make the wrong decision, after all—but necessary for their growth.[26]

In her book *The Romance of Risk: Why Teenagers Do the Things That They Do*, Dr. Lynn Ponton distinguishes between "healthy" risk-taking and "negative" risk-taking, and urges parents to acknowledge that "risk-taking is the major tool adolescents use to shape their identities."[27]

**What my daughter is going through isn't very different from what I experienced when I was an adolescent.**

Not so, says the research. Once again, we turned to Dr. Peter C. Scales of Search Institute who emphasized that, as parents, we do not generally appreciate the way in which the stresses our daughters face are markedly different from those of our own adolescence. He singles out girls because, while the expectations for boys have changed in the last thirty years, what is now expected of boys is more "reactive" than anything else (they are expected to empathize, see girls as their equals, and the like). What is now expected of girls is a challenging expansion of older cultural expectations. As opportunities for women have opened up, so, Dr. Scales argues, the pressure on girls has increased. In addition to the "old" cultural expectations—be pretty, sexually alluring, thin, nurturing, understanding, deferential, and the like—that accompanied puberty, girls are also expected to be strong, athletic, and high-achieving. As he puts it, the challenge is clear: "Now that you *can* do all of these things, why aren't you?"[28] The cultural vision of the "superwoman"—with all of its problems and contradictions—has filtered down to a new generation of girls with little or no modification.

Peggy Orenstein, author of *Schoolgirls: Young Women, Self-Esteem, and the Confidence Gap*, which was first published in 1994 and brought the issue of girls' declining self-esteem during the adolescent years to a wide audience, concurs. In answer to the question of whether girls today are under even more pressure than before, she replied that "I think the pressure on everyone has increased, but the pressure on girls—particularly that of the media—has increased exponentially. The dominant images of what girls should be are so much fiercer, so much more sexualized at a much younger age than ever before. The 'body as battleground' issues—the pressure to become sexually active, and sexual harassment—are so much more intense." She notes that chronic dieting as well as the onset of eating disorders occurs in increasingly younger girls: "Girls start seeing themselves as objects of desire, and worthy through being objects of desire, at younger and younger ages." All of this coexists with what she identifies as "girls' greater sense of entitlement, greater sense of opportunity, and their feeling that they can really do things in the world." Despite all the changes that have taken place in the last twenty-five years, Orenstein notes that "girls still struggle with that divide between the new messages and the traditional definitions of femininity." In the end, she says, "They wrestle with fear and anxiety, and it really comes home in the way that they look at their bodies." (Wryly, she comments that the contradictions can be summed up in a single sentence: "You don't have to be thin and beautiful but no one will love you if you aren't.") At the talks she gives all over the country, Orenstein is frequently asked why girls still struggle with self-censorship and self-doubt, when women have so many opportunities and have achieved so much. The problem, she says, is that the cultural messages about femininity are so deeply fixed that we as women, unwittingly perhaps, perpetuate these conflicts—as much as men or the "culture"—by passing them on to our daughters. She recounts a telling anecdote that she has often repeated in her lectures: She became aware, as she worked with and interviewed groups of young girls, that if she hadn't seen them for a time, she would often comment on their looks as a way of engaging them—complimenting their hair or their earrings, for example. So she consciously made the decision *not* to connect with them on the basis of looks: "How was the soccer game?" or "How are things going in English class?" took the place of "You look great." It was, Orenstein admits, hard and uncomfortable for her, and further proof that the culture's preoccupation with women's looks and attractiveness is buried deep in our psyches.[29]

~ ~ ~

Looking back, my husband and I question one of the choices we made with our eldest daughter. When she was just going into the teenage years, the very thing my child seemed to want turned out to be her cry for the very opposite. At the time, she seemed to want and need space—she said, "I want a phone, I want a television, I want to be in my room"—and we said, "Okay, we'll give you that." She didn't have a bunch of girls to run with and, frankly, at the time, I was just as happy that she didn't because some of the groups I saw forming at school were going to places I didn't want her to run—the makeout groups, the drinking groups, the sex groups with kids twelve and thirteen getting way ahead of where they ought to be. But that left Hannah in her room—watching TV, eating, being on the phone. She got her life experiences from watching the damn television.

We kept thinking it was a stage that would pass—"She'll only do this for a couple of months," we thought. So you leave your kid, thinking that you've actually given her something she's asked for— a chance at being adult, making her own choices, being in control of things herself. Then, in the last year, what we've heard is something totally different—"My brother gets all the attention and you don't pay any attention to me, you do things with him." What she really was saying was, "I really want you as parents in my life," even as she was shutting the door on us. Unlike my other two children, Hannah didn't have outside interests—sports or activities—so there weren't any participatory things we could do to get into her life. And she would get defensive when we tried to create something to do together. I worried about her self-esteem, and giving her what she wanted seemed, at the time, the right thing to do.

Connie, age fifty-two, mother of three adolescents, talking about her adoptive daughter, now sixteen

But, if some things—such as the emphasis on the older stereotypes of femininity—have stayed the same, the world our daughters confront has changed in important ways and we need, as mothers, to begin by acknowledging how these changes will present specific challenges for our girls. We must keep in mind that we have experienced many of the changes one by one, over time, as adults, and that some of the more seismic changes don't affect us in the same way that they do our daughters. Finally, it isn't just any one of these changes; it is their confluence. The older we are as mothers, the more we will find, on reflection, how much the world has changed since we were adolescents. The story that begins this section is not all that unusual; recent studies note that more and more of our adolescent children's activities tend to be "private," behind the closed doors of their bedrooms, away from the circle of the family. Technological advances have changed how our girls spend their time; they have also increased the number of outside influences on our daughters' lives.

**Technological advances**: The amazing growth of technology has subtle and not so subtle effects on our daughters. Their exposure to various kinds of media simply isn't comparable in any way to our experiences as adolescents or even young adults. (As a Kaiser Family Foundation report put it: "While one generation of Americans experienced a childhood in which they shared a single black and white three-channel TV with their parents, the next is growing up with a Walkman glued to their ears, 100 channels in the bedroom, and the World Wide Web of information at their fingertips."[30]) How our daughters spend their time is radically different from how we spent ours. Adolescents spend roughly thirty-eight hours a week—just slightly short of the adult working week—immersed in media, including listening to the radio, watching television, playing CDs and video games, going on the computer, and reading. Girls between the ages of twelve and fourteen spend roughly seventeen hours a week watching television (compared with a little over six hours on homework and a little under four hours reading for pleasure). Seventy-seven percent of sixth graders have televisions in their bedrooms, and 65 percent of all adolescents report that the television is on during dinner.[31] A study released in 2000 by UCLA reported that adolescents twelve to fifteen spent roughly five and a half hours a week on the Internet; by sixteen to eighteen, they were spending just under eight hours a week online.[32] (That, in case you missed it, is a full working day!)

We need, as mothers, to understand the different ways in which the Internet has opened up our daughters' worlds. On the one hand, without question, the Internet has opened up resources unimaginable even as recently as a decade ago: Our daughters can visit the Louvre in Paris without ever leaving home or check out the latest development at NASA with a single click of the mouse. On the other, there are the well-publicized dangers of bringing a world filled with strangers and, sometimes, predators into the confines of your own home.

The growth of the Internet has, in the last years, been exponential and if experts agree on anything, it is that it is too early really to know what long-term effect the Internet will have on our daughters. We turned to Dr. Ilene Berson of the University of South Florida, who has been studying girls and the Internet for the past five years, and asked her to comment. What she had to say was extremely valuable. "One of the things we've found is that being part of the cyberworld gives girls the opportunity to explore behaviors and attitudes that wouldn't necessarily be part of their everyday, 'real world' interactions. There is, though, a 'good news/bad news' aspect to this. On the one hand, because girls perceive themselves as safe—typically, the real-world environment surrounding them when they go online is at home or school—they are more likely to take more risks than they would otherwise. This makes them more vulnerable to online exploitation of every kind. Some girls, when they turn on the computer, don't see themselves making connections with real people around the world, but see the experience as a game which pemits them to explore different things about themselves. Some of these explorations are positive but others are negative in nature." Dr. Berson recounts how some girls use the medium to explore negative behaviors—such as exchanging verbal harassments or having sexually suggestive chats—which were not part of their real-world lives but could nonetheless affect them. ("Is it okay to be engaging in these online fantasies?" Dr. Berson asks. "How will they affect these girls' social and emotional development?")

On the Internet, you can be whomever you want to be—a lonely, pudgy girl can become a willowy blond cheerleader and no one will be any the wiser. In Dr. Berson's words, "It can be a wonderful, make-believe game where you can pretend to be older, smarter, more popular, tougher and more experienced than you actually are." This kind of role-playing can, in fact, put a girl at risk. On the other hand, on a more positive note, the Internet also suspends the more superficial values imposed on girls—the pressures to be thin, to be popular, to be pretty—and thus may allow some girls a place where their authentic voices can actually be heard. And, in Dr. Berson's view, many of the girls she has worked with and interviewed see it precisely that way.

According to Dr. Berson, the ways in which girls use the Internet and the possibilities it offers are directly correlated to parental involvement. In her view, the girls using communication on the Internet to "show who they really are, to be strong, without worrying about the superficial values which sometimes impact on their day-to-day interactions" almost universally have "ongoing and open communication with parents or significant adults in their lives who have been guiding forces in showing them how to make this into a positive medium." Conversely, the girls who are using the Internet in more negative ways are almost universally unsupervised, and tend to be the ones who are online for an extensive period of time, increasing the likelihood of negative interactions and risk-taking.[33]

The Internet may influence our daughters in more subtle ways, the full effect of which will only be apparent over time. How will the cyberworld influence the morals and character development of our adolescents? Will girls who feel it's okay to lie about who they are in cyberspace transfer those attitudes into real-world situations? How will the nature of communication on this new medium affect our children? The instant communication the Internet provides— the Instant Messages, the e-mails, even the e-mail language of adolescence (the shorthand for LOL, gtg, kewl, cya, and the like)— open up equal opportunities for communication and the loss of it. Quite literally, the ways in which our daughters are communicating with their friends and how they see the nature of friendship (particularly friendship on the Internet) are different in kind from the way we communicated as adolescents. Once again, Dr. Berson's comments are both wise and illuminating, as she reminds us that, on e-mail, the cues of tone, facial expression, and body language are missing. Discourse on the Internet is flattened out, without nuance.

Both how our daughters use the Internet and where our computers are located in our homes are issues we need, as mothers, to address.

**Sexualization of the culture**: While the television shows of our youth may seem, in retrospect, quaint and somewhat comical—did anyone believe those twin beds, separated by a night table, on every sitcom?—the amount of specifically sexual material our daughters are exposed to—on television, in the movies, in advertisements, you name it—is staggering, particularly when you consider how much time our daughters spend involved with various kinds of media. For example, a study in 1999 concluded that fifty-six percent of television programs include sexual content and that an average of 3.2 scenes per hour include sexual behavior.[34] (One study estimates that once the sexual content of advertising is factored in, the number probably goes up as high as ten sexual scenes an hour.) The American Psychological Association has estimated that through television alone, adolescents are exposed to 14,000 sexual references and innuendoes a year![35] Most, if not all, of the sexual images aren't balanced by any discussion of consequences or contraception or responsible and healthy sexual behavior, not to mention emotional readiness. (It's been noted that while television executives are reasonably comfortable with sexual references and situations, advertising contraceptives is considered a viewer turn-off.) And should we try to convince ourselves that none of this *really* matters, the statistics about adolescent sexual behavior say otherwise. Twenty-five percent of all fifteen-year-old girls have had sexual intercourse; by sixteen, thirty-nine percent have, and by seventeen, over half.[36] While there is no statistical evidence, it has been reported by both parents and health-care professionals that casual encounters involving oral sex among middle-school-age children—that is, children thirteen and younger—are on the rise. (And keep in mind that 8 percent of children age thirteen have already had intercourse.)

When we were adolescents, the terms "date rape" and "harassment" weren't part of American culture; they are part of our daughters' everyday vocabulary—along with HIV and STDs. Yet as Nathalie Bartle, Ed.D., notes in her book *Venus in Blue Jeans*, "the adolescent community at large displays a lack of knowledge about STDs."[37] Indeed, the profoundly upsetting truth is contained in statistics released by the Kaiser Family Foundation: one-quarter of all new cases of STDs occur in teens, while two-thirds of all new cases occur in people aged fifteen to twenty-four. By the age of twenty-four, one in three sexually active women and men will be infected.[38] It's worth noting that girls and women are biologically and socially more at risk since it is physically easier for a woman to become infected than a man. (According to the Alan Guttmacher Institute, in a single act of unprotected sex with an infected partner, a teenage girl has a 1 percent risk of acquiring HIV, a 30 percent risk of getting genital herpes, and a 50 percent chance of contacting gonorrhea.[39])

*A changed drug scene*: Research has shown that parents—particularly those of the Baby Boom generation—tend, based on their own adolescent and young adult experiences, to view marijuana as a relatively benign drug. But according to the American Academy of Pediatrics, because of selective inbreeding of the plants, marijuana is roughly five hundred times more potent now than the Baby Boomers remember it.[40] Although the use of illegal drugs has, according to national surveys, leveled off slightly, it remains a problem.

Many of the myths and misconceptions about adolescent girls actively prevent us from seeing our daughters whole; they also tend to gloss over the degree to which adolescence is a process, stretched over years. In the human life cycle, the rate of growth and change experienced by our daughters during adolescence is second only to that of infancy. The changes are physiological, psychological, behavioral, cognitive, and social. New and ongoing research at the National Institute of Mental Health, using the latest brain-imaging techniques, has shown that the brain is still undergoing significant development during the adolescent years.[41] And while we can generalize about some of these changes, no two adolescent girls experience them in precisely the same way or at the same time or with the same personalities or coping mechanisms.

We need to use what researchers do know about adolescence to inform the relationship we will have with our daughters during this decade of our shared lives. And we need, as mothers, to work on shedding the unproductive myths about motherhood, adolescence, and "letting go" so that we can do a better job of shepherding our children from one stage of their lives to another.

~ ~ ~

In the last weeks, coinciding with her entry into seventh grade, I see a marked change in my daughter. It isn't that she is constantly fractious—although, at moments, she can be—or that she is determined to fight with me. It's something more subtle, a different kind of behavior; she's engaging me in a new way. A year ago, she would have asked my advice on how to do something or handle a situation—and she would have done pretty much what I suggested, whether it was homework or smoothing out a problem with a friend. She's still asks me for advice but, once it's given, she goes to great lengths to let me know it's "only an opinion, after all." The child in her still sees me as the All-Knowing, Ever-Resourceful Mother; the adolescent part of her is intent on trying her own competence on for size. But at this moment in her life—just a few months away from thirteen—the only way she sees to measure herself is to take a measure of me first, by challenging me. It's a more vocal version of how she used to put her hand up against mine to see how "big" she was.

Peg, my coauthor and mother of Alexandra, age twelve-and-a-half

In her book *Altered Loves*, Terri Apter argues persuasively that, during the adolescent years, contrary to popular wisdom, daughters do not abandon their relationships to their mothers but transform them instead. In Apter's view, girls only choose "separation" from parents—particularly mothers—when they have failed to find a way of "making this relationship flexible, only if they are unable to find any validation of their changing self, only if the once nurturing love turns to strict confinement." Put in other terms, girls separate from their mothers only when the relationship has already failed to meet their emotional and psychological needs.

Apter draws a useful distinction between "individuation" and separation: "Being an individual distinct from one's parents does not imply the absence of a strong and binding relationship to them." She goes further to counter the idea of necessary separation, as Erik Erikson proposed it, by detailing how the continued connection and relationship to her parents, most particularly her mother, is necessary for the adolescent's growth as an individual. Most importantly, she outlines how wresting her mother's recognition and validation of this new self is sometimes neither straightforward nor direct:

> The adolescent needs a relationship with parents to achieve individuality. It is through this relationship that the adolescent can hope to get validation for a concept of self. In particular, the girl turns to her mother for self-confirmation. She fights with her mother to gain validation. She expends much energy, she plots silently and consciously, to wrest from her mother the recognition she needs. She is prepared to shock her mother into submission. She will behave outrageously to get a sharp response—no matter that the response is a protest. She will goad her mother into taking a newly appreciative look at her. She will try to destroy her mother's previous images of her and to impress her with a new adult self.[42]

Contrary to popular wisdom, the problem is not that we want our daughters to stay the same or, even, not to grow up—although certainly we may feel some ambivalence, even anxiety, about our children's ability to negotiate the shoals ahead. Whatever tension exists between mother and daughter, paradoxically enough, is based on intimacy and connection—not separation or abandonment. And these confrontations, when they occur, are painful to us precisely because of our intimate ties. As parents, it is up to us to understand the dynamic and make sure that we can begin to manage navigating the waters.

We've called it the "I-Thou" of parenting.

~ ~ ~

> I think many adolescents choose rebellion as a form of individuation. I believe that if teens are listened to—deeply listened to—and treated with respect and if they are afforded a great deal of both choice and accordant responsibility and if parents don't bail them out or decide how they should be acting, they are much less likely to rebel. If they are safe at home and in school, respected by adults and allowed appropriate levels of freedom and given appropriate boundaries, I think most kids can individuate without severe conflict.
>
> Patti, forty-two, mother of two adolescent girls

A few months ago, a close friend called me, enormously and understandably upset. Awakened in the middle of the night by the muted sound of voices—her husband was away on a business trip and she was sleeping fitfully—she stumbled into the darkened hallway outside of her bedroom, trying to get her bearings. Was there a television on somewhere in the house? Still groggy, her first thought was that her daughter must have fallen asleep while watching. Then, as she neared her daughter's door, she could hear her child's voice and, in the stillness of the house, with the door ajar, she could overhear every word. She stopped dead in her tracks, listening as her sixteen-year-old, talking on the phone, described having sexual intercourse for the first time. Stunned, she stood there, deciding what to do. Should she march right in and confront her?

Should she wait until her daughter "confessed"? What was the "right" way of dealing with this?

The next morning, at breakfast, in as calm a voice as she could manage, she told her daughter what she'd heard, emphasizing that she'd overheard the conversation by accident. Trying hard not to recriminate, she expressed her unease and worry about her daughter's actions. She didn't ask her daughter any particulars but only if she'd been careful—was it "safe" sex? Her daughter responded by saying, "I'm not stupid, Mom"—but went on to tell her mother more of why and how it had happened.

In the months since, the dialogue between them has begun to bear fruit. Her daughter has begun to see how dangerous and precipitous her actions were; in context, my friend has come to understand that her daughter needs even more love and attention than she was getting before. Had my friend acted differently—impulsively, punitively, invasively, or in any way that severed the connection between them—the outcome would have been very different. There is still much to work on between them, but with the lines of communication open, there are lessons to be learned on the parts of mother and daughter alike.

Relationship is at the heart of "I-Thou" parenting.

We've borrowed the term "I-Thou" from the theologian and philosopher Martin Buber not only because his insights into the human spirit are so important but also because the emotional and psychological engagement of mother and daughter during the years of adolescence is all about the process of relation. We use the word "process" deliberately because, first and foremost, we need to acknowledge that our relationships to our daughters during these years will, with effort and commitment, evolve on a continual basis. For this evolution to take place, how we see and listen to our children will also, of necessity, have to change. In his work *I and Thou*, Buber distinguishes between the two ways human beings have of relating to the world around them. Both kinds of relationships have a role to play in human life and each has a legitimacy of its own, but they yield very different results. The first of these he characterizes as "I-It" (or I-She, I-He), which has to do with the world of experience. In these relationships—to people, things, and even ideas—the "I" remains detached from the "It" or "She." In these connections, the "I" remains analytical, experiencing the other person, even knowing the other person, but never being changed by what Buber calls "the encounter" with that other person. The model for the "I-She" relationship is one of control, of distance, and without mutuality; the mother-daughter dialogue in an "I-She" relationship is likely to be one-sided. In parenting, this type of relationship would be characterized by arbitrariness, rules without meaning, or seeing our daughters as either extensions of ourselves or, in the alternative, as completely separate from us. We are likely to fall into this pattern of relating when we see adolescence as a problem to be dealt with, a period to be "gotten through," or when we confuse "autonomy" with lack of attention.

The "I-Thou" relationship, on the other hand, is dyadic in nature. In the "I-Thou" relationship, we allow ourselves to be changed by the encounter with the "Thou"—the "I" isn't closed off or circumscribed. In the "I-Thou" relationship, we actually see the other person for who they are—not as we wish to perceive them.[43] In the dyadic relationship, we allow the interaction with our daughters to redefine our motherhood and permit ourselves to take on new and more aware roles. It is, by its very nature, a relationship that requires us to acknowledge false steps and mistakes, as well as personal limitations and shortcomings. In the "I-Thou" model, we let our intimate knowledge of the changes our daughters are experiencing inform and shape our behavior as mothers. We give ourselves the freedom to change and experience, as they change and experience.

Simply put, the "I-Thou" of parenting marks a conscious transformation of our relationship to our daughters. While our connection to our daughters remains grounded in the shared history of their babyhood and childhood—the roles we have played as guardians, caretakers, protectors, and teachers—the new "I-Thou" relationship is rooted in the present, and explores new ways of communicating. "I-Thou" parenting requires that we become articulate about the decisions we make for our daughters, and requires that we come to terms with our own histories so that they don't get in the way of seeing our daughters helpfully and clearly. As our daughters grow and mature and begin to try out new ways of thinking about and connecting to the world around them, we need to learn to listen, rather than preach. And although we may find it difficult to relinquish the older patterns of mothering, we must grant our daughters the right to disagree with us or argue with us and, when appropriate, allow ourselves to be swayed by their reasoning. At times, we will find that this new relationship—which is different in some important respects from the one we had with our daughters when they were younger—is hard for us to master.

Leaving ourselves open to learning new lessons about parenting is part of the challenge.

We all dream of great and wonderful things happening for our children, from the moment we first hold them. Sometimes it is hard to accept the ways in which our daughters' dreams differ from our own, or how their goals diverge from those we have envisioned for them. Sometimes, our own strengths and weaknesses get in the way of seeing precisely what our daughters need, and when. One of the goals of "I-Thou" parenting is to help us see our daughters not as extensions of ourselves but as individuals in their own right.

Kate surprised both her father and me this last year with how well she did in math. It wasn't always easy for her but she plugged away and, in the end, the B-pluses she earned in math and science made her doctor-mother proud. Just before school started this year, Kate rather innocently asked me if I had heard anything from school about her math class; in fact, I had. I'd gotten a note saying she'd been promoted into eighth grade algebra. To tell the truth, I didn't grasp the significance of the note but it turned out that Kate, along with a small group of students, had tested into upper-level math. I was thrilled, but imagine what I thought when I congratulated her and she responded by asking me to get her out of it! (Get her out? Was she kidding?) She argued that it would be too much work since half the textbook had to be done by Christmas. I have to admit that my response was less than sympathetic, and I was adamant that she take the class.

During the weeks that followed, Kate didn't miss a single opportunity to implore me to call the school and get her out of algebra. She had any number of reasons—it'd be too much pressure and "everyone" told her that if she'd gotten a B+ in regular math last year, she'd likely as not only get a C– in this. I looked her squarely in the eye and had two words for her: "Nice try!" I was pretty sure something else was going on; since Kate already thought of herself as an outsider, I thought she was afraid that being good at math—which she perceived as being uncool for a girl—would push her even farther to the social periphery. I enlisted my friend Esther—a brilliant scholar whom Kate admires enormously—to talk to her. Esther listened to Kate patiently and then said, "Kate, the world is full of underachievers. Why would you want to be one of them?" That seemed to do it, and Kate went into the advanced math class.

Fast-forward two months into the school year: Kate's math turned out to be overwhelming. She struggled with memorizing, retaining facts, and being able to juggle time and prioritize the work that needed doing—things that, somehow, have always come easily to me. But this wasn't about me and my abilities—it was about her—and her other subjects, especially writing and literature, which are important to her, needed her attention too. So we reconstructed her schedule and took her back to the math that the rest of her class was taking. All the adults in her life, especially her mother, thought the advanced math was a terrific idea; Kate, on the other hand, knew from the beginning that this would be more than she could or wanted to handle. For her, going back to basic math has another advantage; since fitting in is important to her, it has meant that she can be part of the larger group. In retrospect, it's now clear to me that there are plenty of pressures in the years ahead, and that she'll take those challenges on when and if she's ready. Once again, understanding how the demands of motherhood change during these years is important. When Kate was younger, I grew used to taking charge when Kate needed guidance, to stepping in and deciding for her; at this stage in her life, as she begins to take on more responsibility and define her own interests and goals, I need both to guide *and* to listen. And to make sure, along the way, that the girl in the mirror isn't my reflection but hers.

We all learn from experience and, as parents, we tend to extrapolate from our own experiences and examples. As our children individuate, the ways in which they are different from us may perplex us, annoy us, or simply confound us. We may find it hard to understand their lack of passion for an activity or a subject that has been enormously valuable or important to us or, conversely, they may engage in activities we can hardly begin to fathom. During the years of adolescence, we may find that the ways in which our daughters are different from us require us, as mothers, to grow and change more than we are willing or even able. Sometimes, the challenges our children's differences present to us prove to be valuable lessons.

Rachel, a psychologist and the author of a number of books, is a scientist by training and a voracious and passionate reader, whose vision of "intelligence" was the kind readily tested and measured by college boards. Her daughter, Ashley, is now nineteen and studying music in conservatory. During her adolescence, Ashley shared none of her mother's interest in science but it became clear that she had prodigious musical talents. Her mother, by her own admission, has none. The differences in their abilities made the journey of motherhood difficult and revelatory by turns, and required her mother to learn new lessons. As she tells it, "For me, the greatest challenge in mothering an adolescent daughter has been the whole process of letting go, of allowing her to be whoever she's going to be. It meant separating my hopes for her and her hopes for herself and, at various points, it was a hard experience for me. I'd been a math major in college and when my daughter was placed, at the age of twelve, in the fastest math class in her private prep school—by the time the kids graduate they have finished calculus—I was thrilled." Rachel went on to recount how, at the very first parent's conference, the teacher's first words were, "Your daughter doesn't belong in the class." Rachel's response was completely different from her daughter's: "I was devastated, absolutely devastated. The teacher decided not to move her but to carry her and, while it was hard for my daughter to be the slowest in the class, she just didn't care about math in the long run. It was much harder for me—every year she dropped down a class. By the end of her sophomore year, it was finally clear to me that her talents lay elsewhere and I went to the head of the department and asked that she be put in an easier class. He remarked that, in thirty years of teaching, he'd never had a parent ask for an easier class." Rachel had to put aside everything she knew about the importance of math and science—"every study ever done tells you you are supposed to encourage them in math and science." Instead, she had to change how she saw things: "The change I made was to respect the direction she was going in, to trust her judgment, and to be her ally. She was the first kid in her class to drop math, the first to drop science. But Ashley has extraordinary talents in music, and she has found her own path. It may not be the path I would have chosen for her, but it is her path. There were points along the way where she would make her own decision, and I would say, "I don't agree with that but I will go along with it and I'll support you 100 percent in it."

Supporting her daughter resulted in growth for each of them. On reflection, Rachel adds, "The world she chose for herself was so different from my own that I learned over time to trust her judgment because she knew better than I did what was right for her. Mothering required that I set aside my own expectations to really see her. Even when I wasn't able to do that completely, I was at least able to trust her judgment. In ninth grade, she began private lessons, and I stayed pretty much out of the loop. Then, one day, I got there early and ended up chatting with her teacher who said 'she could go to college for voice.' I didn't really understand it—I had the liberal arts in mind—but she wanted to go to a conservatory, and she was right. She is perfectly suited for it."

As both of these stories—mine and Rachel's—demonstrate, what makes mothering an adolescent difficult is twofold. On the one hand, sometimes we need to set aside those solutions and answers that have worked for us in the past because they aren't the right solutions for our daughters. On the other, it's also true that, sometimes, we have to put aside the "textbook answers"—and yes, it is true that every study supports the tremendous boost proficiency in math and science, traditional male subjects, give a girl's self-esteem—for answers that address our individual children's specific needs more directly.

There's no question that, sometimes, the task seems daunting, requiring the wisdom of a Solomon and the stamina of a marathon runner. In the pages ahead, drawing on the research of experts and the experiences of other women, we will come to see that, in those moments of crisis, there is tremendous opportunity for us to help a stronger, healthier, and more empowered generation of women come of age.

## CHAPTER THREE

# The Nature of the Journey

I was weight-obsessed from a very young age and, by high school, I weighed myself every day. By then, I was surrounded by weight consciousness—I knew girls who literally took snake venom antidote to make themselves vomit. This was in the late 1960s and bulimia didn't have a name then, but I knew girls who were clearly bulimic, as well as girls who indulged in binge eating and then took speed to suppress their appetites. Think of the models of the day—Twiggy was on the cover of every magazine. If anything, I think things are worse now: women don't just have to be thin—they have to be thin, buff, *and* busty.

I've made a conscious effort not to talk about how I think I'm fat in front of my daughter; I think all the focus on looks is detrimental to healthy habits. For one thing, I didn't want her to develop the sense that overweight people are somehow less valuable and less worthy than thin people. I've tried hard not to reinforce negative eating behaviors—I consciously don't use food as a reward or withhold treats because she hasn't "cleaned her plate." Even though I try not to discuss it, negative comments inevitably slip out, or she'll overhear a conversation I'm having with a friend about weight.

I went on my first diet when I was my daughter's age—by limiting myself to a single serving of everything. Now, when I look at my childhood pictures, I can't find the fat child I was once convinced I was. Even so, it feels as though I've always been on a perpetual, if unsuccessful, diet.

Leslie, age forty-eight, writer and mother to Lily, age nine

EVEN THOUGH NOTHING terrible happened to me in my adolescence, I didn't emerge from it entirely unscathed either. I was a good student and, up until tenth grade, thought I was pretty. But the joke I've told many, many times in the intervening thirty years—that I peaked in ninth grade and that things went downhill from there—reflects more than a little bit of truth.

At fifteen, I was sitting on the top of the world—I was popular in my junior high school and had a boyfriend I was crazy about. He was a football star, an "A" student, and gorgeous. We made a cute couple, and we—and everyone else—knew it. In that relatively uncomplicated time and place (I lived in Fort Wayne, Indiana), the relationship was comfortable and unpressured (think making out to popular music), and I felt loved and admired. We went off to different high schools and then, between my freshman and sophomore years, I gained some weight. Looking back now, it was probably nothing more than normal adolescent fleshiness but what happened as a result is a story familiar to many girls and women in America.

Fort Wayne isn't that large a place, and my ex-boyfriend and I ran into each other from time to time. The Beach Boys' songs were on the radio, and images of California girls—thin blondes wearing blue eye shadow and tiny bikinis—were everywhere. They were national treasures and, whatever else I was, I wasn't one of them. One day, when our paths crossed, my ex-boyfriend wasn't alone and his companion was everything I wasn't—leggy, blond, and from California. (I still remember the pale green eye shadow she was wearing, if you can believe it.) I remember feeling that being smart wasn't all that important.

Then, at the beginning of my sophomore year, I got a letter from him telling me how worried he was about me. I still remember what he wrote me, even though I lost or threw out the letter many years ago: How it would be a pity if I let myself get heavy because I had such a pretty face and how great it would be if I managed to lose a few, much-needed pounds. I was devastated by his comments, and spent the rest of high school feeling terribly insecure about my body and my looks.

What makes girls so easily vulnerable to criticism about their looks? In my case, that letter confirmed something I had already noticed: that I wasn't courted or accepted by any of the "A" groups I longed to be part of—the girls who were cheerleaders or ended up as homecoming queen or part of her court. For me, the transition from my smaller junior high to a larger high school where the cooler kids lived in a different part of town dealt a terrific blow to my sense of self, and that dumb letter became a part of something larger. I was a round-faced girl, largely invisible to the boys who crowded the hallways, and that sense of invisibility marked me for years to come.

I write this in my home office, and on the wall behind me are photographs that symbolize some of the great opportunities my life has afforded me. There is a picture of me with Joan Lunden, Charlie Gibson, and Barbara Walters; another of Diane Sawyer and me; yet another with former president Bill Clinton, a friend from the time I lived in Arkansas. On the right, there is a picture of me in the operating room. In the middle of all these photographs—evidence of a full life—is the framed cross-stitch my college roommate made me my first year in college. The sentiment it expresses is one most women will ruefully acknowledge they've had at one point or another in their lifetimes: It reads, "I know I'm efficient. Tell me I'm beautiful."

Isn't that the sorry truth?

~ ~ ~

What He Says . . . What He Means!
I'll call you tomorrow! . . . Be lucky if I ever call again!
I just wanna be friends . . . This is the best excuse I could
   think of not to go out with you.
Let's go back to my place . . . Let's get it on!
I like those pants! . . . I wonder how fast I can get them off
   of you!
You look a lot better this year! . . . Last year you were a dog!
Yeah, you look cute, I guess . . . You are butt ugly!
I like your shirt a lot . . . but I like what's under it more!

Text of an e-mail forwarded from Nancy's daughter, Rachel (age twelve), to Peg's daughter (then twelve and a half) and, judging from the e-mail addresses on it, forwarded to more than 150 girls in the Pacific, Central, and Eastern time zones in a two-hour period in November 2000

The memory of those years and how I felt about myself makes me wary as a mother; I worry about the lessons from the outside world Kate and Rachel will internalize and incorporate into their senses of self. I worry particularly because life seems so sped up for girls now—just look at the e-mail on the previous page, which was sent to mainly twelve- and thirteen-year-old girls and passes for a cross between humor and popular wisdom! I think of the sock hops, held in the gym on Friday afternoons, when I was their age and compare the sixth-through-eighth-grade dances in my daughters' public school. They start at 8:00 p.m. and end at 10:00, way too late for my taste. Social acceptance, now as then—but even earlier now—is a large part of adolescent life. A part of me would like to keep my daughters out of this loop entirely but I've felt that forbidding them to attend these dances will only serve to make them that much more important.

Last year, in seventh grade, Kate went to every school dance. I would stand at the door after I dropped her off and would watch as she circled the dance floor, looking for a friendly face. The first time I stood there, the pain on my face must have been obvious because one of the teachers came up to me and said, "It's okay. I'll keep an eye on her." But it wasn't really okay; no boys ever asked her to dance and the fact that many of the girls danced in groups didn't console her one bit. Neither could I. More upsetting, perhaps to me, was the evening when a boy from another school did ask her to dance, and when I came to pick her up, she was walking on air. When I tucked her in bed that night, she told me this was the best day of her whole life. It bothered me that validation came so easily and it all hung on whether a boy paid attention to her or not.

It doesn't escape me that, despite the incredible dialogue that has gone on in America for the last twenty years about womanhood, girls, and self-esteem, none of it seems to have changed the experience of adolescence.

The effect on her became clear: This year, Kate refused to go to any of the dances, saying that it was no fun at all to be left out. As a mother, I can hardly think that any of this was a worthwhile rite of passage—what did it teach her? Or her classmates? Is this really how a thirteen-year-old should be "having fun"? For Kate, the experience simply reinforced her vision of herself as an outsider—without any positive focus on how her differences make her interesting or valuable.

On the other hand, my younger daughter, Rachel, found confirmation of what she believes to be true about herself in going to the same dances this year. She could hardly wait for the first school dance and, while her older sister settled in with a bowl of popcorn and a movie at home, Rachel was busy putting on way too much eye shadow and putting her hair up in a marabou scrunchy. (For the record, I made her take off most of the makeup and, in return, she noted that I was, in her words, "a very mean mother.") When we got to school, she shot out of the car even before I had a chance to put it into park, and disappeared into a thundering herd of kids.

When I went to pick her up, I found my youngest daughter in the middle of the dance floor, slow-dancing with a boy who was at least six inches shorter than she. Her hands were on his shoulders and his on her waist. The lights were turned down low and I watched them rock back and forth in each other's arms. It looked innocent enough but it still struck me as a loss of innocence on any number of levels—my daughter is only just twelve, after all. But it was more than that: She was one of the cool kids and she knew it. I wish I could tell you that it made me happy.

Sitting alone in the kitchen, after the girls are in bed, I realize that what bothers me is not that my daughters want to be admired and liked by boys or, for that matter, by girls—to be popular, in short. It's simply that if I have learned anything thus far, it is that a sense of self-worth isn't bestowed on you by anyone else. Our daughters have to learn that the shortcut so many women take in their lives—as I did—of handing over the responsibility for defining the self to someone else never, ever works.

It's up to us, their mothers, women who know better, to help them find another way.

~ ~ ~

By the time I was fourteen, I was in ninth grade and incredibly lonely and insecure: My relationship with my mother had become impossible and, while I wasn't entirely without friends, real popularity eluded me. Then I fell head over heels in love with a boy who was three years older, and a senior. At seventeen, he was much more sexually experienced—I hadn't progressed beyond close-dancing and kissing in a darkened movie theater—and it didn't take long before I was in way over my head. Although the fear of pregnancy stopped me from sleeping with him, I simply wasn't emotionally ready for everything else I *was* doing. Looking back, it's hard to believe that my parents let it go on, or that they didn't object to the fact that he was so much older. For whatever reason, they simply weren't minding the store.

Of course, while the intensity of the relationship made me feel less lonely on one level, it made me lonelier on others. I couldn't tell anyone what I was doing with him—I knew, after all, that it wasn't appropriate—and I was also terrified that someone would find out. "Nice" girls didn't do this stuff. I was also scared of not being able to stop myself from moving on to the next step. I was still a child, involved in an adult situation with all the attendant emotions, and it took me years to undo the damage the relationship caused.

Now, with a daughter who is thirteen, I feel strongly that it's up to me to make sure that nothing like this happens to her—that she never finds herself in a situation for which she is, in every way except perhaps the physical, unready and unprepared. I plan on talking to her about everything and anything and, hopefully, she will listen.

Peg, fifty-one, my coauthor and mother of Alexandra

As I write this, yet another study on how adults and adolescents communicate has been released and, once again, the study emphasizes how the media perpetuate negative images of adolescence, reinforcing the idea of adolescents as "a tribe apart" that wants little to do with adults. We need to understand precisely what the journey that is adolescence entails—in physical, emotional, and psychological terms—so that we can best help our daughters cross the bridge between childhood and womanhood and, finally, into adulthood. First, we need to distinguish between "puberty" and "adolescence," which are vastly different, though connected.

Traditionally, the boundary between childhood and adolescence has been marked by the physical changes that accompany puberty. Sit in a parked car across from any middle school in America and, in seconds, it will become apparent that the age of puberty and rate of physical development vary enormously from girl to girl. In any group, there will be a thirteen-year-old who still looks like a slightly taller version of her fourth-grade self; a thirteen-year-old who looks more like a sixteen-year-old with a woman's body; and a thirteen-year-old who finds herself somewhere in between, with budding breasts and newly rounded hips and belly. "Puberty" refers to the biological process that ends with a female (or male) who is, from the physical point of view at least, fully sexually mature and capable of reproduction. As a process, puberty can begin as early as eight or as late as thirteen, and can take place over a period as short as eighteen months or as long as five years.[1] These are, when you think about it, enormous variations—in which nutrition, heredity and genetics, and perhaps environment play a part.

Puberty is a process that takes place in predictable stages, called Tanner stages, after the physician James M. Tanner, who identified them. While the timing of these stages, as we've noted, varies enormously from girl to girl, it's nonetheless useful for all of us as mothers to familiarize ourselves with the characteristics of each stage, particularly because our girls are concerned with them and their timing. (Remember: Do not use these as an absolute scale and, if you have any questions about your daughter's development, consult your doctor or health-care provider.) The Tanner stages measure a girl's sexual maturity in terms of the separate development of the breasts and pubic hair. Breast development is measured in terms of contour (not size)—the shape of the breast, areola (the ring around the nipple), and the nipple itself. Following are the five Tanner stages of breast development:

1. Prepubertal: no signs of breast development
2. Early breast budding
3. Elevation of the areola and breast, "moundlike"
4. Projection of nipple and areola above breast mound
5. Adult breast—only the nipple projects

Separately, sexual maturity is also rated according to development and growth of pubic hair; again, the Tanner scale has five distinct stages:

1. Prepubertal: no pubic hair
2. Growth of a few (curled or straight) hairs, usually over labia
3. Pubic hair appears darker, coarser, and curlier
4. Pubic hair extends above labia—may be abundant
5. Adult stage: pubic hair extends to thigh

In addition to these changes, during puberty girls will experience a growth spurt and, at some point in the process, the onset of menstruation (menarche). Once again, while the average *age* at menarche in the United States is 12.8 years, the average *range* of ages is between 10.8 years and 14.6 years.[2]

Talking to our girls about the anticipated changes in their bodies long before they take place is extremely important. We will say this over and over in the course of these pages; do not delegate the responsibility for having these talks to your daughter's teachers. Generally, the average age for the onset of puberty has dropped four years—from seventeen to thirteen—in the last hundred years.

But additionally, one in seven Caucasian girls goes into puberty at the age of eight; among African-Americans, nearly one out of every two.[3] The phenomenon of "early" puberty—first reported in 1997 by Dr. Marcia Herman-Giddens—and the subsequent debate over its causes and whether or not it should be considered within "normal" guidelines—has further complicated the experience of puberty for individual girls and for our society in general.[4] While a number of possible factors for early puberty have been discussed and debated in the scientific community—the rising incidence of obesity in America, the overall better nutrition available to Americans and their children, the use of hormones in the raising of food animals such as cattle and pigs, among them[5]—more disturbing to psychologists is how early puberty affects girls.

When puberty takes place and how long a period of time a girl's physical development occupies affects not only the child and her sense of self but also the relationships she has to peers and family alike. The physical changes of puberty alter not only how a girl perceives herself but, equally important, how others—parents, peers, teachers—perceive her. A fourth-grader who finds herself the only pubescent among her peer group—the only one with a period, the only one wearing a bra, the only one with curves—will think of herself as not belonging and, likely as not, will end up with not only the unwelcome attention of older boys but some amount of peer-group exclusion. Among other girls who are clearly still children—at a time when conformity is prized—she will feel singled out. She is also likely to feel as though she has been pushed out of childhood, unready and unwilling, by forces beyond her control. While her looks—the degree to which she is perceived as attractive by the standards of our culture—may affect her self-esteem and her "status" among her peers, the evidence of her physical "maturity" may also affect how the adults in her world treat and judge her. Adults, on the other hand, may well mistake the external signs of being "mature" with an emotional and psychological maturity she is not yet capable of. Conversely, given how our society focuses on the rush to grow up with all of its perceived benefits (independence, decision-making, dating among them), a fifteen- or sixteen-year-old still in the early stages of puberty—still premenarche, with only the beginning of breast development—is equally likely to feel that her biology has made her unnecessarily—and cruelly—different from her peers. Adults may also treat her as somehow less mature, less capable, than her more physically developed peers. In the scheme of things, both the early and the late bloomers are at a distinct disadvantage; importantly, studies over the last decade have noted that girls who undergo early puberty are at high risk as well.[6] We turned to Dr. Annie Rogers of the Harvard Graduate School of Education for advice about the psychological consequences of "early" puberty and her answer was both telling and illuminating:

> Girls at ages nine, ten, and eleven often can't think as complexly as adolescents can. Today, girls are generally so much younger when their bodies start to change, and it is easy for adults seeing a child who looks fifteen or sixteen at age twelve to think that girls this age are adolescents and capable of making the kinds of decisions we expect teenagers to make—but this is not the case. Even if they are mature physically, preteens and young teenagers are really still children in many respects—still in need of close primary attachments and guidance, still in need of someone who knows what is going on. Adolescents can be expected to make more mutual and independent decisions, in part because they can think through the consequences much more carefully. The quality of relationships with parents and knowing what is going on in a girl's daily life is important whether girls mature earlier or later, but when girls mature early, it is especially vital to remember that psychologically they may not have caught up.

How long the process of puberty takes—in conjunction with what chronological age it begins—will also be a factor affecting how our daughters feel about themselves and what is happening to them.

Puberty signals the birth of the sexual self and, in a culture that sends girls so many contradictory messages about sexuality and the female body, it is not surprising that the physical changes that accompany puberty are a watershed moment for most girls, regardless of the age at which they take place. Many separate studies have shown that preoccupation with body image—with thinness, in particular, and with dieting as a solution to unwanted weight—is a psychological component for girls as young as the age of five.[7] (Please keep in mind that we are talking about girls in kindergarten here.) Our culture's preoccupation with the body—the female body, in particular—is so pervasive that many different factors can trigger a young girl's unhealthy response to her own body; chief among them are her mother's own preoccupation with dieting, teasing or other forms of social victimization, the child's perception that thinness is important to either or both parents, and the desire to emulate same-sex media figures.[8]

These messages take on new meaning and importance when, during puberty, our daughters' bodies actually begin to change from the familiar childish contours and become, as our culture has it, "feminine" in nature. At this moment, the cultural stereotypes of female "beauty"—even if not yet directly tied to an individual girl's growing understanding of her sexual self or involvement in a sexual context—become the matrix by which our girls judge themselves when they look in the mirror. The real problem is that our culture has no definition of femininity or, for that matter, the female sexual self except in the context of the "opposite" sex. During the years of adolescence, the postpubescent girl's sexual self is realized solely in relation to her attractiveness to boys and, parenthetically, in other girls' appreciation of that attractiveness—whether or not she is a soccer star or a champion swimmer or rider. In our culture, the "sexual self" has a very narrow definition. It's hard to believe that Naomi Wolf's intelligent, if somewhat belligerent, book, *The Beauty Myth*, was published a decade ago (remember that cultural stereotypes have a long shelf life) but her words contain more than a little bit of truth:

> The questions, Whom do I desire? Why? What will I do about it? are turned around: Would I desire myself? Why? . . . Why *not*? What can I do about it? . . . What little girls learn is not desire for the other, but the desire to be desired.[9]

Seen from the vantage point of a new century, after forty years that have witnessed an extraordinary growth in both female accomplishment and positive female role models—among them soccer players, basketball stars, doctors, lawyers, politicians, television correspondents, engineers, professors—little has changed in how an adolescent girl perceives the connection between self-esteem and (sexual) desirability—or, as Naomi Wolf puts it, "the desire to be desired." This connection is emphasized in song lyrics, movie plots, the figures and clothing of teen stars such as the big-breasted and flat-bellied, size-one Britney Spears and others. As Dr. Annie Rogers observes, "What happens, too, is that girls have really taken in and are vulnerable to the messages around them that are still very there about not connecting with their own wishes and needs in a strong enough, connected way. So when a boy comes on to them sexually, they start to feel the importance of that, and they make a curious kind of trade-off which is to enter into a relationship only on a boy's terms."

Messages that define the standards of "beauty," "sexuality," and "attractiveness" are so ubiquitous in our culture that, like pieces of furniture that have long been a part of our surroundings, they often blend in, unnoticed, in the day-to-day. But consciously noted or not, these messages have the ability to affect us and our daughters in powerful ways, and in some sense, their very ubiquity makes us all the more vulnerable to their influence. These are not new messages, after all—there are simply more media available now to broadcast them. Once again, we offer another one of our decidedly random samples—drawn from magazines in Peg's daughter's room—but the incidence of these ads is so high that the inquiry doesn't even warrant scientific methodology. The tag lines with the message are in bold:

- **Softness: Our Most Surprising Strength. Strong enough for a Man. But made for you.** (Secret deodorant)

- **What smells sweet and juicy and gets your legs smooth and sexy in four minutes?** (New Nair Raz-mat-tazz for totally touchable legs)

- Admiring girl watching a male skateboarder skate away: **Tough. Just the way you like it.** (Baby G watches)

- Image of sexy, female legs with an ice cream cone where the face and body would be: **Fruit Smoothies.** (Skintimate shaving gel)

- Photograph of a watermelon slice: **Juicy from head to toe.** (Softsoap)

- Sexy girl with a come-hither look on her face, curled around an orange: **Your Main Squeeze for Shine.** (Citre hair products)

- Picture of a long-haired girl in a towel transposed against a flower: **You've never been caressed like this before.** (Caress body lotion)

- 1940s-style pin-up girl (big-breasted, long-legged, with a tiny waist), either pouring a boy a cup of coffee or leaning over a jukebox with a guy about to take off his leather jacket: **Get Lucky xxxooo**. (Lucky perfumes)

Sexual desirability—expressed in terms of pleasing a male other and making a girl no more than a sweetened piece of fruit (look at the metaphors!)—animates each and every one of these ads. Sometimes, though, the pitch becomes more even more explicit, when a photograph takes the undercurrent of all of these ads and brings it to the forefront: The ad for Ralph Lauren's Romance perfume features a young woman sitting on a fence—nude save for a beaded ankle bracelet and what looks to be a sheet—who embraces a fully clothed young man kissing her thigh. The ads for Candie's fragrance are, if anything, more direct. One shows a tattooed, bare-chested young man, with the bleached-tip dark hair thought to be sexy and *au courant*, wearing black leather pants. His legs are spread wide and there is a computer screen where his crotch would be—and on the screen is a pair of high-heeled woman's boots, presumably attached to legs and body, lying on a shag rug with two bottles of perfume. Another shows the same young man with different tattoos, standing before a bathroom sink, with just a towel around his waist; a girl—in a dress and wearing high-heeled slides—is seated on the sink and has her legs wrapped around his waist. It's unclear what they are doing. She is looking at him intently; he, on the other hand, is gazing at his own reflection in the mirror.

These messages about what it means to be female—as seen and formulated by the marketers and ad people—take on special meaning for a girl whose body has begun to change. But prepubescent girls—girls just beginning their journey into the years of adolescence—are also influenced by these messages and for them, the pressure to grow up—a cultural trend we've already noted in other contexts—takes on another level of meaning. A disturbing report issued by the Girl Scouts of the U.S.A. in September 2000 confirms what mothers all over the country already suspected while shopping for daughters as young as nine or ten: There has been what the authors call an "age compression," which, in their words, is the process through which "kids get older, younger." (If you have any doubt about this, go to a mall sometime and take a look at the clothes being marketed to girls ages eight to twelve. Try finding a dress that doesn't look as if it has been shrunk down from something a twenty-two-year-old might want to wear to a bar or Britney Spears would throw on for a video. And while you're there, take a look at the underwear, mini-versions of those in the Victoria's Secret catalog. Long gone are the training bras and white cotton panties of my youth.)

Mind you, this does *not* mean that girls are developing or maturing emotionally and socially more quickly than before. The authors point to three "drivers" of age compression: marketing messages aimed at children; exposure to media; and changes in nutrition that have resulted in earlier menarche and accelerated adolescence (the latter is their opinion). "Age compression" may be affected by the early onset of puberty, but it is nonetheless different from it. As a consequence of age compression, the authors assert that the three areas of child development—cognitive, physical, and emotional—have become dangerously out of sync. While girls as young as eight or as old as twelve may dress and talk like adolescents, may be as physically developed as a girl of thirteen or fourteen, their emotional development is still precisely where it should be chronologically. What this means is that those "standards" of attractiveness are being accepted as fact by girls at younger and younger ages; following is an excerpt from the report, with the italics added for emphasis:

> Girls speak about these affectations of popularity in terms of appearance, sexuality, and materialism, describing the value system that will

determine a girl's popularity as a combination of a child's brand own-
ership and affluence (what brands she wears, how much money she
has) and sexual maturation. *Status and popularity, in these girls' opinions, require the ability to attract boys with looks and expensive clothing—
along with a certain degree of emotional callousness.*[10]

"A certain degree of emotional callousness"? Keep in mind that,
while sixth and seventh graders were among those sampled, the preponderance of the girls were in third, fourth, and fifth grades.

American business has duly noted the fact of age compression,
and the magazines that help to create the phenomenon not only
profit from it but promote it. A *New York Times* article, aptly titled
"In the Age of Diminishing Innocence, Magazines for Teenagers
Shift Focus," notes that "underlying many articles is the guiding
premise that teenage girls are swiftly becoming miniaturized ver-
sions of grown-ups."[11]

As you read this, your first impulse might be to imprison your
daughter in a high tower and begin to dig a moat as quickly as possible. (I understand this impulse from the very bottom of my heart
but, trust me, it's not the way to go.) Your second impulse might
well be denial—that may be the way someone else's daughter is
responding to cultural messages but not mine. (I understand this
impulse equally well, but just because your daughter or mine does
not appear to be acting on these messages *now* doesn't mean she
isn't hearing them or being influenced by them.) We are so surrounded by cultural messages that, in one sense, we have no real
way of assessing how powerful they really are, or how much they
influence any one of us—or our daughters—individually. For just a
glimpse of how much they might, we looked at the research done by
Dr. Anne Becker of Harvard University Medical School, whom we
interviewed for this book, to see what we could learn from it. The
story of her research is a fascinating, if disturbing, cautionary tale.

An eating disorders expert and a cultural anthropologist, Dr.

Becker focused her research on the people of Fiji, whom she had studied for twelve years. If your geography is a bit hazy, Fiji is very remote—a string of islands, one hundred of which are inhabited, in the South Pacific, more than one thousand miles from the northern part of New Zealand. Because of their geographic location, while Fijians were able to view movies on VCRs, they did not have access to television until 1995 when a single station—carrying American, Australian, and British programming, in addition to local news— was introduced. Traditionally, food has played an important symbolic role in Fijian society—in the forms of feasting and the generous treatment of family and guests—and more robust body types were socially and culturally preferred. In 1998, a mere three years after television came to Fiji (think *Beverly Hills, 90210*), 11 percent of girls reported vomiting to control weight, as opposed to none in 1995 when television was first introduced. More importantly, testing revealed that the percentage of girls at risk for eating disorders had more than doubled. Sixty-two percent of the girls surveyed reported dieting during the previous month.

In an interview conducted for this book, Dr. Becker emphasized that the results had surprised her: She had assumed that Fijian cultural traditions—some two thousand years old—which stressed consensus and conformity, would "withstand television." But as she points out, there was a "massive influx of imagery" and in addition, Fijian girls lacked the media viewing experience to fully understand that the images—and the people and body types—displayed on the television screen were not "real."

What can we learn from the experience on Fiji? For one thing, Dr. Becker points out, young American adolescents are equally vulnerable to mistaking television characters as role models for real life. As we've already noted, they, too, are subject to a massive amount of imagery. Here's the real question: Is your daughter culturally sophisticated enough to realize that the images she's looking at—in magazines, on CD covers, on television—have been altered and enhanced, digitally and otherwise? Does she realize that the bodies (not to mention the skin, hair, and nails) presented as "ideal" may also have been specially lit, "altered," or "enhanced"? Are her mathematical skills sophisticated enough for her to recognize what a teeny percentage of the female population on this planet actually is born looking this way?

More to the point, are *you* sophisticated enough not to be influenced by the imagery? Pick up any of the fashion magazines aimed at your own age group and, honestly and truthfully, answer the question.

~ ~ ~

> I believe that the way I look affected me in both positive and negative ways. As a teenager I was overweight; my friends would tell me that I was fat and that I needed to diet. I was very self-conscious— I was the only one who was fat—and it affected my self-esteem tremendously. I hated being fat, and never felt in the least bit pretty. I attended a private all-girls high school which was very competitive in every area. During the summer of tenth grade, I lost 25 pounds and entered eleventh grade feeling terrific. I weighed 125 pounds and remember feeling very happy and very pretty. On the positive side, my confidence grew and grew. Staying thin became a huge focus for me and I had to constantly work at keeping my weight down. I learned to eat healthy and I exercised on a regular basis which became my lifestyle. I do believe that you must feel happy with the way you look as a woman and as a girl. When you feel good about yourself, then you project this feeling with almost everything.
>
> "Victoria," divorced, thirty-eight, event planner and mother to "Christina," age twelve

As the mothers of adolescent daughters, we must take into account not only the age compression but the culture in which we live when we parent. As Dr. Anne Becker notes, "Since the 1970s and 1980s, our cultural values have begun to support an investment in the body, a cultivation of the body. Culturally, the body has been increasingly seen as a personal space through which we can project an identity." Again, as you read those words, ask yourself how you feel about your body, why and how you exercise, and locate yourself in the culture. In a book that should be required reading for all parents of adolescent girls and their daughters, *The Body Project: An Intimate History of American Girls*, historian Joan Jacobs Brumberg points outs that while each generation of women experiences sexual development

> a girl's experience of these inevitable biological events is shaped by the world in which she lives, so much so, that each generation, at its own point in history, develops its own characteristic body problems and projects. Every girl suffers some adolescent *angst* about her body; it is the historical moment that defines *how* she reacts to her changing flesh.[12]

From her vantage point as a social historian, Brumberg analyzes how, during the course of the twentieth century, the idea of the "self" shifted from the definition of the Victorians (who focused on the inner self and character, and who worried about vanity and self-absorption) to being organized around the body. In Brumberg's words, "Today, many young girls worry about the contours of their bodies—especially shape, size, and muscle tone—because they believe the body is the ultimate expression of self."

It doesn't take a big leap to move from the body "as the ultimate expression of self" to seeing dissatisfaction with the body (that is, deviation from the norms of beauty promoted by the culture) as dissatisfaction with the self. Brumberg is adept at outlining precisely what these cultural values do to our girls when they actually become women:

> Girls who do not feel good about themselves need the affirmation of others, and that need, unfortunately, almost always empowers male

desire. In other words, girls who hate their bodies do not make good decisions about partners, or about the kind of sexual activity that is in their best interest. Because they want to be wanted so much, they are susceptible to manipulation, to flattery, even to abuse. Body angst is not only a boost to commerce . . . it makes the worst forms of sexual flattery acceptable. . . . [13]

As mothers and role models for our daughters and their friends, we need to look closely at what we tell our daughters about puberty, what we teach them about their bodies and their sexual identity, what we communicate about our sexuality, and the point in cultural history we and our daughters have come of age.

As mothers, we need to recognize that, in the absence of messages that help define what it means to be a person and a female beyond physical appearance, beyond the body as the "ultimate" or "only" expression of self—communicated by mothers, fathers, and other mentors—the messages concocted to sell goods and products will, by default, prevail.

~ ~ ~

How will I talk to my daughters about sex and relationships? Well, I'm full of hope and confidence now, but I don't know what lies ahead. I had unpleasant sexual experiences as a young woman, and that may color how I speak to them—I don't want them to repeat my mistakes. I tend to have high expectations, so I'm going to have to rein in my judgments. I'm also not the best at picking the right moments to talk about certain subjects. When they're on my mind, I want to address them immediately, and immediately is not always the best time. I hope that knowing my weaknesses will help me overcome them and to be the mother a daughter would come to with concerns, questions, fears. It's certainly one of my greater goals. My mother told my best friend and me about menstruation at about nine because my friend wouldn't ask her own mother. My mother was comfortable and smart about it. But I didn't talk to my mother about my unhappy sexual experiences. Once when I was seventeen, she said—shyly, I thought—"I'm afraid you're probably too young to be having sex." It was already a done deal at that point, so I just quietly reassured her and changed the subject. We were both uncomfortable. I don't remember resenting her then and I don't now, but I want to have a different, better, relationship with my daughters regarding their sexual lives.

"Michelle," married college professor, mother of two girls, one age seven

While we and our daughters are surrounded by sexual imagery and suggestion, every study indicates that we—individually and as a society—are not very good at talking about sex. And in a prime example of what can only be called cultural dissonance, despite all the messages about "femaleness" and sexuality bombarding even the youngest of our adolescent daughters, only slightly more than half of the schools in the United States teach sexual education in the fifth and sixth grades. Of those that do, most focus on the "nuts and bolts" of sexuality: Puberty and its attendant physical changes are taught close to 93 percent of the time. While three-quarters of teachers discussed how alcohol and drugs affect behavior, fewer than half discussed how to resist peer pressure to have intercourse. Only one-third taught how to recognize and resist media pressure regarding sexual behavior. And while in the higher grades—seventh through twelfth—93 percent of schools report that sexuality education is taught at some point, researchers conclude that what is offered "is increasingly focused on abstinence and is less likely to present students with comprehensive teaching." (Forty-one percent of sex education teachers cited abstinence as their most important message; in contrast, 3.6 percent cited self-esteem.) In addition, there is a large gap between what teachers think should be taught and when, and what actually takes place in the classroom. For example, while 88 percent of teachers thought that resisting peer pressure to have intercourse should be taught as early as seventh grade, it was only taught in 70.4 percent of classes. (By ninth grade, it was taught in only 82.4 percent of classes, and by tenth through twelfth grades, it was taught, on average, only 62 percent of the time.[14])

Recent studies show that in the absence of information provided by schools and parents, adolescents will turn to other sources of information, including television, to learn about issues important to them.

What all these statistics mean is simple: We *cannot* leave it to the educators or, by default, the marketers and television producers to talk to our daughters about what it means to be female and sexual, no matter how difficult talking may be for us personally. We *cannot* wait until our girls are "ready" to talk to us.

We *can* learn how to initiate an ongoing dialogue, just as we *can* take what we have learned from our experiences to help our daughters make a healthy and safe transition from childhood into adulthood.

But first we need to look at ourselves a bit more closely.

~ ~ ~

I think the mother-daughter dynamic is a more intimate and intense and emotional one than the father-son relationship. I think there's something elemental about it: Mothers labor mightily to bring their daughters into the world and from that moment forth there is a powerful and intimate bond that the father-son relationship can only approximate. I should add that I do not have a son so I can't make any comparisons in that respect, but I think that my wife is closer to both of our daughters and probably more "attached" in all senses of the word than I will ever be.

I think that part of the intensity of this relationship is a gender thing. Girls know how to "get" to their mothers and Mary certainly knows how to get to her mother, in part because girls are just more like their mothers: sexually, emotionally, physically. I think it's also true that Mary (and I suspect all daughters to some extent) is able to hurt her mother in ways that she could never hurt me, precisely because she knows on a primal level how intimate the attachment is.

"Tim," age fifty-three, married media executive, father of two adolescent daughters, "Mary," age fifteen, and "Jane," age twelve

In *Mending the Broken Bough: Restoring the Promise of the Mother-Daughter Relationship*, a book aimed primarily at adult mothers and daughters who seek to improve their connection, Barbara Zax, Ph.D, and Stephan Poulter, Ph.D., write:

> The way a mother interacts with her daughter, and how she "models" for her what it means to be a woman, has a strong influence on how her daughter lives, loves, and works. When a daughter looks out at the world, much of what she sees is colored by what she has learned and absorbed from her mother. Her mother's moods, behavior, and point of view can alter not only how a daughter views the outside world but how she sees herself. . . . For each woman, the early relationship with her mother is the foundation upon which she will build *all* her future relationships. A young girl may bask in the bright sun of her mother's approval and internalize those good feelings, which, in turn, become a positive part of her self-image. Or she may habitually get the message that mother is disappointed in her, which also becomes a part of how she views herself. As a child grows, each interaction with mother, both positive and negative, has the power to impact a daughter's emerging self-portrait.[15]

I read these words and suddenly feel an enormous burden of responsibility. Surely, I think to myself, it cannot all be about *me*; surely, the relationships Kate and Rachel have to their father, to each other, to their brother, their grandparents, aunts, uncles, cousins, friends, teachers, coaches, and the rest of the world matter too. Those relationships do matter, of course, but at the same time, there is no denying the special influence and importance of the mother-daughter relationship, particularly during the years of adolescence.

I'm not alone, of course, in feeling both the burden of responsibility and a certain amount of worry about how I will handle the challenges presented by these years of mothering. Recently, both as a result of working on this book and by virtue of my own two ado-

lescent daughters, women—friends and strangers alike—have confided how uncertain they are about when they need to talk to their
daughters, what the nature of the conversation ought to be, what
boundaries they should draw pertaining to their own experiences,
and how much "interference" is appropriate or necessary as their
daughters begin the journey that is adolescence. For my own part,
with a new awareness of the special challenges of raising two adolescent girls—each one an individual in her own right, after all—I've
started to puzzle through some of my own personal definitions,
among them what it means to be a woman.

And in both thinking about it and talking to other women, I've
come to see that among the mixed messages our girls receive about
being female may be those we ourselves send our daughters. Self-
examination doesn't come easily to most of us, and perhaps the
hardest things to be articulate about are those that lie closest to our
own sense of self. Before we can talk to our daughters about issues
of substance, we must be able to face those issues ourselves. For
some of us, becoming articulate will involve coming to terms with
our own mothers and our own adolescence; for others, the journey
will involve locating ourselves in the present, putting into words
what we really feel and think about the issues of selfhood that will
begin to be addressed by our daughters.

Definitions of the female self have always, in some sense, been
fluid since, during the course of a lifetime, women move from
one biologically-defined stage of life into another; both our ever-
changing bodies and the finiteness of our fertility guarantee that
our sense of self cannot remain static. In our lifetimes though, these
natural evolutions of self have been compounded by changing social
definitions of what it means to be female, along with changes in
attendant obligations and responsibilities. Most of us have had to
reinvent how we define ourselves in literal ways that are quite different from exercises in soul-searching. Many of us come from traditional backgrounds—with stay-at-home moms and wage-earner

dads—and during our own adolescence, imagined growing into similar lives only to find ourselves later in entirely different circumstances. Some of us have had to give up the primary labels that defined us in earlier parts of our lives—"wife" and "housewife" among them—for new ones such as "custodial parent," "worker" and "primary wage-earner." We may have begun the journey of motherhood in one set of personal and economic circumstances and found ourselves, when our daughters reached adolescence, in another place entirely. Others among us—who were working women in one part of their lives but who later chose to stay at home with their children—may, as their daughters become more independent, find themselves feeling suddenly "jobless" and faced with their own crisis of self-esteem. (For more on this, see Ann Crittenden's book *The Price of Motherhood*, and its discussion of how "nonworking" mothers are viewed by our society and what happens when they try to re-enter the workforce.[16]) Still others—now that their children are older and need different kinds of care—will be making new choices about careers and jobs, and even personal relationships.

The female self—long past the years of adolescence—continues to evolve on many different levels. The older mothers reading these words—those who came of age in the 1960s and 1970s as I did—may feel as though, all through their adult lives, they've had to shed preconceptions about what it means to be female, the way a snake sheds its skin, to make way for new growth and to thrive or survive in a changing world.

I am, in many ways, a case in point. Even though my becoming a doctor constituted a departure from traditional female pursuits, I carried a tremendous amount of emotional baggage about "femininity" into college, medical school, and beyond. Like most women of my generation, during my girlhood I learned lessons about the incompatibility of outspokenness and femininity, which guaranteed that I knew better than to speak my mind or "talk back." Ironically, this actually served me well in medical school, because the med school hierarchy doesn't encourage talking back, but I already knew that as a female. In other areas of my life, though, the ways in which I was quiet, modest, and deferential worked only to my detriment. My assumptions about "femininity" often canceled out the benefits of my independent achievements. Even though I entered a profession that made it possible for me to take care of myself financially, I never thought of myself as either a primary wage-earner or caretaker; I remained on the lookout for, as the song puts it, "someone to watch over me." The proof of this? The way I handed over my paychecks to my second husband. Men, I thought, not women, handled money. My untraditional achievements coexisted with more traditional definitions of femininity and attractiveness and, at various points in my life, I certainly thought that "womanhood" was something conferred upon a female by a man, marriage, and (perhaps) children.

Now, at almost fifty, my vision of "womanhood" is something else entirely. Womanhood has, in my opinion, little to do with having a period (or, as a perimenopausal woman, not having one) or breasts, or even raising children but is instead a slow, ripening evolution into selfhood. I have finally given myself permission to talk back, to give voice to what I think and need, and, harder still, even to make demands—to be, as I like to say, as reasonably "sassy" as I want. I am a woman who is, by turns, a doctor, a cook, a television correspondent, a horseback rider, an author, a mother, a folder of laundry and consultant on homework, a wife, a lover, a friend, a sister, an aunt, and a daughter. Each of these roles is inextricably tied to my definition of self. For me, womanhood—a synonym for true personhood—is a culmination of all of my life experiences; it is a stage of life I finally grew into in my fifth decade, years that, in many ways, have been the most fulfilling and productive of my life and that coincide with the years of my daughters' adolescence.

The guidance I offer my two girls at this stage of my life—guidance about what it means to be female, what it means to be a woman—is inevitably shaped by where I find myself now. Had I lived my life differently—had I been a decade younger when my daughters began this journey, had I made different life and career choices, had I not unlearned the definitions of "femininity" I grew up with, had I not grown into having a voice of my own—what I had to say to them might have been very different. For this reason, among others, I think it is crucial that the dialogue between mothers and daughters be informed not just by our own personal experiences but those of other women, who can help us fill in the gaps where our own self-esteem or awareness falters or stumbles.

In his book *The Moral Intelligence of Children: How to Raise a Moral Child*, renowned psychiatrist Robert Coles makes a point that is applicable to the work that mothers need to do with their daughters during this crucial period of time. Coles discusses and describes the "moral imagination"—the "place" in our heads where, as he puts it, "we ponder the meaning of our lives" and of "ethical" challenges— which can be understood to illuminate the process that is parenting as well:

A reflecting and self-reflecting mind at some point gives way to a "performing self": the moral imagination affirmed, realized, developed, trained to grow stronger by daily decisions, small and large, deeds enacted, then considered and reconsidered. Character is ultimately who we are expressed in action, in how we live, in what we do, and so the children around us know: they absorb and take stock of what they observe, namely, us—we adults living and doing things in a certain spirit, getting on with one another in our various ways. Our children add up, imitate, file away what they've observed and so very often later fall in line with the particular moral counsel we wittingly or quite unself-consciously have offered them.[17]

While Coles is talking about "character" in a very specific way, what he has to say is equally applicable to "character" in its broadest sense—our very nature. Our femaleness, our personhood—that part of ourselves our daughters look to to inform their own expectations, the authority they look to for permission to give voice to their own inner selves—is also expressed not just by the reflecting mind—the part of us that thinks theoretically and becomes teacher and lecturer to our girls—but by the "performing self," the conscious and unconscious ways we express what it means to be female by how we live and what we do. While it is important for each of us to be able to be articulate about what it means to be female—letting the "reflecting mind" do its work—we need to become consciously aware of how we express ourselves in action.

We can help ourselves become better mothers to our daughters by seeing the other women in our lives as resources of perspective, vision, and information.

This is one part of the journey we do not have to make alone.

~ ~ ~

What I remember most about my adolescence is the complete and desperate confusion about who I was supposed to be, and the utterly contradictory messages that were communicated by society. I went to a small, private girls' school and while there was pressure to be smart and get good grades—it was an excellent school and I had very smart classmates—there was also terrific pressure to be pretty and popular with boys. I downplayed my intelligence with guys—it wasn't, in the mid-sixties, considered a particularly attractive trait in a girl—and worried about my looks continually. This continued through college where I ran for Miss University, heaven help me, and stayed mum about making dean's list and Phi Beta Kappa. Then I went on to graduate school in English where the conflict between looks and smarts continued, albeit in a different form.

The low point came after an interview with the faculty for a prestigious position as a teaching assistant at Columbia College. I was standing in the hallway, outside the room where the all-male group debated the comparative merits of the graduate students. In one of those odd moments, when there is a sudden lull in background noise, from behind the closed doors, I heard one of the professors say, loudly and distinctly, "Streep teach young boys? Hell no, she's too pretty to be a preceptor."

And that pretty much sums it up. I was twenty-three or so at the time, feminism was in full bloom, and the basic message was still the same one I had learned in my adolescence.

My co-author, Peg, mother of Alexandra, thirteen

This I noticed from the beginning: Parenting is calculated to undermine one's self-confidence and self-esteem. There is no other aspect of our lives that complete strangers feel as comfortable commenting on as how we raise our children. And because no one brings any prior job experience to the process, we are very vulnerable to this criticism. We question ourselves as parents from the start. All babies cry, and there are always problems of some kind; there is no child so "perfect" that there is never a reason to question our choices. Consequently, it has been very difficult to be told that I was harming Sam by not fostering his independence at an earlier age. I think that if the principles suggested by "conventional wisdom" were even remotely palatable to me, I would have made other choices simply through lack of self-confidence.

Abby, age forty-two, computer expert and mother of a boy, age thirteen

I'm told, on reasonably good authority, that in Chinese there's a single character for both "crisis" and "opportunity," and perhaps that's precisely how, as mothers, we need to look at the years of adolescence. If we're going to cut bait on the so-called popular wisdom about the "inevitable crisis" of adolescence and ignore the messages about "necessary separation" between mothers and daughters, then perhaps we will be able to see our collective way clear to the unique opportunities this period of life offers us and our daughters in terms of personal growth. Perhaps then, rather than seeing this period of life shared by mother and daughter as something to be gotten through or managed or, in the popular parlance, "survived," we can see it instead as a time of mutual growth, one that permits us, the mothers, to learn new skills as people and parents and perhaps uncover new aspects of ourselves, even as our daughters begin the journey toward selfhood.

It's interesting that, as Elizabeth Debold, Lyn Mikel Brown, Susan Weseen, and Geraldine Kearse Brookins note, little research—save Terri Apter's, which we've already mentioned—has actually studied the *positive* aspects of the mother-daughter relationships.[18] Yet psychologists readily acknowledge the mother-daughter relationship as "a critical arena" for girls' healthy development, one that contributes to their "hardiness" or ability to cope with the questions and situations that arise in adolescence. One interesting study, conducted by Leslie A. Gavin and Wyndol Furman, compared adolescent girls' perception of "harmony" in two different relationships, those between mothers and daughters on the one hand, and best friends on the other. "Harmony" was defined as "frequent supportive interactions and infrequent conflictual interactions." The authors found that girls with more harmonious relationships with their mothers "displayed more cooperative relationship skills, more positive affect, more attunement to mother, and better ability to negotiate power."[19] More to the point, while literature on adolescence tends to emphasize the differences between peer and parent relationships, the authors found a common process among all close relationships. In other words, harmonious mother-daughter relationships *do* provide a template for other relationships.[20] Most important, the study found that one factor that distinguished the mother-daughter relationship from the peer relationship was the degree to which "harmony" in the mother-daughter relationship depended on problem-solving. In the authors' words: "Compared to peer dyads, mothers and daughters are more likely to have more experience and spend more energy discussing problems and working out day-to-day hassles, perhaps making it a more important skill in this domain."[21] Once again, the point is made that a working dialogue is absolutely key to the relationship.

But what form should that dialogue take? We turned once again to Dr. Annie Rogers to discuss how the dynamic between mothers and daughters changes during adolescence, and what she had to say was both reassuring and illuminating:

> I think there are two things going on. First, if a girl has had a close relationship with her mother, they are going to remain close, even if there is some renegotiation of closeness. Second, because girls begin to understand themselves and their experiences differently in adolescence—much more in terms of internal experiences—they will want to be recognized in new ways. That's certainly true in their peer relationships but also in their relationships with their mothers. Some mothers will be able to come forward and really meet that girl, while other mothers will have difficulty. Girls are psychologically trying to discover who they are and testing their mothers to see if it is possible to be someone new in that relationship. There will be some mothers who don't take that personally and can remember their own adolescence and can combine being firm and very clear about their limits while maintaining a sense of humor about this process with their daughter. And there are other mothers who simply can't do that, become defensive, or give up their own voice and power when they are tested by a teenage daughter.

"Testing," of course, takes on many forms during these years—from the sullen folded arms and uncommunicative body stance, familiar to me from one of my daughters, to the open sniping and raised voice favored by my youngest and countless variations on the theme. But, Dr. Rogers counsels, if we learn not to take our daughters' ways of "testing" us personally and if we can tap into our own memories of struggling with self-definition, if we can maintain both our firmness and our sense of humor, we perhaps can meet our girls face to face. In a separate interview, Terri Apter made a similar point about our vulnerability as parents:

Mothers sometimes experience a crisis of confidence when a daughter goes through adolescence because the tactics that worked so well when the daughter was a child no longer work. A mother who could comfort her moody or weepy ten-year-old may find that her efforts to comfort her fourteen-year-old are counterproductive: Instead of comforting her, she increases her irritation. If a mother then concludes that her daughter doesn't want her anymore, or doesn't need her, she feels useless. A change in perspective in which she sees that her daughter still needs her would inspire her to keep trying to find new ways of offering her comfort and understanding.

But how, you might ask yourself, am I really supposed to do all that—standing in my kitchen with a sink full of dirty dishes, after an eight-hour day at work, face-to-face with a sixteen-year-old I can't seem to get through to? How can I figure out the best way to mother when what she wants from me seems to change from minute to minute, day to day? How am I supposed to magically "change perspective"? Isn't this the Perfect Mother thing all over again?

Actually, it isn't. What it involves is coming to terms with *your* part of the mother-daughter dynamic—of focusing on yourself, the older part of the dyad standing in the kitchen—and one way of doing that is taking a hard look at how you are reacting to the sullen, withdrawn, or apparently angry adolescent who seems to be facing you down. This goes to the heart of what we have called "I-Thou" parenting.

Becoming conscious of our assumptions about *why* our daughters are acting the way they are is the first step. Once again, we turned to Terri Apter for guidance, who reminded us that "the myth of necessary separation" is not only harmful to the mother-daughter relationship but to all parent-child relationships:

If parents believe that their daughters are quarrelling with them in order to separate from them, then they are likely to respond either by letting them go (thinking that is what is best) or by feeling rejected themselves. However, if they see quarrels and tension with a daughter as stemming from a daughter's need to readjust the relationship, they will respond in a very different way. Instead of withdrawing, they would work to improve the connection. The harm of this myth continues past adolescence, too, as parents feel that their daughters should stand on their own two feet. Parents are sometimes critical of a teenager or young adult who still needs closeness and support.

Depending on our personalities and our "style" of parenting, each of us will react differently to the manner in which our daughters try to "readjust" the relationship. Some of us may feel vulnerable or insecure; others may equally feel threatened by what feels—rightly or wrongly—like our daughters' constant criticism of our every thought and every action. Some of us may resent the "no-win" situation in which we seem to find ourselves. Some of us may become fearful as we see our daughters begin to experiment with new ideas and ways of acting and try to assert excessive control over them, their thoughts, and their behavior. (Keep in mind here that we are referring to behavior that is not clearly self-destructive or inherently dangerous, but behavior or ideas that we may disagree with or that make us feel uncomfortable. For more on distinguishing the warning signs of real problems from normal patterns of behavior, please see page 255 and following.)

Research shows, for example, that the African-American experience of the mother-daughter relationship during the years of adolescence is markedly different from that among whites. African-American girls not only hold their mothers in high esteem during these years but consider their relationship to their mothers central to their lives.[22] In an interview, Dr. Jacquelynne Eccles expanded on the research for us, saying, "We are finding a very interesting difference between African-American families and white families, particularly around the mother-daughter dyad. The evidence from the field is that the conflict between mothers and daughters accelerates during the early adolescent period. It looks like that may be linked to mothers' fears—and our data suggests this—about their daughters getting involved in behaviors or in peer groups that are going to get them into trouble. These fears are focused around sexuality, dating, drug and alcohol use. As the daughter begins to look like an adult because her body begins to change, many white mothers become increasingly concerned and clamp down on their daughters in ways that are likely to increase, rather than decrease, the likelihood that the daughters will engage in these behaviors. The daughters perceive the control not just as a lack of trust but as an inappropriate shift in their parents' restrictiveness. The daughters think they are going to get more freedom and the parents clamp down and give them less, exactly at the time that the girls, in fact, think they are capable of taking care of themselves." In contrast, she notes, "In black families, it looks like puberty signals to the dyad that the mother and daughter can become closer. The data confirm this: Black mothers are more likely to give their daughters birth control information, rather than clamping down on them. They really see puberty as an opportunity to have a different kind of relationship, a more positive relationship, a more companionate relationship." Even though the level of conflict between mothers and daughters increases in African-American families, it does not to the same extent as in white families and is centered in different kinds of issues. Black mothers focus on problem-solving and respecting their daughters' maturity.[23]

While "separation" is neither normal nor necessary, the daughter's need to establish herself as an individual—to individuate—is. No matter how awkward (or belligerent) our daughters' methods of "readjusting" the relationship are, it is absolutely crucial that we, their mothers, be able to recognize and respect their need to transform it. Terri Apter delineates the degree to which "tension" between mother and daughter is a necessary, even beneficial, part of the journey toward selfhood:

> The tension between mother and daughter does help the daughter define herself. Even highly individual girls look at their mothers as they might look at a possible future self. Some of this is comforting and inspirational, but girls also want to be different. When they refute what a mother says, or criticize her for what she does, they gain confidence in their own self-boundaries. If a mother punishes or threatens a daughter who asserts her difference, then the daughter's anger may increase—or she may buckle under. I think if mothers felt less threatened by an antimother culture, they would find the strength to accept a daughter's differences.

Accepting our daughters' differences—that's the hard part, I think. Being adult enough, secure enough, to accept that our daughters' differences are legitimate—to put away the disappointment or even the anxiety those differences may instill in us and not to feel threatened by their disagreement—is a goal each of us needs to set for ourselves. Recognizing that their attempts at argument aren't necessarily challenges to our authority but exercises in growth is another. Moving away from an attitude that sees the ways in which our daughters are changing as ones that need to be "controlled" or "straightened out" is another. We've talked about how "I-Thou" parenting encourages us to see the mutuality of the mother-daughter experience. Examining how we parent—our individual style of parenting—can also help further develop our awareness. Experts distinguish between four distinct styles of parenting, the first of which is most directly related to positive adolescent development. "Authoritative" parenting combines emotional warmth and a clear-cut set of demands on the adolescent's behavior with an atmosphere that permits the adolescent to express her ideas and opinions and establish herself as an individual. "Authoritarian" parenting, on the other hand, presents high-level demands (rules and controls) with little warmth and no room for psychological autonomy. The "indulgent" style of parenting has high levels of warmth and a low level of demand, and what Dr. Laurence Steinberg has called a "laissez-faire" attitude toward decision-making. Finally, "uninvolved" parenting has low levels of demand and warmth, as well as a laissez-faire attitude toward decision-making.[24] We'll be turning to the positive benefits of "authoritative" parenting again and again.

One way we can make sure that we are not confusing what is a necessary part of growing up—redefining the boundaries of the self and discovering personal likes and dislikes by measuring oneself against one's mother through a variety of strategies—with either a personal attack or a power struggle is to enlist the help of other women. As Dr. Annie Rogers puts it:

> The most important thing is for mothers to make contact with one another and with likeminded women—to really explore the cost of their own growing up and their strengths and then, from that experience, to really talk about how they need to connect with their daughters and what they really need to learn from one another to do it better. When the idea of "framing resistance" is put into popular terms, it is often mistranslated—it can sound as though mothers need to be better mothers than they are being, as if any of us can leap over old injuries and become different people. The emphasis too often is put on "for the good of the girl," which is really not the point at all.
>
> I think that if teenage girls look at their mothers and they don't find a person of strength and integrity with some weaknesses and imperfections who can be real with them—then who else can they turn to? I think then the most important thing for a mother is to come into the strength, integrity, and authenticity of her own experience and to turn to those other women for support and to know

themselves and their own personal development so they can come forward and meet their girls in a way that is truly different. It's not so much for the good of the girl as it is for the good of the relationship, including the mother's side of it.

In the pages that follow, we'll be looking at how each of us—possessed of strengths and weaknesses, integrity and imperfections—can come forward and meet our girls in ways that are, in Dr. Rogers's words, "truly different."

~ ~ ~

Self-esteem: Pride in oneself; self-respect.
    *American Heritage Dictionary of the English Language*
Self-esteem: A confidence and satisfaction in oneself; self-
    respect. . . .
        *Merriam Webster's Collegiate Dictionary*, tenth edition

While our own self-esteem might not be an issue when we are mothering a baby or a toddler—confidence doesn't really factor into diapering or reading a picture book—how we feel about ourselves, whether we are aware of it or not, becomes part and parcel of both our "style" of mothering and the example we set for our daughters. "Self-esteem"—or better put, the lack of it—has become a buzz word of sorts in our culture (one search engine yields more than three hundred thousand web page matches to those two little words!) and it's worth taking a look at what it means and how it matters.

During the months we've been working on this book, because we happen to live on opposite coasts of the United States, Peg and I have spent literally hours and hours on the telephone, not to mention exchanging countless e-mails, along with sharing the occasional lunch. Most of the time we talk about our girls—exchanging notes on how each of us has reacted to the most recent parenting challenge posed by one or the other's child, or marveling at the ways our daughters are growing and changing—but we also talk about ourselves and the degree to which issues of self-esteem have affected us both. Despite all of the differences between us—different family backgrounds, growing up in very different parts of the country, different personal interests and goals—there is, nonetheless, a bond of shared experience of not having believed in ourselves at some basic level despite all of our "outside world" achievements. Each of us has had to, in our own ways, grow into self-confidence; it is a journey that has, for each of us, literally taken decades. Between us, we are hard put to name a single woman we know who hasn't struggled with some variation on the self-esteem problem at some point in her life—and we know some very high-powered and gifted women. It's bewildering to us that the outward signs of success—in fields as various as business, medicine, academia, administration—can so easily coexist with an often persistent lack of self-worth. We are both old enough now to recognize the difference between the butterflies-in-the-stomach feeling that gears each of us up to meet challenges in work and life from true lack of self-esteem.

We've talked at length about why something so basic to peace of mind, productivity, and happiness continues to be so elusive for so many girls *and* their mothers. It isn't as though lack of self-confidence is a specifically female problem—it is a human problem, and both genders suffer from it—nor is it true that all adolescent girls will necessarily face a crisis or inevitable loss of self-esteem. It is worth noting and remembering that not every adolescent girl is an "Ophelia" in the making, to borrow the term Mary Pipher popularized in her bestselling book. Many, many adolescent girls negotiate the passage between childhood and young adulthood without serious mishap, and remain reasonably confident of their strengths and abilities. Some, in fact, emerge with a strengthened sense of self-esteem. *But*—and this is an important but—research suggests that there still remain specific areas of concern to girls and their healthy development that we, as mothers, need to pay attention to, and that continue to affect not just daughters but ourselves.

Here is what scientists *do* know about girls and self-esteem:

- The ethnic culture to which a girl belongs is an important factor. Different studies have shown that declines in self-esteem in adolescent girls are noted mainly in white (European-American) populations. One study that focused on both black and white girls for a five-year period, beginning at age nine and ending at fourteen, noted that black girls' sense of self-worth did not decline, perhaps in part because of racial differences in attitudes toward physical appearance.[25] Other studies confirm that self-esteem in African-American girls stays stable and that they tend to be more satisfied with their physical appearance and retain confidence in their abilities more than their white, European-American peers.[26]

- Although the decline in self-esteem in preadolescent and adolescent girls has garnered the most publicity—thanks to the important work done by the American Association of University Women, Peggy Orenstein, Carol Gilligan, Mary Pipher, and others—in fact, the decline in girls' self-esteem begins as early as kindergarten. Part of this seems to be attributable to the conflicts girls feel between cultural "feminine" goals—being kind, modest, or, in the alternative, not seeming overly aggressive—and high achievement.

As mothers, we need to attend to how we reinforce those "feminine" goals, which may be at odds with the overall goal of living a productive, happy *human* life.

- Cultural gender stereotypes about ability—for example, "girls are better at English and boys are better at math"—influence girls and their parents and teachers, *despite* objective evidence to the contrary. For example, with the exception of high-anxiety-provoking standardized tests (girls manage anxiety less well than boys), girls, in fact, do just as well at math as boys do.[27] A sobering, if fascinating, study at Stanford University revealed precisely how powerful these stereotypes are, even within a pool of gifted and talented students. (The authors called this phenomenon "stereotype vulnerability.") College students were given a difficult math test, and two separate groups of males and females were given different information before the test was administered. One group was told that males outscored females on the test and the other that males and females performed equally well. Women who took the test thinking that males would do better were, in fact, outperformed by their male peers—a variation on a self-fulfilling prophecy.[28]

We all need to look closely at not only the gender stereotypes communicated to our daughters by the culture at large but also those we promote ourselves.

- Girls view academic success differently than their male counterparts, attributing success to hard work and effort rather than innate ability as boys do.[29] In a corollary, while girls tend to underestimate their abilities, boys, in fact, tend to overestimate them.[30] *But* even though there is nothing inherently wrong with attributing success to hard work, studies have shown that this attitude—not one favored by American culture—does undermine girls' confidence in their ability in the long run and discourages the risk-taking that is part of high achievement.[31] For more on visions of what constitutes "intelligence," see page 307.

We need to look closely at how we encourage our daughters in their academic pursuits.

- Overall, girls are more affected by failure and fear of failure than boys, and in different ways. While boys tend to externalize the reason for failure ("The test was stupid" or "Who cares about the test anyway?"), girls, in contrast, tend to attribute internal or personal reasons for failure. According to various studies, when confronted by failure, adolescent girls tend to lower their expectations and are more likely to avoid challenging situations than are boys in the same age group.[32]

- Girls demonstrate what Dr. Susan Nolen-Hoeksema of the University of Michigan and Dr. Joan Girgus of Princeton University have called a "ruminative style of coping with distress"—or, in their words, "passively and repetitively focusing on the symptoms of distress" and their causes and consequences. Before the age of eleven, girls and boys are equally at risk for depression. During adolescence, however, girls' rates of depression escalate rapidly until, at the age of eighteen, the rate of depression in females is twice that of males. (This gender difference stays stable throughout the adult lifetime.[33]) Nolen-Hoeksema and Girgus studied adolescent girls and boys and discovered significant differences in what girls and boys focused on when mildly distressed. While boys tended to think about things outside the self (recent events, or a television show or sporting event), girls, on the other hand, turned inward. Girls not only worried more than boys did but— despite some areas of shared and equal concern such as school, getting along with parents, and what to do when you are older—worried about different issues. With the exception of worrying about looks, the focus of worry was relationship— with friends, with family, boys. Much more than their male counterparts, girls worried about "what kind of person I am." In view of what Carol Gilligan and others have found about girls' identities being formed "relationally," these findings are not surprising.

We need to help our daughters develop different and new coping skills when they deal with stress. We can begin by considering our daughters' worries worthy of discussion, and by listening to our children thoughtfully and respectfully. For more on helping your daughter develop her "emotional intelligence," see page 307.

- While it is true that gendered patterns and stereotypes are dying off—girls *are* entering traditionally gender-typed, all-male professions, though not in record numbers—they are dying off slowly. Most disturbingly, in a conclusion offered in a chapter of *Beyond Appearance: A New Look at Adolescent Girls*, the authors write:

    . . . many young women still believe that there is an inherent conflict between feminine goals-values and highly competitive achievement activities. Belief in this conflict creates added ambivalence and anxiety when these young women find themselves in competitive achievement settings.[34]

There is, as we've already noted, a blizzard of media messages that reinforce unhealthy and unproductive stereotypes about not only how girls should look but how they should act. As adults, many of us may, in fact, feel some measure of confusion about what "feminine" goals—not to mention "feminine" behavior—constitute. One way each of us can help bolster our daughters' self-esteem is by offering them what Dr. Jacquelynne Eccles calls "counter-information" to those stereotypes.

But to do that, we first need to figure out, one woman at a time, what we mean when we use the word "feminine."

~ ~ ~

Subject: Goddess Woman

Age 3: Looks at herself and sees a Queen!

Age 8: Looks at herself and sees herself as Cinderella/Sleeping Beauty.

Age 15: Looks at herself and sees herself as Fat/Pimples/Ugly ("Mom, I can't possibly go to school looking like this!")

Age 20: Looks at herself and sees "too fat/too thin, too short/too tall, too straight/too curly"—but decides she's going out anyway.

Age 30: Looks at herself and sees "too fat/too thin, too short/too tall, straight/too curly"—but decides she doesn't have time to fix it so she's going out anyway.

Age 40: Looks at herself and sees "too fat/too thin, too short/too tall, too straight/too curly"—but says, "At least, I am clean," and goes out anyway.

Age 50: Looks at herself and sees "I am" and goes wherever she wants to go.

Age 60: Looks at herself and reminds herself of all the people who can't even see themselves in the mirror anymore. She goes out and conquers the world.

Age 70: Looks at herself and sees wisdom, laughter, and ability, goes out and enjoys life.

Age 80: Doesn't bother to look. Just puts on a purple hat and goes out to have fun with the world.

Maybe we should all grab that purple hat earlier! In celebration of Beautiful Women's Month, send this to five phenomenal women you are grateful to have as friends. If you do, something good will happen: You will boost another woman's self-esteem.

e-mail forwarded to adolescent girlfriends and received by Peg's daughter, Alexandra

What do *you* see when you look in mirror? The question is one that, on the surface, sounds pretty easy and straightforward but, when you think about it, is much more complicated. In a real sense, what we see is determined not only by what we are looking for but what we are, at any point in our lives, ready to see and capable of seeing.

What I see in the mirror is different than it was at any other point in my life. In my early thirties, the outside was all I cared about—

did I look pretty and thin, would people (men) find me attractive?—which reflected how little of me existed below the surface. Then, when I was in my early forties, the unforgiving light in an airplane lavatory—on a flight from New York to San Francisco—brought home a different kind of truth about aging and the end of girlishness. I was shocked to see that the woman who stared back at me looked haggard and old. Now when I look in the mirror, I see an accomplished person, no longer young, who is in the middle of the journey. It's not just the lines and wrinkles that make me look different; my face is more angular, less soft than it was years ago. (That softness—was it vulnerability or neediness, or was it just youth?) What there was once has been replaced by a steady gaze, a confidence that comes from within and spills over onto the surface. I see a woman comfortable in her skin, accepting of her weaknesses and flaws and willing to cut herself some slack.

When our daughters look to us for hints of the people they'll become, they will both look and listen. What does it mean to be female, after all? How can we become articulate about what the female self is or what it should be? To that end, we asked a number of women, all of them mothers, to tell us what they thought was meant by "womanhood." For the record, each one of them was surprised by how hard the question was to answer but, in the end, each of them answered the question in the most individual and personal way. The pace of life doesn't really give most of us the time or leisure to ponder the Big Questions, but we need to try to make time because, whether or not we put them into words, our thoughts about the Big Questions underlie a great deal of our behavior.

These remarkably diverse answers are a testament to precisely how in flux these definitions are in our society.

We offer them to you as examples of what happens when, to use the psychiatrist Robert Coles's distinction, the "self-reflecting mind" comments on the "performing self." These aren't the only answers to the question, of course, but we hope they will help stimulate you into thinking about what you mean when you describe yourself either as a "female" or a "woman," and what, consciously or unconsciously, you are teaching your daughter about both or either. At the end of this section, we've included some questions to start you on your way.

~ ~ ~

I don't like the concept of "womanhood" all that much. Not to sound too 1970s feminist, but "personhood" strikes me as a much better concept. I'd hope that my definition of coming of age would be much the same for a son as for a daughter. Of course, there's a sexual connotation—that's at the very essence of coming of age. But there's also the concept of responsibility—I'd like my daughter to understand that "womanhood" means she'll be responsible for herself, for other people, for the world, and for taking out the trash.

When I was younger, I certainly equated my femininity with my looks and my femaleness with being attractive to men. Now, I associate womanhood with specific qualities—stamina, flexibility, nurturance, openness, among them. This is not to say that men do not display these qualities but I honestly believe that by virtue of living in ever-changing bodies, women have a different capacity for these traits. On an emotional level, what I perceive as my womanhood is inextricably tied to being a mother. If I hadn't had a child, I would have had to define myself differently, I suppose, but I don't think there's any question that, in addition to other messages about being a woman, I am both consciously and unconsciously teaching my daughter about the role motherhood can play in a woman's life.

I don't define womanhood, I define being human: living by the golden rule, do unto others, and all that jazz. There just happen to be two genders. I hope I'm something of a role model to my daughter of what an open, honest and neurotic woman is.

My seven-year-old asked me what appeared to be a simple question: When is a person an adult and what does it mean to be an adult? I was totally flummoxed! I was babbling about being eighteen and being able to drink wine. And all the while, what I was also thinking—even though I didn't say so—is that you can be tried as an adult and be punished or fined in a more severe way if you break the law. I just barely managed to get it together to say something like being an adult is partially about how you treat other people, understanding what empathy means and how to have it. In time, I will have to find ways of defining something even more elusive, "womanhood." How will I begin? I do believe there's a physical aspect to womanhood, but no menstruating twelve-year-old is a woman in my book, nor is every sexually active sixteen-year-old (though she may have some womanly traits). I would tell my daughter it's about maturity, and seeing where you fit into the world, having an understanding of your own strengths and a growing acceptance and love of the "real you." And all of that can begin to come at the time of your physical changes, or much later.

Over the years, I have always tried to teach my girls about the feminine and masculine principles in their lives—saying that they need both to be balanced people, and encouraging them to see that both men and women have access to these traits. I have shown them through various conversations how there is strength in gentleness and how a warrior needs to be receptive to be the best warrior. We have talked a lot about how the feminine is about being a container, how it is about creating safe space for people and things to exist. I was trying to show them how the masculine needs a safe container to act within and that the feminine needs to be honored by the masculine. We have talked a lot about how in a contest of power the masculine principle can always overpower the feminine but how just because you win something by misusing power doesn't make what you did right, nor does it mean that you really win. We talk a lot about using our personal power in ways that respect the power of others and that overpowering others is always a mistake. Also we have talked in great detail about how we need to balance our lives with strong "doing" (active, masculine efforts) with strong "being" (receptive, nurturing feminine principles). We have looked at what happens when one of these two gets out of balance and how that makes us feel inside. I always encourage the idea that no one is whole without expressing both of these traits. These conversations are always grounded in the reality of our days—the examples arise in our conversations about real things. I also have spent a lot of time showing them what kind of trouble our culture gets in when we value only one principle—namely the masculine principle.

Each of these answers is, of course, "personal" in every sense of the word, and there are as many possible answers to these questions as there are women on the planet. Read them and see if you can locate bits and pieces of your own thinking in their words, or feel free to challenge and disagree with them. Just the process will bring you a step further in the journey toward "I-Thou" parenting.

We offer you the following questions and directions as a starting point for a dialogue—it can be an inner dialogue or one you can initiate with a friend, relative, or even the members of your reading group or church. Remember that there are no "right" answers to any of these questions. Nor are these the only questions; feel free to add in your own. We hope they will help you see what really informs your "performing self."

- What is the most important, defining aspect of "self"? Is it physical, spiritual, intellectual, moral, or a combination of several aspects?

- How important is your physical appearance to you? Have your looks been an important factor in your life?

- What does being "female" mean to you? Do you have a personal definition of "womanhood" and, if so, what is it?

- What traits or characteristics—of your personality, manner, habits, or anything else—do you think are most likely to get in the way of a meaningful dialogue with your daughter?

- What traits or characteristics are the assets you bring to your relationship with your daughter?

- Describe the dynamic between you and your daughter's father, whether you are still married to him or not. How does that dynamic affect your relationship with your daughter? How does that dynamic affect her relationship with you?

- Are you happy with yourself, and where you find yourself now?

- Are there issues or conflicts from your own adolescence that still spill over into the present?

- Define your relationship to your own mother. Can that relationship serve as a positive or negative model for you and your daughter?

- Describe a trait or quality of yours that you want your daughter to emulate. Then, describe a quality or trait that you would *not* want her to emulate.

Asking ourselves these questions opens up the possibility of engaging our daughters in a different kind of dialogue, one in which we can meet them "face to face."

~ ~ ~

Did I feel abandoned when my mother went to college when I was thirteen? I do remember feeling some resentment that she was away a lot. She'd often be out at night with new friends and often when I came home from school, there'd be a note on the table saying what was for dinner and when she'd be back. She often used abbreviations and always a heart with an "M" next to it for Mom. Once my older brother wrote on it, "No name, no date, poor spelling: D-" We all laughed about it but it stuck with me and I wonder if she ever saw it as a comment on something about our family life. I'm feeling traitorous talking about this because I don't begrudge her having a life—and that's what she began to have when she went back to school. She went from being a kind of sad and accommodating person to someone who began to understand what she wanted in life. She struggled with big questions, she began to have preferences, ideas, opinions, and I think she was both thrilled and frightened by it all. It was really a five- to six-year transformation. The fact that hers came at the same time as my own, teenage, transformation interests me still, and I haven't sorted it all out yet, but I know I'm glad she's the woman and the mother that she is now. If she'd stayed in her cocoon, we wouldn't have the great relationship I have

now, and maybe I wouldn't be a working mother, which I love being.
I must say that the irritation of not having my mother at home after
school is more than made up for in the fact that she became a fuller
person herself. And I didn't end up derailing as a result.

"Michelle," thirty-eight, married college professor, mother of two daughters,
one seven

In her wonderful memoir, *An American Childhood*, Annie Dillard
describes the way a child gets to "know" her mother, as imagined
from the child's point of view:

A young child knows Mother as a smelled skin, a halo of light, a
strength in the arms, a voice that trembles with feeling. Later the
child wakes and discovers this mother—and adds facts to impressions, and historical understanding to facts.[35]

As daughters, we know that the process of discovering "Mother,"
which Dillard describes so lyrically, is an ongoing one that continues throughout our lives; we see our mothers differently as they and
we age. We adjust our visions of our mother not only as they reveal
more of their own histories but as we acquire histories of our own;
our understanding of their stories and their choices shifts over time.
As mothers, we experience the process from another point of view
entirely as our adolescent daughters begin to refine their childhood
impressions of us. That process will have special meaning for our
daughters, as they look to both our reflective selves and performing
selves as possible templates for their own definition of self.

Michelle's story, which begins this chapter, illuminates one
aspect of this particular stage of parenting: the way in which the
mother's "performing self" can provide a daughter with a model for
her own self-expression. Her mother's own effort to become a person in her own right—a human being with ideas, preferences, and
opinions—validated Michelle's own journey into selfhood. What
her mother became—a stronger, more confident, more authentic

person—confirmed Michelle's own best thoughts about herself and, moreover, laid the groundwork for a supportive relationship that has continued to grow over the course of time—a benefit far outweighing whatever measure of adolescent irritation Michelle felt at the time.

The "performing self" is, in fact, more complex than the reflective self; our performing selves send our daughters (and, for that matter, everyone who comes into contact with us during the course of an hour, a day, a week, a year of our lives) literally thousands and thousands of messages. We've already talked about how research confirms that girls learn from their mothers' example—they take their cues from us on matters as various as dieting, politics, and relationships, and evolve their own definitions of gender roles by the division of labor in our households. They learn equally from our forthright statements *and* our silence on important issues; they absorb the lessons learned from the arguments we have *and* those we avoid at all costs. We teach them all manner of skills and attitudes, both consciously and unconsciously, from cooking and driving to managing responsibility and expressing anger. They watch what we do with our lives, the choices we make, the priorities we set—whether we work or stay at home with our children—and begin to draw their conclusions about what women "do" in the world.

Like roughly three-quarters of the women reading these pages, I work—though, unlike most of them, I travel a great deal. I don't relish the idea of being away from home but travel is part and parcel of the job of being a network correspondent. I am lucky in that I am able to have good help and that, more important, my husband stays at home, but there is no question that my daughters' experience is very different from that of my own childhood. My mother was the fulcrum of the children's daily routine. My parents did, of course, take the occasional trip and there were a few times when I came home to an empty house after school but they were, as I recall, rare.

I know that how much I travel is an issue for my girls, and that the void that they feel when I'm gone—despite the other caring adults in the household—is real. (My six-year-old son is only now beginning to talk about it.) Kate lingers in the driveway as I pull out, and Rachel sighs that I am gone too much. In the last few months, Rachel, my middle child, has been irritable and grouchy and has complained repeatedly that her siblings get more attention than she does. To a great extent, she is right; of the three children, Rachel is the most self-sufficient, a self-starter by nature, and the first to say that she can do it—whatever *it* is—on her own. And so the two others tend to move to the head of the line. The last time I had to fly to New York, she seemed genuinely sad and I resolved to do something about it.

I had a book signing in Santa Barbara and thought that the perfect antidote might be a mother-daughter weekend alone. I called the airline, cashed in some miles, and got her a ticket to travel with me. I planned to surprise her on the way to school on Friday. The surprise, though, was on me: She declined the offer, saying that she had "other plans"—a sleepover with a girlfriend on Saturday and a morning run with someone else on Sunday. So I offered the ticket to my older daughter, Kate, who was delighted to go, and we had a wonderful time. We got home on Sunday even before Rachel got back from her friend's house.

Sitting alone in the car that Friday morning after she went off to school, I felt it was a no-win situation. On the one hand, I was trying to be sensitive to Rachel's complaints about both my schedule and the amount of attention she gets, both of which have a real legitimacy. On the other, I can't stop traveling—it's part of what I do—nor can I wave a wand and change the ways in which my other children need me. The solution I came up with—a weekend for two—was one she rejected out of hand. I was annoyed, and I immediately wondered whether she was, somehow, paying me back and showing me that, if I had my schedule, she had hers too. I took a deep breath and kept my counsel: Maybe, I thought, the gesture was enough for her. Maybe it showed her that I was listening and sensitive to her needs.

I have no doubt that, sometime soon, Rachel will complain about my not being home when she wants me there. When she does, I won't bring up the Santa Barbara weekend but I'll try to see if we can carve out some time together, in a busy household, in which she doesn't have to "share" me with anyone. It's hard for me not to feel guilty when the girls complain or to second-guess myself when they tell me how much they miss me when I'm gone. I have to accept that, at this and at other points in their lives, there will be aspects of my "performing" self that don't quite mesh with their vision of a perfect world and a perfect mother—a mother eternally on call in the kitchen. I know that there are times when my nightly phone call from another city or the homework help I fax doesn't quite cut it for them. At the same time, I also know that having a mother who is recognized for her accomplishments is important to them and that, equally, they appreciate the financial security my work makes possible. But as they move toward adulthood, they will use their views of my choices to shape their own.

Culturally, the euphoria of women's "having it all" has given way to a sobering discussion of the costs of women's choices, and an examination of the real-life conflicts between work and family, personal ambition and emotional commitments, for women and men alike. These conflicts are not likely to be resolved anytime soon. As mothers, we can only do our best to make sure that the lessons we communicate to our daughters through our performing selves are, in fact, those we wish them to learn. We need to be sensitive to the fact that our choices may not always make them happy.

A large part of adulthood is about making choices, and our daughters will, likely as not, begin that process by examining ours in all areas of life, starting with what we do with our days. Challenging a mother's choices—no matter what they are—is often part of the process of growth. One fifteen-year-old girl, the daughter of a commuting lawyer, never fails to mention how her mother is "always" late for every school function, even when her mother shows up on time; when I *can* make it to a soccer practice, my daughter is quick to point out another mother who has "never" missed one. Alternatively, our children may fault us for having work that is not interesting, high-paying, or prestigious enough. One stay-at-home mother of three adolescent girls is routinely castigated for being "just a housewife" who "doesn't know anything." "Why don't you do anything real?" another fourteen-year-old asks her mother, who stays at home caring for three children and an aging mother.

Whether we acknowledge it or not, every choice we make has a cost. When we work outside of the home, we trade something of value—financial security, independence, personal satisfaction, intellectual stimulation—for something else of value—being home after school, helping our girls with their homework, going to soccer practice or just meeting their friends. When we choose to stay home with our children, we pay the price of having a more narrowly focused definition of self than we might otherwise have had. We give up financial independence as well as other less tangible benefits that working in the world might have given us in exchange for uninterrupted time with our daughters and the kind of day-to-day involvement that is often elusive for the working, commuting parent.

Each choice has its own, distinct cost. Unless our society changes more rapidly than it has in the past, the conflict between work and family will be a factor in our daughters' future. Adolescent girls still believe they can "have it all"—a belief that, from their point of view, gives some validity to their criticism of their mothers' choices. As Dr. Jacquelynne Eccles remarks:

When you ask girls and boys what they are going to do with their lives, the vast majority of girls think they're going to do it all. They do not see that the conflict between the demands of work and family is out there. They have to deal with it in college and later on. Our data suggest that adolescent girls are, in fact, even more career-oriented than boys are, and they want higher-paying and high-prestige jobs and certainly have higher educational aspirations than boys do. They also assume they will be mothers—that they can do it "all".

The tension between high achievement and other "feminine" goals emerges, according to Dr. Eccles, when girls are older—between eighteen and twenty-two—when the high aspirations held in high school are modified or even replaced by less demanding goals. The data confirms that the real challenge is having girls keep a broad array of occupations in mind during college and after.

Perhaps one way we can help our daughters hold on to those high aspirations is to give up that phrase "having it all," which, in the end, may be neither useful nor productive. Choice, invariably, involves giving up something else that is potentially valuable. Not too long ago, I gave a talk to residents at a prestigious medical school. The number of young female doctors in the audience testified to how opportunities have opened up for women (and how girls have broadened their sights and horizons) since my own residency over twenty-five years ago. The question of "having it all" came up in the context of women who became mothers during their residencies. I was asked what I thought, and my answer disappointed more than a number of them. In my opinion, residency is a focused and necessarily intense learning experience that is incompatible with motherhood. In this context, motherhood is a distraction from the work that needs to be done by the physician-in-training. Before you groan, as the young women in the audience did, I will answer the next question they asked me: Don't male residents become fathers, after all? Yes, they do—but they have wives who are not residents. Being a doctor and a mother are not mutually exclusive—but there is the question of timing. There is no getting around the fact that the years traditionally devoted to a man's building a career coincide with the years of a woman's fertility; like it or not, our biology pretty much dictates that our choices will always be different in kind from those of men.

Let's teach our daughters about "having what they want" rather than telling them about "having it all" without ever discussing the costs. If we, our daughters' mothers, can begin to have an open dialogue about women's choices—and if we can finally set aside the judgmental tone that has characterized the American discussion of women's priorities—we can, perhaps, begin to take advantage of the variety of women's experiences. Then if we find ourselves unable to meet our daughters' needs during these crucial years of adolescence, we can turn to other women for support and help.

And then, perhaps, we can work together to raise daughters who hang on to both their self-esteem and their high aspirations, and who will be, by the time they reach adulthood, ready to make their own choices.

What, then, is the nature of these two separate but intertwined journeys of mothers and daughters?

For mothers, the journey is one out of old ways of mothering into new ones. First and foremost, it is a journey of adjustment— adjustment to the changes in your child, to the different demands put upon you as a source of guidance and reason, to the challenge of supporting your daughter in her growth, to her demands for a new kind of relationship and communication. Among the goals are:

- **Understanding adolescence as a process that takes years.** We need to try to reconcile our perception of our child's external growth—the way in which she appears to have crossed the line into adulthood physically—with what we know about her psychological and emotional maturity, stage by stage. Our daughters want us to be perceptive advocates, not sideline critics.

- **Becoming conscious of the ways in which our "performing selves" teach our daughters about themselves.** We need to become more aware of what and how we model attitudes toward attractiveness, weight, sexuality, and relationship, as well as standards pertaining to morality and character.

- **Becoming secure enough to give our children the room to disagree or even criticize us and remembering that setting standards for their behavior and a set of immutable rules designed to keep them safe does not mean parenting without dialogue.** Listening, at this stage of a daughter's life, is every bit as important as talking to her.

- **Understanding that true dialogue is not a single talk about sex, drugs, or high grades, the confessional favored by talk-show hosts, or a lecture, but an ongoing discussion that should change over time as our daughters mature.**

- **Getting rid of the preconceptions we have about adolescence as a time to "get through" or the adolescent girl as one who needs "straightening out."** We need to focus instead on the needs of the individual girl in front of us, and to respect the ways in which she is different from any other girl you know or knew, yourself included. Paying attention— understanding her areas of strength and weakness—will also help us identify real problems or difficulties she may be experiencing, and to seek professional help for her when she needs it.

- **Involving ourselves in our daughters' lives in ways that are meaningful to them and to us.** As parents and communities, we need to recognize that, despite the cultural babble about a "tribe apart" and "separation," our daughters need us for more than just spending money or a lift to the mall. We need to look at our daughters' adolescence as a time when the "work" of parenting isn't "easing up" but simply changing in kind.

- **Combining a realistic assessment of the dangers in society with an appreciation that appropriate, healthy risk-taking is part of learning responsibility.** At the same time, we need to make sure the risks our daughters take are appropriate—and that their judgment and ability to make decisions are well developed enough to support them.

Last but not least, because mothering an adolescent girl requires an evolution of our parenting skills, we have to look at ourselves honestly and identify those areas where we have difficulty, and to seek out help and support when we need them.

For most girls, even if the journey through adolescence is not overtly painful, it will feel, at times, stressful and challenging, daunting and uncomfortable. The daughter's adjustment—to a changing body, to new feelings, to new demands in school and in her peer group, to the pressure to establish herself as a person in her own right, to wresting validation from those she loves and cares about, to having to form judgments and thoughts on her own, to finding her place in a complicated world—is even more dramatic and unsettling than the one her mother experiences. The same myths and cultural stereotypes that encourage mothers (and fathers) to turn away from their daughters at this crucial time may also wrongly encourage our daughters to look away from the support and love the adults in their life can give them, even though the research overwhelmingly confirms that this is *not* what they really want.

The Harvard School of Public Health has recently delineated the "ten tasks of adolescence," the areas in which our children need to meet the challenges posed by growth. These are also the areas in which they will need our support. In the following chapters, we will look at most of these "tasks" in close detail but we offer them to you as a useful summary of the "work" of adolescence from the daughter's point of view:

- Adjusting to a sexually maturing body, establishing a sexual identity, and developing the skills for romantic relationships

- Developing and applying abstract thinking skills, including constructing philosophies and beliefs

- Acquiring a more complex view of relationships, as well as developing skills in resolving conflicts and problems

- Developing new coping skills as well as strategies for decision-making

- Identifying meaningful moral standards, values, and systems of belief

- Understanding and communicating more complex emotions

- Forming friendships that are mutually close and supportive

- Establishing key aspects of identity

- Meeting the demands of increasingly mature roles and responsibilities

- Renegotiating relationships with parents and other adults[36]

With all of these tasks at hand, our daughters will, over the course of the years, look into the mirror of their mothers' faces, looking for validation of their progress, of their growth, of their inner selves.

For our parts, just a glance at these tasks makes it abundantly clear that there are any number of areas of potential conflict and disagreement.

It is up to us to make sure that the mother-daughter dialogue is a productive one.

~ ~ ~

It hurts to say this, but I felt closer to my daughters a few years ago when they were "little girls." I certainly love them just as much (if not more) now, but it feels as if I have fewer avenues in which to express that. I can help them with their schoolwork, encourage and help them with sports, but I am not the "go to" parent when it comes to their emerging hormonal changes and all the attendant new interests that accompany them. It's hard, if not outright impossible, for a father to engage his eighth grade daughter in conversation about starting menstruation. I can't relate. Our sixth grader has started to notice boys (and vice versa) and counts among her new obsessions ear-piercing and makeup. I playfully tease her about the boys (all the while keeping my fingers crossed that it's the innocent puppy love it seems to be), but I can't for the life of me conjure up a thought about makeup. I take that back—I came up with one: I told her no sky-blue eye shadow, never. Beyond that, I have no opinions, interest, or experience in makeup.

As they've begun to develop, it almost seems as if a gender barrier has risen between us. The odd thing is, it feels equally frustrating and natural. My spouse continually refers to the girls' current and imminent hormonal changes and the changes in their behavior; I feel almost as if I simply have to take her at her word, suspend my skepticism, and try to be understanding and supportive. I know that I can and will—that is, if my daughters feel they can confide in me—guide them in understanding young boys and their motivations (no advanced degrees necessary for that, to be sure), but in understanding themselves? My maleness will almost surely get in the way.

Doug, Nancy's husband, and father to Kate, fourteen, and Rachel, twelve

And what about fathers? What is the father's role during the years of adolescence, whether he lives with his daughter or not?

Once again, cultural contexts are important. Father-child relationships—both father-son and father-daughter—have undergone enormous changes since the older mothers among us (and even most of the younger ones) were adolescents. For most of the last century, particularly through the 1950s and 1960s, the role of American father was largely defined as "providing for" the family—shouldering responsibility for the family's economic welfare but little of the minutiae of day-to-day parenting. Generally, fathers were called on for larger decisions, crisis management, and administering punishment, as well as teaching boys and, to a lesser degree, girls the specific skills considered part of the "masculine" domain. Since the father's role was seen as pertaining to the family (not the children), apart from earning power, there were no cultural definitions of what made a "good" father, much less a "perfect" one.[37] (Culturally, mothers were and, for the most part, are held to a very different standard.)

The changes in the American family and the greater involvement of mothers in the work force have altered our vision of what fathers "do." Paternal involvement varies enormously from family to family; in some families, husband and wife are true "coparents," while in others, both child-rearing and household tasks are performed along more traditional lines. The involvement of divorced fathers no longer living with their daughters on a day-to-day basis varies just as dramatically from household to household.

~ ~ ~

How do I see my role as a father? I would like to be an alternative confidant, friend, adviser—a good deal more than I am at present. Perhaps this is just wishful thinking on my part, but I would like to be more than the provider of treats and events and the chauffeur and allowance-giver, which is very largely the role I now play. To a degree, this is inevitable for the non-residential parent, but I suspect adolescent girls in general may have trouble sharing with their fathers and so tend to keep them out of their loop.

Peter, age sixty-seven, writer, Peg's ex-husband and Alexandra's father

But, during the years of a girl's adolescence, while research underscores the numerous benefits of a father's active presence in a daughter's life, it also confirms that many girls neither actively seek out their fathers' help nor do they feel close to them.[38] The intensity that marks the mother-daughter relationship is, for the most part, largely absent from the relationship with the male parent. In her book *Altered Loves: Mothers and Daughters During Adolescence*, Terri Apter notes that the relationships between daughter and mother and daughter and father were not only markedly different, but that

> these differences covered every aspect of the relationship—her feelings, her sense of trust, and her sense of self. For what was remarkable was how she saw herself to be different in the company of each parent, and how she proved herself to be different by exercising a different level of maturity in the way she viewed each parent.

Among the significant differences Apter notes are not only different expectations—girls neither expected to "talk" to their fathers nor did they expect to take their fathers into their confidence—but different ways of arguing with them and resolving those arguments. Most important, perhaps, Apter writes that, in contrast to the mother-daughter dyad, "few girls assumed that they had this reciprocal power—to hurt and to heal—with their father." Apter concludes, with not a little bit of wistfulness, that "the strange, disturbing, and sad picture of father and daughter seems to be that during the daughter's adolescence, the distance between them increases."[39]

The physical changes of adolescence seem to signal a sea change in the relationship of father and daughter. Once our daughters stop looking like little girls and begin looking like women, our culture's alternate obsession and discomfort with female sexuality often translate into an awkward self-consciousness on the parts of daughter and father alike. As their daughters' bodies change, men used to hugging and kissing their little girls may back off; girls, on the other hand, conscious of their newfound physical maturity, may distance themselves because they can't think of a better solution. Without the physical component that may have been a childhood fixture of closeness, many father-daughter relationships may begin to founder. In families composed along more traditional lines—with an "authoritarian" style of parenting—the father who takes the role of the disciplinarian "straightening out" his adolescent daughter may be the parent the daughter resents most. Sometimes paternal influence can actually lower a young girl's self-esteem; fathers may, unconsciously and unwittingly, reinforce the cultural biases that encourage girls to identify, in Dr. Joan Jacobs Brumberg's words, "the body as the ultimate expression of self."

Fathers may find themselves not just mourning the closeness they once enjoyed with their little girls but feeling progressively disenfranchised as parents. The father of a nineteen-year-old girl confided his experience of loss after an important conversation with his daughter: "I remember the occasion well. Last spring, my daughter asked me to take her to the emergency room for the treatment of what by her description sounded like a urinary tract infection. On the way, I asked whether she was having sex. She hesitated, then said, 'Ye-e-e-s,' in that way that older girls or young women do when they mean to convey the sense that it's no big deal and they know all about it. I asked whether she peed afterward and, by her expression, it was clear that she thought my question was very strange. I had just enough time to explain the importance of urinating after sex to flush bacteria out when we got to the hospital. When she came out of the examination, she said I was right. That exchange, her revelation that she was having sex, my powerlessness to do anything other than accept it, affected me profoundly. Her innocence was gone without my having been included anywhere along the way in her decision-making process. It was the first really important decision she made entirely on her own, and it marked a change in our relationship. I would not characterize it as 'losing my little girl'; for me it was more a sense of having been forced to realize that she was making her own life and that I would be increasingly left out of it."

And yet fathers are important to our daughters' development and, as mothers, we need to help the fathers of our daughters initiate and maintain their own dialogues. Fathers, too, need to realize that individuation is different from "separation," and that continuing to talk with their daughters—on any number of subjects—is important to their well-being and their sense of connectedness to both of their parents. In fact, it's been suggested that "although we have little idea of what girls want or expect from their fathers or the men in their lives, the comfort men have with the rules of patriarchal cultures may provide girls with a perspective on, as well as experience with, negotiating male worlds. Indeed, fathers' involvement in their daughters' lives is positively associated with girls' work success, occupational competency, and sense of comfort in and mastery of the world around them."[40]

One father of two adolescent girls whose daughters are, at the moment, prone to challenging his every view, had this to say: "I feel very strongly that being able to disagree with one's parents is critical for adolescents of both genders, but perhaps even more important for girls than for boys. It is vitally important that we, the parents of daughters, make them feel that it is absolutely safe for them to disagree with us, argue with us, and sometimes even rebel against us. I say this as somebody who wasn't permitted to disagree and I feel that I paid a heavy price for that."

"Tim" believes that being able to disagree with your parents provides an important element of self-definition. As the father of girls—and an experienced corporate executive—he feels it is even more important for girls to be encouraged to question than it is for boys, because, "even though society and culture have changed enormously in the last forty years, it still seems that we expect and demand that girls behave with more restraint and control and mod-esty than boys do. If women trying to claw their way up the corpo-rate ladder act aggressive and demanding (which is the normal behavior of men making their way), they are seen as 'threatening' and 'bitches,' instead of being seen as acting in the way you are sup-posed to if you want to make it in American business. Since we still have this pernicious double standard about how boys are allowed to act without giving girls the same kind of freedom or latitude, I think it is absolutely critical that we give adolescent girls even more free-dom than boys to do battle with any authority they encounter."

Fathers, too, need to focus on becoming "authoritative" par-ents—and to consider their continuing and evolving relationship to their adolescent daughters an important part of their daughters' healthy development. While this book is mainly concerned with the "mirror" that is the mother's face, we all need to keep in mind that our daughter catches glimpses of herself in other places as well.

In the chapters that follow, we'll be taking a closer look at how we—mothers and fathers alike—can best help our girls on their journey.

## CHAPTER FOUR

# Blossoming—Forming the Self

For as long as I can remember, I had been transparent to myself, unselfconscious, learning, doing, most of every day. Now I was in my own way; I myself was a dark object I could not ignore. I couldn't remember how to forget myself. I didn't want to think about myself, to reckon myself in, to deal with myself every livelong minute on top of everything else—but swerve as I might, I couldn't avoid it. I was a boulder blocking my own path. I was a dog barking between my own ears, a barking dog who wouldn't hush.

So this was adolescence . . .

Annie Dillard, *An American Childhood*

Ask a seven-year-old girl who she is and the answer you'll get is concrete, tethered to the real world ("My name is Amy, I am seven, my mommy's name is Linda, and I have a baby sister named Jessica") and the realm of action ("I like drinking apple juice, drawing, and I play Barbies"). Ask a fourteen- or fifteen-year-old the same question and the answer, likely as not, will not only be contradictory in places ("I'm outgoing but kind of shy," "I think I'm focused but not always," "I'm cheerful but a little moody," "I care about how I do in school but grades aren't everything") but will describe parts of her private self—inner thoughts and feelings—that are unshown to the world. To borrow Annie Dillard's brilliant phrasing, a seven-year-old is "transparent" to herself—she is "un-self-conscious" both in being unaware of her "self" *and* in lacking those feelings of awkwardness and embarrassment that define the other meaning of "self-consciousness."

The fourteen- or fifteen-year-old, on the other hand, is in another place entirely. "Self-consciousness"—in both senses of the word—is part and parcel of her everyday existence. Her "self" may feel like the "boulder" Annie Dillard described or it may feel, to her, as though it's the object of everyone's attention. (Psychologists have a name for this—"imaginary audience"—and it can play a big part in the dynamic between you and your daughter. Because her own preoccupation with her self is so intense, she may wrongly believe that others examine her—both her behavior and her looks—with the same amount of scrutiny.) Thus, she is likely to be acutely aware of the degree to which her "self" is on display—in the hallways at school among her peers, at the dining room table with her parents, even in a public place surrounded by total strangers. I was reminded of this when, on a recent holiday, I bought Kate a two-piece bathing suit to wear on the beach. She looked, to my mother's eye, absolutely lovely in it but she flatly refused to leave the hotel room wearing it. At seven, she would have slipped into it without a thought and headed for the ocean; her almost-fifteen-year-old self was too "self-conscious" to wear it.

If adolescence is, in part, a process of finding answers to new questions, then surely the question that most occupies the adolescent girl is "Who am I?" Experts agree that a key task of adolescence is the formation of identity or the definition of self. These are familiar terms—"identity" and "selfhood" find their way into dozens and dozens of conversations, magazine articles, and books—but what precisely is meant by them? While forming an identity is described as a "task," it isn't work you can do by learning a specific skill—the way you learn to tie your shoes as a toddler, read a book at the age of seven, or drive a car at sixteen or seventeen. Defining the self is a different exercise entirely. While for the adolescent, the process of defining the self may feel (at times) like the most isolating of experiences, it doesn't and can't happen in isolation. The stereotype of the adolescent—sitting in her room behind closed doors, music blaring and diary open, the floor a jumble of discarded outfits and shoes—"finding herself" by shutting herself off from family

and their influence is no more accurate than any of the other adolescent mythologies. In fact, paradoxically, giving voice to the adolescent self—the first of the many definitions of self that are formed
over the course of a lifetime—needs a public forum for it to happen. As Susan Harter writes in *At the Threshold: The Developing
Adolescent*:

> Experimenting with one's persona, and determining whether this
> brings affirmation or denigration from others, is typically an emo-
> tional experience for the adolescent preoccupied with the challenge
> of self-definition. Such self-reflection is not limited to the present
> but extends to one's future self, what one would like to become.
>
> These processes do not occur, however, within an introspective
> vacuum. The self is a social construction. For example, the peer
> group looms large as a source of values, directives, feedback, and
> social comparison. Parental expectations, evaluations, and exhorta-
> tions also play a major role and may well conflict with the values of
> the peer culture. "In Search of the Self," therefore, defines a major
> drama that unfolds on center stage during adolescence, with a com-
> plicated cast of characters who do not always speak with a single
> voice.[1]

Answering the "Who am I?" question will, for many adolescent
girls, be like being asked to paint a self-portrait without a mirror
handy—they will have to imagine themselves before they can even
pick up the paint brush. The line in the sand our culture draws
between "childhood" and "adolescence"—recognized by parents
and daughters alike, and institutionalized by the educational system—may make it hard for our daughters to make use of their
familiar childhood definitions of self as they begin this new part of
the journey, leaving them feeling adrift. When old childhood passions—frogs, stuffed animals, dolls, even soccer or bike riding—
begin to seem "babyish," our daughters may begin to cast about for

new "passions" that either set them apart or identify them with a crowd or a clique. Sometimes, they will indeed find that "passion"; other times, they will pretend to have found it to satisfy others or for perceived social benefits, even though the "passion" isn't heartfelt.

Seen from this point of view, defining the self may feel, to our daughters at least, more like an act of invention or imagination than a task. They will try on identities for size—and the changes in them may take us by surprise: The athlete will morph into the actress, the ice skater into an aspiring model, the ebullient joker into a thoughtful and introspective poet, and back again. In this context—even apart from the emphasis our culture puts on the connection between a girl's "self" and her physical appearance— it's not hard to understand why the game of dress-up they played at six or seven suddenly becomes a real-life game as they begin to experiment with the easier, more accessible aspects of "self-invention." In search of the broad brush stroke, the adolescent will define herself in the small detail: One fourteen-year-old suddenly demands that her parents call her "Christi" rather than the name they'd chosen for her; another mother comes home from work to find both her daughter's hair *and* her bathtub dyed mauve; the captain of the soccer team quits at fifteen and gives up the comfortable, preppy clothing she's worn all her life for short skirts and high heels, much to her parents' chagrin and disappointment; another, from a churchgoing family, declares herself a Buddhist; a bright but quiet sixteen-year-old becomes the expert on "green men" and UFOs. Clean-scrubbed faces give way to eyeshadow and makeup; long hair is cropped, short hair grown long; names are changed, handwriting altered; bedrooms are redecorated and childhood toys banished. Books, magazines, movies, conversations on the Internet become the palette and brush for a self-portrait: "I am exactly like Drew," says one girl and, to make her point, she mimics Drew Barrymore's hairstyle and expression. Posters and pages cut out of magazines are tacked and taped up on bedroom walls—possible models for the "self" in the making.

More dangerously, a girl may begin to diet constantly or literally begin to starve herself; her dissatisfaction with how she looks may become a hallmark of her new self. Hiding her behavior from her friends and family may, in turn, compel her to lie and isolate herself even more. She may engage in dangerous behaviors—such as smoking cigarettes or taking drugs—that, in her eyes at least, make her appear more individual or more "adult." She may decide that being a straight-A student no longer suits the "self" she wants to cultivate, or that taking piano lessons is "a waste of time." She may begin to disassociate from her own true thoughts and feelings in order to please others—parents, peers, teachers—and to provide them with "the self" she thinks they want or expect from her or will make her an object of admiration. (This is called a "false self," as opposed to a "true self.") In a parallel pattern, she may engage in sexual behaviors that she hopes will establish a sense of self and validate her maturation but, in fact, do nothing more than make her feel degraded or, worse, put her at physical and psychological risk.

One part of the problem for many of our girls may well be that there are, in our society, limited venues in which the adolescent girl can actually explore and define the boundaries of self. It's been noted that both the organization of middle schools and junior high schools (which reduces the one-on-one contact between student and teacher, at a time when adolescents "have a great need for guidance and support from nonfamilial adults") and the shift in the school environment (emphasizing "competition, social comparison, and self assessment") may be detrimental, if not downright harm-ful, to the task of self-definition.[2] As already noted by Dr. Peter Scales elsewhere in this book, at the very time that adolescents need to find places where their autonomy and independence can be expressed in healthy ways, school environments tend to stress teacher control over student decision-making.[3] Work and employment constitute a large component of mature self-definition and in generations past, work—and the economic contribution made through work—helped the adolescent emerge into personhood. In the early part of the twenty-first century, Americans are likely to spend most if not all of their early, middle, and late adolescence in school; if they are employed, they often do menial work unassociated with their plans for the future, which contributes little to building their sense of self. (The money they earn may give them a sense of at least partial independence, but because whatever money they earn is usually for discretionary purposes, self-affirming "independence" is limited.) Since a college degree is considered as necessary as a high school education was in earlier generations (84 percent of adolescents plan on attending a four-year college), many will postpone taking care of themselves literally and financially until the years of early adulthood and, in doing so, delay the very activities that help define self throughout the adult lifetime. In previous generations, the formation of permanent romantic relationships—precursors to getting married and setting up an independent household—was another important marker of the self; that, too, for this generation of girls is put on hold until sometime in the first decade of "adulthood"—somewhere between twenty-five and thirty.

In her book *The Myth of Maturity*, Terri Apter notes that the implications of these sociological changes, in fact, stretch out far past the years of adolescence, for "the transition from teenager to adult has become fragmented and unpredictable."[4] "Leaving home" is often a temporary thing; according to Apter, 40 percent of young women (and 50 percent of young men) return home after college. Careers are no longer consistently launched independently; 58 percent of young people between the ages of twenty-two and twenty-four live with their parents, and 30 percent of those between twenty-four and thirty do. Ironically, as she notes, "while 'self-sufficiency' and independence and autonomy are more highly valued than ever, they have become increasingly difficult to attain."[5] The ramifications for young women (and young men, for that matter) are profound as they confront the stress of postponed or adjusted expectations; Apter cites the increasing rates of suicide, eating disorders, illicit drug use, and alcoholism among eighteen- to twenty-four-year-olds, as well as depression, anxiety, considerations of suicide, lowered expectations, and loss of confidence. The situation is often compounded by parents who, in an extension of the myth of separation, ascribe to what Apter has called the "myth of maturity" (and its corollary, the "myth of the spoiled child"). Believing in separation and unqualified independence, they may withhold the help and support their child actually does need to make the transition into adulthood successfully.

There are other ways, too, that changes in the social fabric of the United States have made it harder for girls to do the work of healthy self-expression. Recent research suggests that, as adolescents begin to open up their worlds and try to reformulate the self in a broader context than just that of the family (and begin, at the same time, to recast their relationships to their parents), they in fact want connection with other adults who can provide guidance, new points of view, and a dialogue about ideas, personal thoughts, and opinions. Unfortunately, not only are most American families geographically scattered—making it hard for an aunt or an adult cousin to become a constant in a girl's life—but most communities are no longer closely knit. With the exception of some after-school programs, it's often difficult, if not impossible, for girls to find adult mentors or "othermothers" as they are sometimes referred to. (The exception to this appears to be in the black community, where "othermothers" play a significant role.) In addition, the popular misconception that adolescents "want" to be left alone actively discourages adults from reaching out to them. In truth, researchers suggest that adolescents turn to their peers for guidance and support disproportionately precisely because they have, quite literally, nowhere else to turn.[6]

Put another way, while, on the one hand, our daughters are under pressure to define themselves "now"—to not only formulate their selfhood but demonstrate their independence and autonomy—there are few areas of life where they actually can. For all the evidence of "age compression"—with the pressure to "grow up" starting earlier and earlier—nonetheless it is taking many young people longer and longer to do precisely that. From that point of view, it's no wonder that the area of relationships with peers and family—one of the few arenas available to articulate the self, save academic and athletic achievement—is often perceived by mothers as full of tension and intensity.

~ ~ ~

Usually, other than feeling like a real wimp sometimes, I feel like I'm a pretty good mom. The wimp part happens when my daughter, through her superior (at times) negotiating skills, can cut me down to a mere shadow in minutes. Over fourteen years with a usually amiable child, I've learned several crucial things: Criticism doesn't work and my opinion is often not wanted (although I must say, when shopping, she knows that I have the attributes of a personal shopper, and will tell her honestly and accurately whether something looks good on her). Somehow she knows that I know what is going on in her life—I've instilled what I think is a healthy paranoia in her, backed up by some judicious observation into her business. I would grade myself 9 out of 10 as a mother, therefore.

What are my strengths? I am smart, I've been there (though not exactly where she is, since times are so different and I never wore those tight tank tops), and I've got a really, really good sense of humor.

And my weaknesses? She does have the ability to put me over the edge at times, times when my husband will literally have to separate us. She seems to me sometimes to be rather hard-hearted, which gets me very upset and I show it.

Some things I keep to myself—mainly about friends whom I think to be possibly inappropriate. This does not happen too much. For the most part, I find that the less I mess with her, the better we get along. I don't know if she'd agree with this.

"Martha," fifty-two, artist, mother to an adopted daughter, now fifteen

For centuries, poets, philosophers, psychologists, psychiatrists, and scientists have all tackled the question of what we mean when we use the word "self," and have offered up possible answers. A small digression into what we and the experts mean by "self" is worthwhile because it illustrates the conundrum of self-definition the adolescent girl faces, taking those first baby steps on the road to defining her "self," and illuminates the degree to which the mother's own self-definition is changed by the experience of her daughter's adolescence.

In his book *Altered Egos: How the Brain Creates the Self*, Dr. Todd Feinberg, professor of neurology and psychiatry, offers a theory of how the brain creates the "unified" self. He posits that "relatedness" is central to the definition of self, and goes on to show the degrees of relatedness by which we define our "selves." For example, he writes that "we all have a natural sense of where we as selves end and our environments begin." This may sound pretty rudimentary—that is, you are separate from the chair you are sitting on and the page you are reading, I am separate from the computer screen and the keyboard on which I am typing—but as Dr. Feinberg points out, the distinction between the boundaries of the self and the environment are "actually more dynamic than rigid." Or, as he puts it, "Things or other persons can be relatively close to the inner core of the self's experience, or they can be quite removed."[7] Dr. Feinberg uses a homely example about shoes, which is relevant to what you might well experience with your adolescent daughter as she negotiates some aspects of self-definition through clothing and hairstyles. He points out that while someone else's shoes have no relevance to your self, the shoes on your own feet may, in fact, have different degrees of relation to that self.[8] Picture your own shoes and think about them for a moment while I go through the exercise on the page. I have two pairs of shoes, one a new pair with high heels and the other my old red clogs. My new shoes are significant to me only in that they are new and I need them to conduct an important television interview. On the other hand, my favorite red clogs have a very different significance; they are, as the saying goes, "me," even though both of my daughters have forbidden me to wear them when I pick them up from school.

Dr. Feinberg goes on to describe the relationship between "self" and the "environment":

> The persons, places, objects, and events that one's self experiences are imbued with feeling—the feeling of how one relates to things in a personal sense. Our identities are built around this sense of relatedness. Personal relatedness provides the structure within which the self is anchored in the world. The self is a continuum of relationships. An individual's own body, spouse, and family members are "ego-close." They bear a particular personal relationship to the self, identity with the self; we care about these items, these events, these people, in particular ways. They are significant. The objects of the world, which for us have no personal significance, could be considered "ego-distant." The impersonal world, the stranger on the street, is less likely to be imbued with any sense of personal significance.[9]

Dr. Feinberg labels those people, places, and things that have personal significance to us "ego-close," in distinction to those that have no personal significance, which he calls "ego-distant." *But* because the relationship between the self and the outside environment—people, places, objects, and events—is dynamic rather than rigid, an object or a person can go from being "ego-close" to "ego-distant." This process—called alienation—depends, as Dr. Feinberg wisely puts it, on a single condition: "To become alienated from something, we first have to be close to it."[10] (The reverse process, although he doesn't name it, in which "ego-distant" becomes "ego-close," could be called friendship, empathy, or even love.)

Dr. Feinberg goes on to say that in the psychologically healthy individual, there is "an integrated and comfortable relation of the self and the world," and that the "boundaries between the world and other people are held in delicate balance," a balance that is maintained "automatically and in large part unconsciously." In fact, he observes, "We are not generally aware of these boundaries until they are violated, until someone or something gets too close or too distant, until one feels merged with or alienated from the world."[11] As adults who have experienced the waxing and waning of all manner of relatedness during years of living—relationships formed or abandoned, connections to events and places refined and redefined—we understand how the dynamism of those boundaries shapes our sense of self. But what about our daughters who are just beginning the journey?

Dr. Feinberg's discussion helps us understand how, in one sense, as our daughters begin to formulate their sense of self, the boundaries between the self and the world—people, places, objects, and events—suddenly become fluid. As they begin to explore what relatedness means to them—both in literal and theoretical terms—they may appear, to the adults around them, as capricious or changeable, as people and things become "ego-close" and "ego-distant" by turns. In fact, what they are testing is the boundaries of self and "the world." What follows is a true story of two mid-adolescent girls, which demonstrates how what Dr. Feinberg describes may work in an adolescent's life.

"Meghan" and "Sarah" were inseparable, best friends since nursery school when they were four. Even though they went on to different schools, they played together nearly every week. They always said they were sisters—without all the fights and squabbles. They were a study in opposites—blond, athletic, and outgoing Meghan was a born leader, while dark-haired Sarah was shy and introspective, a storyteller at heart—and that suited them just fine. They invented games together—one year, they were both enchanted by the book *Harriet the Spy*, and so spies they became—their "spy box" was labeled "Top Secret" and held all manner of things essential to the art of spying on parents and anyone else around for their sleepovers. Their friendship went through stages and phases—the shared bubble bath in third grade and the dress-up mode in fourth gave way to collecting Beanie Babies, diving contests, and whispered secrets in fifth. They spent hours speculating who would get her period first and bought matching first bras—stretchy triangles that they didn't need but that made them feel grown-up. Their identical picture frames, necklaces, even the keychains that dangled from their L.L.Bean backpacks, all read "Best Friends."

They ended up in the same middle school, but in different home-rooms, and celebrated by wearing blue nail polish. They had the same schedule a day apart and, as they turned twelve, their friend-ship was an everyday thing. They phoned every night and e-mailed back and forth; they went to their first school dance together. Then, subtly, things began to shift. Meghan worried constantly about being popular, and sought out new friends who did too. The old twosome became a foursome of girls, with Meghan as the unofficial leader—she'd choose the table where they ate lunch, set up the Fri-day afternoon excursions to the local drugstore and shops, organize the four-way playdates that rotated from house to house. Sarah didn't like the other girls in the group as much as she liked Meghan and she didn't care about the things the others spent hours talking about—the "A" list of kids, gossiping or putting other girls down, "going" with boys. Summer came, and Sarah began to set new goals for herself. She wanted a bigger circle of friends, she thought—new friends with different interests.

September came and seventh grade started. Sarah was in a brand-new homeroom with four girls she hardly knew but thought she could get to know better. Meghan's homeroom was, by her lights, a "disaster"—no one "cool" or "fun"—so she focused on seeing her old friends at lunch and during recess. The first confrontation was at lunch: When Sarah brought over her classmates, Meghan insisted there wasn't "room" for them, just for Sarah. Sarah said, "No thanks." The same scene played out the following day, and then the day after that. Sarah ate with her new friends; Meghan expanded her group to include a fourth. Then, six weeks before Halloween, Meghan demanded that Sarah make up her mind about who she was joining for trick-or-treating. It was, she explained, an "either/or situation"—her group, just the five of them—or not. Once again, Sarah refused. The pattern over the next few months stayed the same: The more Meghan tried to control Sarah, the more determined Sarah was to do things with other people. For Sarah, it was a year of discovery—she made new friends, found new interests. She tried to talk to her old friend about what was happening but Meghan didn't see a middle ground: Either Sarah was in her group or she wasn't.

After eight years of friendship, these two thirteen-year-old girls now walk down the same hallways without exchanging so much as a glance or a greeting. Sarah sometimes misses having one "best" friend to share things with but she genuinely likes how all of her friends are different. Even though they eat lunch together, go to one another's birthday parties, and have sleepovers and play dates in groups of two, the five girls aren't really a clique or a group. Each of them is into something different: One does Irish step-dancing, another loves soccer, a third crafts earrings and is teaching herself to make clothes on a sewing machine, and a fourth enjoys reading and spending time alone. Sarah's new passions are Buddhism, art, and opera—in no particular order. Boys are, for her, something she'll get to when she's older—she explains, solemnly, that she's "not going with anyone this year"—and at the moment, she likes the variety the more loosely formed friendships offer her.

This story characterizes adolescence, and may echo your own daughter's experiences with shifting allegiances. Each of these girls unconsciously took the first step toward defining the self by testing and changing the boundaries of "relatedness." In their case, moving forward to define the "self" involved letting go of a friendship formed in and maintained throughout childhood when the differences between them were perceived as neither meaningful nor important. The two very different ways they've chosen to define themselves—one closely identifying herself with a clique or group and the other with more loosely defined friendships—may again change in time as they each seek out different ways of self-expression.

While the boundaries between the self and the outside world are always dynamic, during the course of adolescence, they are even more so—sometimes even uncomfortably so. An adolescent girl's changeability—often popularly but wrongly ascribed to "raging hormones"—is, in fact, a function of the developing self. If, as Dr. Feinberg tells us, "the self is a continuum of relationships," we can imagine how unanchored the adolescent feels as she begins to explore what is and isn't important to her, what she does and does not believe, the things and people she does and doesn't care about, who she is now and who she wants to become. Because the self is a social construct, according to Dr. Susan Harter, Professor of Psychology at the University of Denver, "socialization pressures require teenagers to develop different selves in different roles."[12] But as a result, the answer to "Who am I?" may seem, at times, hopelessly out of reach when the adolescent tries to reconcile not only the sometimes contradictory aspects of her emerging self but the contradictory assertions of the culture about "feminine" behavior. Is she the concentrated but reticent girl she shows to her English teacher? ("Why am I such a wuss around her? She scares me a little.") What makes her pick on her younger sister when being nice to people is so important to her? ("I don't know—she just drives me crazy.") How can she be so quiet around her friends when her parents are always telling her to "pipe down" or "ease up"? ("Being liked at school is really important to me. I worry I might say the wrong thing. My mom and dad say I mouth off too much.") Why does she act so "dorky" around boys? ("I don't know. Talking to guys makes me nervous.") Is she stable or flaky? Shallow or deep? Nice or self-effacing? A leader or a follower?

For girls, these contradictions may present a crisis as they try to combine all those various pictures of self reflected in all the "outside world" mirrors that surround them literally and figuratively into a single, consistent theory of self. The question of "Who am I?" is complicated by the other questions that crowd into the adolescent's mind: "Who do I want to be?" "Who should I be?" "Who can I be?" "Who will they let me be?" "Who will I become?" The answers to these questions are as fluid as the world of relatedness in which the adolescent operates.

Understanding that testing those boundaries between the self and the outside world is part of the work of adolescence may make it possible for each of us to weather the sea changes which, to one degree or another, will characterize our relationships to our daughters. We will not be exempt from the process for the simplest of reasons: We are central to how they see themselves.

~ ~ ~

I met Linda when I was thirteen, at the beginning of eighth grade. I'd just moved from suburban New Jersey to Manhattan and was entering an all-girls private school for the first time in my life. Needless to say, I suffered a certain amount of culture shock, but it was lessened considerably by the fact that I made a good friend almost instantly. I think Linda had always felt a bit left out—and I was the proverbial fish out of water. So that's how we ended up gravitating toward one another but we became good friends because we just seemed to be on the same wavelength. An awful cliché, I know, but it really sums it up perfectly—we weren't all that much alike on the surface, and yet we had the same sense of humor, the same snide teenage worldview, and absolutely the same taste in clothes (think slutty Beatnik, with a little Carnaby Street thrown in for good measure). It was one of those friendships where you were always happiest in the other's company—I spent almost an entire summer with her, and it didn't seem like too much at all.

What inserted a wedge between us was, I guess, competitiveness—for boys, definitely, but also competitiveness that revolved around our looks. I was very insecure about my looks in those days—particularly about my glasses—and Linda seemed to have a need to be the Prettiest Girl in the World. (Who knows? Maybe we all do at that age.) In any case, she'd do things like talk up her own beauty (and her Devastating Effect on Men) at the expense of my own.

Which is all really sad. By tenth grade, we were no longer best friends. Years later—easily over a decade—she called me out of the blue and she started telling me this story about her fear of flying, and it was so funny, and I remembered vividly how very much on each other's wavelengths (there's that cliché again) we used to be. And I thought, Wouldn't it be great to be friends again? And of course, we have gotten back in touch since then, and had some terrific conversations. But I'm still guarded. I still don't entirely trust her, much as I'd like to.

"Beth," age forty-eight, and mother to "Eleanor," age nine

When mothers of adolescent daughters sit down to talk, one of the things they're likely to talk about is peer groups (and of course, sex, drugs, and violence). The focus by the media on peer groups—which is largely and often frighteningly negative—feeds maternal worries; we are likely to see our own girls as falling prey to potential bad influences, expert opinion notwithstanding. But even though peer influence is not uniformly negative, at the same time we need to pay attention to the social environment of the schools our girls attend. We've already noted that harassment—specifically sexual harassment—is a real issue that needs to be addressed by parents with a certain amount of watchfulness. Bullying—while most often associated with boys—is another area in which some of our daughters will find themselves at risk. A study in the *Journal of the American Medical Association* published in April of 2001, reporting a study of sixth- through tenth-graders in the United States, revealed that 35 percent of girls reported being bullied in school. While being bullied about looks or speech was common for both sexes, girls reported more incidences of verbal bullying—through rumors and sexual comments—than physical harassment. (With boys, bullying takes on a more physical form.) Soberly, the authors concluded that bullying, in the United States, is an important problem.[13]

It goes without saying that instances of sexual harassment or bullying must be taken seriously and investigated by every mother, even if your daughter protests that she does not "need" your help. Do not assume that coping with either harassment or bullying will make your daughter self-reliant or more resilient, or teach her how to stand up for herself; the research is absolutely unequivocal on this issue. Just because verbal forms of harassment and bullying are both more commonplace—they may even have been part of your own adolescent experience—and appear less alarming than their physical counterparts does not make them acceptable. Become proactive, and find out by talking to teachers, counselors, school authorities, *and* other parents to what degree—if any—your school tolerates these types of incidents. (Same-sex bullying—girls on girls, for example—may be wrongly considered as relatively harmless. And in certain parts of the country and in certain schools, there is still a "boys will be boys" attitude toward verbal sexual harassment.)

When it comes to peer groups, most of us bring our own emotional baggage from our own adolescence along for the ride. Who among us doesn't remember the exclusionary cliques of junior high or high school, or the terrible fear of peer rejection? Who doesn't remember longing to be part of a specific group—and never quite getting the invitation? (I do, and I still remember how much it hurt then, though I sometimes wonder what happened to all of those girls I thought "had it all.") The "why" of cliques and crowds—their sudden emergence in the social environment of early adolescence—is complicated and intimately connected to the adolescent's search for the self. Research reveals that cliques and "crowds" perform both positive and negative functions in an adolescent's life. According to Dr. B. Bradford Brown, Professor of Human Development at the University of Wisconsin, the changes in peer groups are affected not only by psychological changes and puberty (the new interest in the opposite sex) but by the environment of the larger middle and junior high schools composed of what he calls "a much larger and shifting array of peers" compared to the stability of the elementary classroom. Thrust into a new, more diverse environment, cliques and crowds not only help the adolescent to sort out her identity but permit her to categorize other peers, making it easier to negotiate relationships with peers she hardly knows. According to Dr. Brown, a "clique" performs the function of identifying an adolescent's friends. "Crowds," on the other hand, are usually based on broader stereotypes; they may break down among socioeconomic, racial, or ethnic lines, or reflect activities and interests— "cheerleaders," "social types," "brains," and so on. If "cliques" serve to categorize friends, then "crowds" tend to identify the individual from the peer group's point of view. Crowds are larger than cliques and are what Dr. Brown calls "reputation-based"; the individuals in a crowd may or may not socialize with one another. Because crowd affiliations reflect "a personal evaluation," most adolescents resist being labeled as part of a crowd.[14]

There are many variations on the theme of how the adolescent girl uses crowds and cliques to bolster her sense of self; some girls will feel comfortable being labeled within a certain clique or crowd while others will work hard at changing the peer perception of who they are. Still others will deliberately define themselves as being outside of any particular crowd, or aspire to a different crowd than the one they are perceived to belong to. As Dr. Brown points out, "For teenagers who successfully locate an acceptable niche, who form a supportive network of clique mates and settle into a crowd whose image is compatible with their activities and aspirations, peer groups promise to be a highly adaptive context in which to negotiate adolescence. For those who either falter in these tasks or choose a dysfunctional crowd, peer groups can have maladaptive consequences."[15] These peer group affiliations are fluid over time.

For many mothers, peer influence—particularly that of a girl's inner circle of friends—will emerge as an area of concern. Over coffee, one mother complains that ever since "Ella"—a high school junior with straight As and a member of the swimming team—has become friends with a girl whose parents have little or no expectation that she will go to college, her daughter has not only stopped going to practice but has let her grades slip. Night after night, mother and daughter do battle over homework, undone college applications, and the amount of time spent on the Internet and telephone. With each successive argument, each becomes more recalcitrant; each time the mother disparages the new girlfriend, the daughter's loyalty to her deepens. Another woman expresses concern that the crew of girls her fourteen-year-old has taken up with is too "social" and too "fast" for her taste, and that the Friday night parties the eighth-graders attend are largely unsupervised. Her worst fears are confirmed when she calls the mother who is supposedly the official hostess of one Friday night gathering; the parents are, in fact, out for the evening, their seventeen-year-old son tells her. My own twelve-year-old makes friends with a girl who is socially quite precocious and whose mother, a stunning former model, is proud of her precocity. Without much ado (and without confrontation), we adopt a new house rule pertaining to the friendship: All sleepovers are to take place at my house. Another mother takes a more extreme stance when her adolescent gets involved with a crowd of kids she doesn't approve of; she pulls the child out of school entirely, and begins a homeschooling program. The daughter perceives this as no different from being under house arrest and, in response to her mother's decision, literally stops eating.

Friendships become a special concern for mothers for a variety of complicated reasons. It's true that the negative media portrayal of peer groups—often depicted only slightly better than dangerously coercive—increases parental anxiety, without ever balancing the positive effects peers and friendship can have in encouraging and supporting our children throughout adolescence. The research, though, reveals the importance of peers to the formation of self; in *At the Threshold*, Ritch C. Savin-Williams and Thomas J. Berndt write, "For many adolescents relations with friends are critical interpersonal bridges that move them toward psychological growth and social maturity."[16] Friendship takes on a different aspect for girls than it does for boys; the research notes, for example, that girls have smaller circles of friends than boys but spend more time with them. The model for female friendship—which won't come as a big surprise to any woman reading these words—is different in kind from that of adolescent males. Girls' friendships are self-disclosing, and place a high degree of importance on loyalty and trust; the sharing of confidences and "secrets"—as any mother will attest—plays a significant role in the formation and maintenance of girls' friendships. In that sense, friendship offers yet another mirror for our daughters in which to catch a glimpse of their present and future selves, a safe forum where they can begin to give voice to themselves. More negatively, though, these friendships often become in some sense exclusionary, with the girls showing an unwillingness to let others into the inner circle. Viewing these friendships from a feminist perspective, some researchers, among them Lyn Mikel Brown, Niobe Way, and Julia L. Duff, have speculated that, "read against the backdrop of a dominant culture in which making it to the top of a hierarchy is valued, whereas competition, conflict, and strong feelings like anger are unacceptable for girls, adolescent girls' preoccupation with loyalty, and, conversely, with betrayal or 'backstabbing' behavior is perhaps understandable."[17]

Most women readily acknowledge the important role female friendship plays in their lives, yet many mothers also express concern and dismay about the importance their adolescent girls place on friendship. Why is that? For one thing, the combination of the "separation" myth (and its corollary, the "necessary rebellion") and the standard vision of negative peer influence set an adolescent's friends and parents up as diametrically opposed, each vying for a position of influence, despite the more nuanced and more complicated picture painted by research. In fact, most adolescents, while conforming to peer expectations about more superficial matters such as clothes and entertainment, tend to hold the same opinions and support the same values as their parents on important issues such as basic moral principles, educational and career goals, and the like. Indeed, friends tend to influence important aspects of behavior—morals, goals, and the like—only when the adolescent perceives her relationship to her parents as negative or deficient in support or guidance. In the void created by lack of guidance, absenteeism, or inattention on the part of parents, peer group pressures may also negatively influence an adolescent's behavior as she first attempts a romantic relationship.[18] (Even more dangerously, studies on delinquency, for example, reveal that "adolescents are not so much being pulled away from adults by the deviant crowd as driven to this crowd by parents' ineffective child-rearing practices."[19] But the popular mythology tends to have a longer shelf life than the facts, and it's not surprising that many parents are quick to view and evaluate their daughter's circle of friends with a critical and wary eye. There are other, more subtle, factors at work as well. A mother's concern with the intensity of a friendship may reflect her own memories of how emotionally vulnerable she was at her daughter's age or her own experience with a failed friendship. Or there may be something else: Seen from the mother's point of view, the coincidence of her daughter's attempts to reshape the mother-daughter relationship while cementing her relationships with girlfriends may feel like an emotional rejection. This may be particularly true of single mothers raising daughters alone who have come to see their daughters as both companions *and* fellow travelers on the journey of life.

Other than sexual development and the first efforts at romantic relationship, there is perhaps no sea change as dramatic in an adolescent girl's life as that pertaining to friendship. Friendships in elementary school tend to be monitored and organized by mothers who make the play dates (or by caretakers who are acting *in loco parentis*) and, often as not, choose the children of like-minded mothers for their daughters to play with. Parents meet and check each other out either at school or when children are picked up or dropped off. By and large, "play dates" are just what they sound like—opportunities to play—and friendships are based in shared likes and dislikes. By the time girls reach eleven and twelve, the basis of friendship begins to shift, and girls are apt to begin to spend as much time talking as they spend "doing." Friendship—particularly same-sex friendship—plays an important role in the formation of self. Some of this has to do with the literal fact that, after elementary school, American adolescents spend more time with their friends and peers than they do with their parents.

During adolescence, friendships offer girls an opportunity to explore the boundaries of the self in the context of relatedness. By mid-adolescence—thirteen to fourteen—a girl's sleepover will often consist of watching a movie or television show with a friend or friends, and then spending the rest of the time sitting on a bed or cuddled in a sleeping bag, talking. Sharing secrets and disclosures—particularly self-disclosures—is very much a part of adolescent friendships; girlfriends, like mothers, are another "mirror" into which the adolescent girl gazes for glimpses of her true self. In the words of Ritch C. Savin-Williams and Thomas J. Berndt:

Close peer relations are essential during adolescence. Friends seek a shared understanding, openness, trust, and acceptance. In addition, emotional and social needs are met, and problems are worked out. This "consensual validation" is "a reciprocal process whereby two persons seek to understand their world through a mutual exchange of ideas, feelings, and thoughts that are offered to each other for comment, discussion, or evaluation." Because the process requires equality in give-and-take, friends are the key to consensual validation. The ultimate developmental outcome should be individuation, a feeling of being separate from and yet connected to others. One should discover in friendships one's uniqueness.[20]

But at precisely the same time that friendships become more central to our girls' lives—when they enter middle school or junior high school and then go on to high school—mothers are not only less likely to know all of their school friends (this is particularly true of working mothers) but also less likely to be involved in the formation of those friendships. (Since parents of children this age are also less likely to be involved with school and school activities than parents of younger children, they are also less likely to know the mothers and fathers of their children's friends.) Friendship, then, is an area that begins under a mother's control and, during the years of adolescence, shifts out of it—creating an area of potential conflict. Not surprisingly, the choice of friends becomes an arena in which girls may choose to demonstrate their independence of their parents, particularly their mothers; by the same token, it is an area in which a mother might feel most pained by the changes in the mother-daughter dynamic. For some women, this perceived loss of closeness with her daughter—who may suddenly seem to shift her allegiances from her mother to her girlfriends and who may no longer share confidences with her mother as she did before—may be hard to accept. For others, losing control over her daughter's choices may feel more like a challenge to her authority than anything else.

Since the area of peer friends is one of potential conflict, as mothers we need to:

## Support and honor their need to forge friendships

Recognize the important role friendship plays in your daughter's development, and support the friendships you think are valuable and healthy. Friendship teaches many different lessons, among them the need for reciprocity in talking and listening, taking responsibility, respecting boundaries, being supportive, and the like. If she has discussed her plans with you, support and honor your daughter's commitments to her friends; do not consider them less important than commitments you or another adult family member has made.

If you disapprove of a friendship, force yourself to be articulate about why you disapprove of it, and sit down and talk to your daughter directly. Rely on your own first-hand knowledge about the friend in question—not what you've heard about her. Try not to extrapolate from outside appearances; in today's world, a tight-fitting tank top and pants may not mean what it did when you were growing up. (Same goes for nose rings and the like; you may not like them but they don't necessarily represent what kind of a person the girl is.) Talk about the things that concern you using concrete examples so that your daughter understands why you feel the way you do. Give her room to talk about what she finds valuable or interesting about her friend, and be open to hearing her out.

If you believe that your daughter and her friends are engaging in dangerous behavior, take action. Speak to the parents of her friends and keep in mind that it is easier to blame your daughter's behavior on the bad influence of others than it is to confront the more complicated truth.

## Manage whatever sense of temporary loss of intimacy we feel

Resist the impulse to see yourself and your daughter's friends as mutually exclusive forces in her life. If you do feel shut out of her life, be direct by telling her how it feels to you; don't express your own feelings of loss or pain by forcing her to choose between time spent with friends or family, by denigrating or criticizing her friends, or by making her feel guilty about enjoying her friends' company. Try to find different ways of spending time with your daughter and use that time creatively.

### Talk to our daughters honestly and openly about the experience of friendship

Despite the important role girlfriends play in most of our adult lives, many of us remember our own adolescent friendships with a certain amount of ambivalence, particularly those from the time when we first started to date and form romantic attachments. One woman confessed that, "There was only one captain of the football team, and he was cute and smart to boot, and all of us—my whole circle of girlfriends—were dying to go out with him. He knew that, of course, and played one girl against the other. And what did we do? Were we smart enough to figure out that maybe this guy wasn't worth it? Not on your life. Instead, we ended up turning on each other—saying the worst things about each—to win points with him."

Friendships can actually provide a certain amount of protection, and function as a buffer for girls when they do begin to date. In their decidedly feminist book *Mother-Daughter Revolution*, Elizabeth Debold, Marie Wilson, and Idelisse Malavé wisely suggest that, "When a mother lovingly accepts her daughter as she is, a daughter learns to expect acceptant, affirming love from others. As girls enter the competitive world of dating boys, a mother can also encourage her daughter not to abandon her friends as girls trash each other. By letting a daughter know that keeping her commitments to girlfriends is important, a mother gives a daughter another way of thinking and behaving amidst the world of men's desires, which typically leaves girls defenseless."[21]

### Help and support them when friendships become difficult or painful

Engage them in conversation when a friendship breaks up, or changes significantly. While it's true that your perspective on relationships has been informed by experience and that you are doubtless right that "this, too, shall pass," try not to marginalize your daughter's feelings of pain and disappointment. If your daughter has trouble making friends or keeping them, take it seriously. Talk to her about it—without sounding critical or anxious about it—and find out how she feels. If you think that the exclusionary tactics of a clique have crossed over into bullying or harassment, discuss it with your daughter's teachers. The exploration of identity often feels isolating to girls, and being lonely will only exacerbate those feelings. Explore other venues—after-school activities or enrichment programs, for example—that will give her an opportunity to meet other girls.

### Remember that there is room in her life for more than just one kind of closeness

Do not feel as though the "girlfriend" model is the only one that will permit you to stay close to your daughter. She does not need another confidante; she needs a mother. For more on this, see page 216.

### Find ways of involving yourself with your daughter and her friends

Don't assume that they want to be a "tribe apart" or that you are required to be the silent chauffeur when you drive them places. If you show respect for certain of your daughter's boundaries—her ability to have a private conversation or to close the door some of the time when her friends are over—and you have acknowledged how important friendships are to her, she will be far more likely to want to involve you with her friends. Remind yourself that girls want to be heard and that, all appearances to the contrary, they like to listen.

~ ~ ~

> I remember the moment distinctly, standing in the checkout line at the grocery store with my daughter; the clerk was asking me all the questions—did you find everything, is there anything else we can help you with—but his eyes never once left her and never once did he really look at me. It reminded me of the first three months of her life, when all my friends and family seemed to forget how to say "Hi, Donna" and the greeting of choice became "Oh, there's that pretty baby." During that first moment of invisibility I was highly enamored of her myself; the second time, there was already multi-layered tension in our relationship. Part of me was pleased and proud of her and her new Woman status but part of me felt she had just done something that would make my life more complicated and less appreciated and it felt final. The shift in attention is inevitable and it is hard not to resent, just a little bit, because that second invisibility defines—with a sharp degree of permanence—a social perception of you as the older woman, the somehow less important mother. For me, it started a long internal dialogue about age, aging, and physical appearance. It was the beginning of a redefinition of self.
>
> Donna, artist, age fifty, mother to Katie, age twenty

Timing, as they say, is everything. Because the mother-daughter relationship is a dynamic wherein each is affected by changes in the other, the growth of our daughters' physical and inner selves will affect each of us in different ways. One woman, a stay-at-home mother of three for fifteen years, confided feeling liberated in some sense; she's out in the world, exploring her own interests now that her youngest daughter is an adolescent. Another goes into crisis as she enters perimenopause and her beautiful daughter emerges into womanhood; her own looks, she says, have always been a large part of her identity and her daughter's blossoming throws the issues associated with aging into high relief. Peg, my coauthor and a single mother, hears a wake-up call when she does the math and realizes that her daughter will be off to college in a scant five years. It is time, she realizes, that she needs to prepare for a life without mothering at its center.

Unless you had your daughter when you were comparatively young, it's likely that your own daughter's attempts at self-definition will coincide with your own entry into midlife and the feelings that new part of life's journey engenders in many of us. In our looks-conscious culture, aging, for many women, is a difficult process—a time of needing to let go of certain assumptions about self-worth and forging new ones—and may feel even harder to deal with as our daughters blossom. Witnessing a daughter's burgeoning sexual self may release contradictory feelings about one's own sexual self and attractiveness. Even imagining the possibilities that lie ahead for our daughters may make us feel disappointed in the paths we have chosen for ourselves, the decisions we've made, the work we do. Alternatively, we may find ourselves putting pressure on our daughters to fulfill the dreams that somehow proved to be beyond our grasp—and find their active disagreement with our visions for them painful and disappointing.

In his book *Crossing Paths: How Your Child's Adolescence Triggers Your Own Crisis*, which documents the results of a study of two hundred families, Dr. Laurence Steinberg examines the coincidence of parental midlife and a child's entry into adolescence, and posits that some of the concerns raised by midlife are exacerbated by the changes in one's child. The areas he delineates as the most likely "triggers" are puberty, sexuality, dating, independence, emotional detachment, and deidealization. According to Dr. Steinberg, some of these triggers—such as sexuality and dating—may create inner turmoil for a mother as she compares and contrasts herself to her daughter, both physically and in terms of her own choices and experiences. Other triggers may reinforce feelings or anxieties brought on by the normal stresses of midlife but compounded by the changes in one's child. As he writes:

> Accepting the adolescent's need for independence on an intellectual level is one thing; coping with it emotionally is quite another, however. As the adolescent becomes less dependent upon the parent and assumes greater control over his or her own activities, the parent is no longer in the role of one who governs the child's activities. The majority of parents are nervous and ambivalent about permitting the freedom that the teenager wants. Most have invested a great deal in their child, and they have a lot of hopes and dreams tied up in his or her future. Further, parents derive a great deal from keeping their child dependent—a sense of control, the security of knowing their child is safe, the child's adulation, companionship, and so on.
>
> The paradox, then, is that the very thing parents are supposed to be helping their child toward—growing up and becoming independent—is precisely what they deep down don't really want to happen.[22]

Openly acknowledging that we may feel ambivalent about certain aspects of our daughters' development is the first step we each have to take as we adjust to the ways in which the mother-daughter relationship is recast during adolescence. "I-Thou" parenting permits us to see that there is nothing wrong with or unnatural about feeling ambivalent as long as we recognize our feelings and take a hard look at how they affect how we parent our daughters. The mother-daughter relationship is not one of equals, and it is our responsibility—and ours alone—to make sure that the bits and pieces of our own emotional reactions don't cloud our judgment.

Talking about those areas that give us trouble is the first step toward making sure the dynamic between us and our daughters stays healthy. We need to remember that the myth of the Perfect Mother is just that—a myth—and having some amount of difficulty with the changes in ourselves and in our children is par for the course. Do seek professional help if you are having trouble managing all these various transitions on your own.

And if there are areas that are likely to leave us profoundly ambivalent, chief among them will be our daughters' own burgeoning sexuality and their first efforts at forming romantic relationships.

~ ~ ~

> Some things are really easy for me to talk with them about. Others are harder. Values are very easy for me to talk about. The emotional parts of relationships and of being intimate are also easy. Laura doesn't say much back but listens. Becca was like that until she started having her own relationships, and then our conversations became more of a dialogue. Sex—some facets are easy. General things. My ideas about the spiritual aspects of physical intimacy are very easy for me to talk about. But we have never really talked about specifics that much. They haven't wanted to and they know the door is open if they want to. Steve has talked with them more about the "body mechanics stuff." Being the doctor and all, he just worked a lot of things into other conversations. I have not talked to my kids at all about my own sexual experiences. It hasn't seemed appropriate yet. Maybe someday. But then, I kind of doubt it. I think some things are better discussed with friends and not mothers. It feels like a boundary violation for me to talk about some things with them. Perhaps if I was not married to their father and was currently having relationships with other men, these conversations would feel more appropriate. I don't know. I usually try to stick with speaking about things that feel right in my gut to talk about.

> Patti, age forty-two, married, mother of two adolescent girls

The problem, of course, is that we've all, in one way or another, been there and done that, and when our daughters begin to express and explore their own sexuality and form their first romantic attachments, who among us can really be calm and sanguine? For one thing, roughly half of us reading these pages will have lived through the ultimate romantic disappointment—divorce. Then, too, it's not simply that our daughters' sexual emergence makes us focus on where we find ourselves now; it is also, watching them begin their journeys, that we remember where we were then. Looking back at

her own late-adolescent self—coming of age in the early 1970s—
one mother sees a sad history of looking for love and validation in
all the wrong places, and finding nothing more than a series of emotionally empty sexual encounters. Another remembers the terrific
high of being in love at sixteen and, equally, how she felt when, two
years later, he moved on to someone else without even as much as
an explanation. Another recalls her feelings of despair and humiliation at being, as she puts it, "the only one in my group at sixteen
who'd never been on a date and never had a boyfriend." At midlife,
it is very clear to me that my own adolescent notions of romantic love, a destructive cross between "Cinderella" and "Sleeping
Beauty," were a function of my own lack of self-esteem, and helped
propel me into two failed marriages and a number of other damaging relationships. (You know the story: The prince or the knight
falls in love with the girl and, because he does, she is made whole,
recognized for who she "really" is, and lives happily ever after. It
took me over twenty years to give up this damaging fantasy for
something else, which formed the basis of my third marriage.)

Western culture's continued fascination with and idealization of
romantic love—the kind that is supposed to leave you breathless and
your legs feeling like jelly, in which the "self" finds its ultimate expression by "losing" its sense of separateness through connection—is
reflected everywhere in the adolescent's world: in popular songs
(roughly three out of four), television shows, movies, novels, and
countless magazine articles. While the basic concept of romantic love
hasn't changed much since we were adolescents (or, for that matter,
for centuries), it's worth noting that it has become increasingly sexualized; star-crossed lovers, even young adolescent ones, are likely to end
up in bed together nowadays. Paradoxically, Western culture's idealization of romantic love is inseparable from an appreciation of its rar-
ity, its fragility, and, not coincidentally, its capacity to cause pain and
suffering and to induce anxiety, jealousy, or anger. Thus, doomed
lovers are a staple of Western culture's vision of romantic love, from

William Shakespeare's fourteen-year-old Juliet and her Romeo to James Cameron's Rose and Jack in *Titanic*, which became the top-grossing film of all time because adolescent girls all over the globe returned to movie theaters to see it again and again. (My own daughter Kate, at age twelve, saw it three or four times.) "True love"—breathless, heedless, all-consuming, and most important, life-changing—is the rare diamond every adolescent girl is taught to yearn for.

Our girls are primed for romantic relationships long before they are old enough to act on their impulses by more than just the media. In their study of the peer culture of third- through sixth-graders (mainly white boys and girls, ages nine to twelve), sociologists Patricia A. Adler and Peter Adler discuss the importance of "popularity," and isolate the telling differences in boys' and girls' "popularity factors." Contributing to popularity are not just socioeconomic factors (symbols of prestige such as designer clothes, big houses, and other material possessions), physical attractiveness, and academic achievements but superior social development, which, importantly, includes interest in boys from the earliest elementary years. Remember that the focus here is on the youngest of adolescents; in fact, in their book, the authors call them "preadolescents." In closing, the authors note:

> From an earlier age than boys, girls are attracted to the "culture of romance" . . . They fantasize about romantic involvements with boys and become interested, sooner, in crossing gender lines for relationships, both platonic and otherwise. They absorb idealized images of gendered ways of relating to boys based partly on traditional roles. This fosters passivity and dependence by encouraging them to wait for boys to select them. Girls who accomplish romance successfully, by attracting a boy who will actively pursue them, gain ascribed status among other girls.[23]

Elsewhere the research suggests that "beginning around the sixth or seventh grade, American adolescents find themselves spending much time in a world of peers where romantic involvement is increasingly expected."[24]

The real problem is that our cultural vision of what constitutes romantic love hasn't proved to be very good for us—and there's not much chance it will work any better for our daughters. Think for a moment about the metaphors that animate our vision of romantic love—being "swept off" your feet, being "consumed" by feeling, "becoming one" with someone else, and the like—and it becomes clear that what's actually being described is a giving up of "self." (Obviously, sexual intercourse is also usually described as "becoming one" with another but, out of bed, there are always two separate people, even if they are intimately connected to each other.) In the romantic love fairy tale, movie, or song, the prince often takes over the responsibilities of the self by becoming the "rescuer." (Think *Titanic* and its message: True Love—and a session in a literally steamy automobile—save the heroine from an abusive mother and fiancé so that she finds her "true" self. There's really not much new there.) Visions of romance in our society usually follow traditionally cast gender roles, if slightly exaggerated ones. It's not surprising that, faced with the sometimes painful, often confusing work of defining the self—not to mention the ambivalence adolescent girls sometimes feel about autonomy—romantic involvement can seem like an attractive, if ultimately unhealthy, alternative. In this context, it isn't much of a stretch to understand how an otherwise strong, intelligent, and seemingly empowered sixteen-year-old daughter can suddenly and alarmingly seem to give up her voice just to become "Johnny's girl," or, alternatively, how a girl who feels on the outside of the cliques and popular groups in school will take unreasonable risks to prove her attractiveness.

While the cultural vision of romance isn't new, what is even more confusing to our daughters is the way it coexists not just with other, more progressive definitions of gender roles but with a widely broadcast view of male-female relationship as being difficult or impossible to sustain. This is not just a function of the divorce rate—with which our daughters will have at least secondhand, if not firsthand, knowledge—but the media focus on relationships as problematic at best and hopeless at worst. In American culture, the strains of "Some Day My Prince Will Come" are background music for countless talk shows and articles detailing how—to quote the title of a best-selling book from the last decade—"men are from Mars, women are from Venus." It is, from the adolescent's point of view, more than a little confusing.

In the main, though, for adolescent girls, the idea of romance seems to have more staying power. What the adolescent girl experiencing the "glow" of falling in love for the first time doesn't recognize is that these notions of romantic love will not teach her, as they didn't her mother, anything about lasting and healthy relationships between women and men that require two "selves" to function. Romantic fantasies don't include any notion of the real work and commitment relationship requires, or the issues of intimacy and boundaries. As adults, most of us—with a certain amount of regret, perhaps—realize that it's not nearly as simple as the song would have it; love *isn't* "all you need." Even so, the idea of the swept-off-your-feet romance seems to die hard in every woman's heart, spawning an industry of its own in magazines, talk shows, books, and websites. ("Put the romance back in your life!" "Recapture those first moments!" "Discover your own inner Venus!") Is it any wonder that our girls, too, are drawn to it?

The romantic fantasy and its connection to sterotypical beliefs about femininity work to girls' detriment in other ways as well. A study conducted by Dr. Deborah L. Tolman, a researcher at the Center for Research on Women at Wellesley, suggested that "conventional femininity ideology may function as a barrier—and, conversely that critique of femininity ideology may offer a booster—to adolescent girls' sexual health." She points out that "holding conventional beliefs about femininity" has been "associated with health risks and outcomes in women, including eating problems, risk for HIV, smoking, and breast reduction and augmentation."[25]

This isn't to say that we (or our girls, for that matter) don't need love or that attachment isn't important, or that sexuality isn't vital to the self. It's simply that the models of romantic love don't work in our or our girls' best interests; they encourage us (and them) to let someone do the work of defining us and of taking care of us.

Romantic attachment and the awakening of sexual desire are the adolescent's brave new world, the unexplored territory. Like all explorers—both literal and metaphorical—adolescent girls first imagine and then approach this new world of romance and desire with a heightened sense of possibility, the promises of emotional riches and a sense of belonging, and a belief in what looks like a once-in-a-lifetime chance to earn the admiration of their peers. In the bright light of anticipation, it may be easy to discount what they know intellectually to be the risks and dangers of such explorations, particularly where romance and sexual activity intersect. While certainly the physical changes of puberty (and the body's biological readiness for reproduction) contribute to the adolescent's desire to form romantic attachments, "cultural scripts" as sociologists and anthropologists call them also affect how adolescent girls (and boys) view not just the idea of romantic attachment but its relative importance in their lives.

To engage our daughters in meaningful dialogue and to help them negotiate this complicated part of the journey, we need first to look at how romantic attachment and sexual identity contribute to our daughters' sense of self and, parenthetically, how they have contributed to our own.

~ ~ ~

I was nineteen going on twenty and in college when I finally slept with someone. I'd done my fair share of making out and petting but I was worried about my reputation—despite the fact that a fair number of my friends, both in high school and college, were no longer virgins. It was the late 1960s, after all, and once the university banned curfews and other rules, sexual connection was pretty much the norm. But, even so, there was still a double standard; the age of Aquarius didn't stop guys from dumping on women who slept around. I think I finally said "yes" because I was tired of fighting when I did say "no"—more like battle fatigue than anything else. I tried to pretend that it was about love but, in fact, it wasn't about anything weightier than being lonely and wanting this guy to care about me. Needless to say, it was hugely disappointing physically and, worse still, I was disappointed in myself for doing it. When my daughter gets older, I plan on telling her about it. I don't want her to make herself as actively unhappy as I did myself.

Peg, fifty-two, my coauthor and mother to Alexandra, thirteen

In search of self-definition, spurred on by the changes in their bodies, our daughters leave the relative androgyny of childhood behind and begin to explore two separate but related aspects of identity: gender identity and sexual identity, each of which, psychologists tell us, is a key developmental task of adolescence. The words "relative androgyny" are important because studies show that the formation of gender identity and gender roles begins long before adolescence and may, in fact, influence behavior not simply during adolescence but into adult life. For example, the authors of a recent study of preschool and kindergarten girls and boys found that children not only segregate themselves by sex when they play but formulate "appropriate" gender roles, even in situations (such as a preschool class at a university) where teachers are encouraged to promote gender equity. In other words, children younger than six already begin to define what is "masculine" and "feminine." Interestingly, the longer children spent time with same-sex peers, the more both boys and girls were likely to engage in gender-typed behaviors.[26] Other studies confirm that traditional gender roles—particularly in girl-boy interactions—tend to structure the behavior of young adolescents just as strongly.[27]

These studies tell us that, despite all the efforts made at inculcating gender equity and the spate of books asserting that girls no longer need "special" attention or support, old ways of thinking die hard, and coexist, if uneasily, with both women's achievements and high expectations for adolescent girls.

How an adolescent girl discovers her own personal definition of what it means to be female and formulates what she believes are the roles and responsibilities of her gender—think of it as a sentence that begins, "A woman is someone who . . ." and then fill in the blanks—is thus more like making a patchwork quilt than anything else, bits and pieces taken from here, there, and everywhere, including her childhood. Our daughters will take their cues not only from the behaviors we model for them, but from the reactions our behaviors garner from others, including their fathers and stepfathers. A father's implicit and explicit way of finishing that same sentence— "A female is someone who . . ."—will be part of the various alternatives a daughter can consider, as will be the pattern of praise and criticism, support and argument, she receives from him. Teachers— and we use the term broadly to include not only their teachers in school but coaches, camp counselors, ministers, and rabbis—explicitly and implicitly communicate information about gender identity, not just by how they treat our girls but by how they treat the boys around them. Peers, too, influence our daughters as they look for successful formulations of self that will increase their social status in the peer group and make their connections to others more secure.

Our daughters' formulation of gender roles will affect not only the goals they set for themselves in school and, later, in the outside world but the assumptions they make when they begin to form romantic attachments and explore their own sexual identity.

Nowhere else does the culture conspire as actively against our girls than it does in the area of sexuality and romantic relationships where contradictions abound. The idealized vision of courtship and marriage—premarital abstinence followed by a lifetime commitment to monogamy—manages to hang in as "normative" despite the increased rate of sexual activity among adolescents and the divorce rate among adults. Female desire—save in the context of marriage—still is off-limits as a subject, and is often presented as unhealthy, dangerous, or predatory in nature. Despite the high percentages of adolescents engaging in a variety of sexual activities by the age of eighteen, as a culture we still tend to see any sexual activity as deviating from the norm. (This represents, as one expert puts it, "a schism between the current realities of adolescent life and traditional societal expectations."[28]) Although there are individual exceptions to the rule, sex and sexuality remain, for many, a difficult area of discussion, as it was for many of our parents; perhaps, absent the model in our own lives—the talks with our own mothers—we remain unsure about what we should say, and when. It may be, too, that few of us actually get to this stage of life without some negative experiences, which make it all the more difficult to approach the issues of sex and relationship openly.

Societally, attitudes toward female sexuality, in particular, remain oddly contradictory. While we are relatively permissive in terms of allowing our daughters to engage in boy-girl activities, and while we recognize that sexuality is a part of the adult self, we nonetheless continue to have different expectations for our daughters than for our sons. As the watchful parents of adolescent girls, we are likely to become more conservative in our thinking, and may even revise our own histories. As Sharon Thompson notes in *Going All the Way: Teenage Girls' Tales of Sex, Romance, and Pregnancy*, "Adolescents traditionally see themselves as the first of a radically more sexual generation, a view that adults often support by casting the past, and their own youths, as good—pure, nonsexual—examples."[29] Parents do this for any number of reasons—among them personal reticence or discomfort, fear that their own past conduct might set a bad example, or the wish to stay reasonably idealized. For women, the recasting of the past may have to do with some amount of ambivalence about past sexual behavior; the desire to be seen as a "good" or "perfect" girl dies hard. Experts consistently report that the double standard—familiar to us from our own adolescence—is alive and well in America, untouched by the "sexual revolution" of the 1970s. Ask any adolescent girl and she'll be quick to tell you that a boy who tries to attract girls is, in the parlance of the day, a "stud" or a "hottie"; a girl who tries to accomplish the same goal—either by wearing suggestive clothing or by acting on her impulses—is a "slut." In the aptly-named chapter "Studs and Sluts" in *The Sex Lives of Teenagers*, Dr. Lynn Ponton offers an explanation:

> The questions remain: Why are gender stereotypes being strongly enforced for young people? Why at earlier ages?
>
>     The pressure from the media is, I believe, only part of the story. The double standard so evident in the 1950s has resurfaced in the 1990s. Expecting and enforcing strong gender roles for children and young teens offers a sense of security to adults. If the gender model is there, then parents don't have to talk about it, and they can continue the strong taboo around discussing sexual matters. Teens follow their parents' leads. Exploring options becomes nearly impossible in such a rigid environment. If adolescents question, they do so in private, hiding their activities and protecting themselves.[30]

The earlier onset of puberty has also further complicated what has long been a difficult area of discussion. Our daughters' biological ability to become pregnant, their susceptibility to being physically overpowered or otherwise seduced, and more recently, the alarming rate of STDs have thrown America into a defensive crouch. To protect our children, our school systems teach abstinence, thus depriving the adolescent girl (and, of course, the adolescent boy) of a potential forum for discussing sexual and emotional responsibility, the intersection of sexuality and relationship, and of romantic connection and selfhood, and other important issues. As Peggy Orenstein writes in her book *Schoolgirls*, "we protect our daughters by exacerbating their vulnerability, by instilling them with what we know are the perils of sex: the fears of victimization, of pregnancy, of disease."[31]

Much is left out of this equation—some of it vital to a young woman's sense of self and well-being. Left undiscussed are the different degrees and kinds of emotional and physical intimacy, the legitimacy of female desire, and other subjects of importance to our daughters. Consistently left in, though, is the definition of the "good" girl. As feminist scholar and researcher Deborah Tolman notes, "Good girls are still supposed to 'just say no,' are not supposed to feel intense sexual desire, and remain responsible for the sexual desire of boys, and for protecting themselves from harm."[32]

The turmoil these contradictory attitudes create becomes clear when we look at what the culture simultaneously teaches adolescent boys—the boys who talk to and sometimes flirt with our daughters at recess in sixth grade and who eventually will take them out to a party or movie—when they confront the parallel issues of self and "masculinity." Patricia A. Adler and Peter Adler note that by fourth to sixth grade, boys and girls see sexual interest from opposite ends of a spectrum:

> Not only were boys interested in sexual exploration for its own sake, but they sought it to enhance their social status. Boys derived peer prestige for 'scoring' with girls and talking about it. It is at this age that the 'baseball' analogy of sexual exploration (first base, second base) surfaced, leading boys to talk about sexual matters they barely understood.
>
> Girls, however, were socialized to derive their social status from having boys pay attention to them, from having boys do things for or give things to them, and *from resisting sexual pressure*.[33] [emphasis added]

The facts of girls' earlier maturation and the body changes that signal the birth of the sexual self further complicate the issue. As William Pollack, Ph.D., notes in *Real Boys*:

But there is no change in boys' bodies that directly lets them know they're capable of sex and reproduction. Indeed, the only real way for boys to know that they can have sex is to have it. This increases the pressure to have sex as proof of maturity and amplifies the anxiety surrounding that first act. Boys worry that they won't be good at making love, and the fear of impotence—the ultimate humiliation— runs through every boy's mind.[34]

Seeing it from the boy's point of view, Dr. Pollack points out how intimidating the adolescent girl, who matures several years earlier, appears; the boy's response, he ventures, will be an exhibition of "compensatory bravado" so that "hence, there is locker-room talk, reducing girls to objects, and bragging about conquests." The conclusion Dr. Pollack reaches is unlikely to warm the heart of the mother of a daughter:

> And even worse, the motives of a young boy and a young girl thinking about having sex for the first time are very different. Girls tend to look at sex as signaling an act of love and the ultimate connection. Boys tend to view it, at least partially, as a way of confirming their masculinity. Boys only relax and become emotionally vulnerable after they are able to feel secure about their sexual ability and feel secure that the act of sex won't shame them in any way. Girls want boys to be emotional and loving, *before* sex. Boys, with a very different pace and philosophy around emotionality, often find that they can't open up until *after* sex—sometimes long after sex. Before that time comes, it looks to girls as if boys don't care.[35]

Sharon Thompson, in her book *Going All the Way*, ventures that girls and boys approach teenage romance at cross-purposes "with boys developing a sense of masculine identity to a significant degree by separating from girls whose identity development depends on affirming relationships." She concludes by saying that boys face a contradiction in teenage sex: "Having sex proves masculinity like nothing else, but girls' insistence on merging sex with love brings back the danger of being trapped in the homey, mergey, infantilizing world of childhood they must escape in order to be men."[36]

You may, once again, be ready to dig a moat or drag your adolescent daughter off to an uninhabited island. But even amidst all these contradictory social visions, neither fear nor feeling powerless is justified. When our daughters are emotionally and cognitively ready, both romantic attachments and explorations of sexual identity are an important part of "finding the self," and in the best of all possible worlds, when they are ready, they should be able to turn to us—not their peers—for advice and support.

In the pages that follow, we'll be looking at precisely how we can accomplish that goal.

~ ~ ~

> I did not handle her first few dates very well and neither did her father. We had just invested all this time and love in helping shape a whole healthy young woman and then we were expected to graciously turn her over to the most reckless and irresponsible element in our society, a teenage male? It didn't happen that way—we were nervous wrecks, parents who wanted phone numbers and times and addresses. The young men she chose seemed like geeks and were all, without exception, totally transparent liars when it came to time and place. But both John and I got better with time and experience; she proved trustworthy for the most part and lots of interesting young people came through our doors. I personally was very uncomfortable with the dating thing; I felt I was in uncharted waters partly because my first date was after I graduated from high school and just before I left for college, so I had never watched any other parents handle this aspect of growing up. Dealing with our daughter's emerging sexuality caused both of us to rethink lots of issues.
>
> Donna, artist, age fifty, mother to Katie, twenty

For the preponderance of girls, reconfiguring their relationship to the opposite sex will be an important component of the task of self-discovery—and a source of concern, if not worry, for their mothers. Explorations of these relationships will inevitably and altogether normally involve some degree of sexual behavior—whether that is kissing, touching, or, more alarming from the parents' point of view, sexual intercourse. The rite of passage we call "dating" will likely as not fill our hearts and heads with trepidation and concern for our daughters' emotional and physical well-being; not surprisingly, the whole question of when, where, and with whom often becomes a battleground between mothers and daughters. Girls first see "going with" a boy and then dating—as recognized rites of passage—not only as ways of establishing their maturity and independence, but as marks of prestige and status. The "age compression" of our society encourages girls to form romantic attachments earlier and earlier, and they will probably want to go out on dates earlier too. Because parents have remarkably diverse attitudes about what kind of activities are appropriate at any given age—going to the movies in girl-boy groups, going to girl-boy parties, dating—as well as different standards for parental supervision, it's likely that, sooner or later, we'll find ourselves being unfavorably compared to someone else's mom or dad. Inevitably, we will also find ourselves uttering the words we swore—when we were adolescents—we would *never, ever* say as mothers: "I don't care what the other mothers think. I'm your mother and you'll do as I say." The degree to which this continues to be a hot topic in adolescent circles is reflected in the number of articles in teen magazines and chat rooms on websites devoted to strategies for changing a parent's mind about dating.

Because romantic attachment and relationship—like sex—are pervasive subjects and themes in the media (and an important subject of discussion among adolescents), adolescent girls (and boys) are likely to overestimate what they know about them, just as studies show they do about sex. (Adolescent misconceptions about sex are well documented, particularly the confusion about the safety of various sexual practices and transmission of sexual diseases, where the gap between what they think they know and the facts is alarming.) There is no reason for any of us to believe that their information about male-female relationships—of which sexual behavior is only a subset—is any more complete.

Because the societal focus on romantic connections between adolescents tends to be on sex and its dangers, the whole question of relationship is usually given short shrift if it's discussed at all. But relationship and its connection to sexuality—the healthy (and unhealthy) contexts within which sexual activity takes place—is precisely what our daughters need to learn about to become healthy, functioning, and happy women. Talking about relationships and the culture's ideas about romance is vitally important, particularly if you share our view that what the culture teaches our daughters actually puts them at risk. For any number of reasons—her wish to be perceived as mature, her assertion that her experiences are unique, her protestation that she doesn't need your advice—your daughter may brush off your attempts at a discussion. Keep in mind that, as your daughter begins to formulate her idea of self, her relationship to you will be ambivalent in the true sense of the word. As Terri Apter writes in *Altered Loves*:

> The adolescent's romanticism about the self—that it is unique, unknown, misunderstood, that its truth can be revealed only through secret rites of diary writing or solitary confidences among friends— conflicts with her need for her mother to know, to acknowledge, to validate. But in the area of sex she takes special care, knowing that knowledge, understanding, validation here will not confirm but impede her individuality.[37]

Remember that even if you have already set rules about what's appropriate, and even if your daughter is not permitted to date, she is still beginning to sketch her own vision of relationships and romance from here, there, and everywhere, if only realized in fantasy. Experts agree that even when adolescents are not literally sexually active, sexual fantasies are not only a source of arousal and substitute for the satisfaction of sexual needs, but "provide an opportunity for teenagers to confront their sexuality."[38] Similarly, "adolescents spend time thinking about romantic involvements long before they spend time with romantic partners, and negative feelings, such as worry, disappointment, and jealousy are often associated with these thoughts."[39] Once again, the rule of thumb is simple: If you don't talk to her, she will get her information elsewhere.

Many of us will find it hard to be objective as our girls begin this part of the journey. Our own adolescent experiences with boys—good, bad, or indifferent—will certainly help shape the rules we set for our daughters, along with our perceptions of our child's maturity, readiness, and our attitudes toward the role of risk in the development of self. It's important that we confront and examine our own experiences thoroughly, and take a look at the more meaningful differences, as well as the similarities, between where we were then and where our daughters are now. More subtly, our daughters' first involvements with boys may summon up some of our strongest feelings about men and relationships, particularly if our own experiences, including our adult ones, have been painful or disappointing. Without discounting the value of our own past experiences and the lessons they've taught us, it's nonetheless important that each of us pays attention to the messages about men and relationship—implicit and explicit—we communicate to our daughters. The information the culture communicates to our daughters is already enormously contradictory and confusing, and it's important that we try to etch out some balance between positive expectations and reasonable cautions.

The issues relating to dating and romantic relationships may be further complicated by where we find ourselves in life. We've already mentioned that Dr. Laurence Steinberg has identified dating as a potential "trigger" for midlife crisis in mothers and fathers alike; he found that, among mothers, "having a child date dramatically increased their feelings of self-doubt, their regret over past decisions, and their desire to change their lives." Divorced mothers may feel a variety of mixed emotions, depending on their circumstances. One mother admitted that she was horrified to realize that she felt competitive with her seventeen-year-old when she noticed her own date paying attention to her daughter; another mother, still scarred by an acrimonious divorce, allowed as how she was, in her words, "unreasonably strict" with her sixteen-year-old because she was "terrified" her daughter would get hurt.

Not one of us gets to this stage of life without a certain amount of emotional baggage, and we all need to keep in mind that our daughters learn from both our "reflecting mind" and our "performing self." Before you initiate a discussion with your adolescent daughter about relationships between girls and boys, and women and men, at different stages of their lives, spend some time thinking about what you want her to learn from you. It goes without saying that the lessons you'll want to impart to a fourteen-year-old should be different in kind from the discussion you may have with a seventeen-year-old or even an eighteen-year-old going off to college, and you must assess your daughter's emotional readiness to hear what you have to say. Before you talk to her, think about whether or not you have a consistent philosophy about male-female relationships or just a scattering of opinions. Ask yourself how applicable—or useful—your observations will be to her. If you are married to your daughter's father or her stepfather or living with someone unrelated to her, think about your own relationship—and what it is teaching your daughter. If you are single and still recovering from the failure of a marriage or relationship, you need to take a hard look at all the information you impart about male-female relationships. If you are dating, you need to pay close attention to what your daughter is learning from your life.

For most of us, these will be difficult and somewhat uncomfortable observations to make. It's hard to let go of wanting, somehow, to be "perfect," and each of us, deep down inside, longs for some fairy godmother to perform a miraculous makeover on one part of our lives or another. But seeing ourselves whole will help us help our daughters to see themselves whole too. Once again, it may be helpful to air your views with other mothers, or with a friend, or even with a professional counselor. Remember that your goal isn't to justify your own life choices; it is to help your daughter negotiate the sometimes difficult but necessary shoals of selfhood.

~ ~ ~

> While fathers and sons can be emotionally bound together, as I was with my father, the bond—at least in my case—was largely interiorized. That didn't mean it wasn't very strong, but it didn't get expressed very often. We had difficulty talking about important things. (My father never once talked to me about sex.) You and Alexandra have an accordion of a dynamic, or I think will have, in which you separate out—in conflict or rebellion or simply peer-bonding on Alexandra's part—only to come back close together again as the music plays on. My father and I were more like opposite ends of a string—tied together, yes, but straining (on my part) to get away.
>
> Peter, age sixty-seven, Peg's ex-husband and father to Alexandra, thirteen

What we remember about adolescent relationships from our own experiences needs to be adjusted and amplified by what we can learn from expert opinion and research. Our impulse to protect our daughters from potentially harmful or emotionally painful experiences needs to be tempered by an understanding of how romantic relationships help shape an adolescent's developing self in important ways. Romantic relationships represent a difficult transition for most mothers (and fathers); finding the right balance between parental supervision, on the one hand, and some amount of freedom for our daughter's experiences, on the other, is rarely easy.

First and foremost, romantic relationships in adolescence are significantly different from those in adulthood not simply because of the relative inexperience of the girl and boy involved. Typically, romantic relationships have separate stages—beginnings, middles, and, often, endings. According to Dr. Willard H. Hartup, what distinguishes adolescent relationships—relationships that begin in prepubescence and extend into adolescence, straddle early and late adolescence, or extend from adolescence into adulthood—is the "complex interactions between the development of relationships, on the one hand, and the development of individual human beings, on the other."[40] Even short-term relationships during adolescence will show some measure of this interaction, making them different in kind from relationships between adults. Moreover, an adolescent's emotions are very different in kind from both those of a preadolescent and those of an adult. Studies show that adolescence is "a period of strong and frequent emotion." While, on the one hand, adolescents do experience more negative emotions than preadolescents, they also "report higher rates of *both* extremely positive and extremely negative emotions than adults."[41] Not surprisingly, research confirms that adolescent romance is, more often than not, romance on a roller coaster.

Comparatively little formal research has been done on adolescent romantic relationships. This is partly a function of the push to focus on sexual development, the reticence both among adolescents and their parents, whose permission is needed for minors to talk about their relationships, and the very nature of adolescent relationships. They are often so short-lived—lasting days, weeks, or just a few months—that, as one researcher wryly notes, "Studying adolescents' romantic ventures is something like chasing a greased pig."[42] Nonetheless there are valuable insights to be drawn from the work that has been done, which lend perspective to common worries and concerns.

The establishment of romantic relationships connects to the formation of self in a number of ways. Like friendships, romantic relationships serve to establish an adolescent girl's autonomy, and provide another medium for the work of self-definition. Insofar as they establish her as "mature," they also help to redefine her connection to her parents and family. Romantic relationships, for better or worse, provide different endings for the sentence that begins, "I am . . ." Romantic relationships expand an adolescent's social skills, as well as providing a beginning template for managing and understanding emotions. ("Emotional intelligence," as it is called, "involves not just debunking illusory infatuations, it involves learning to accept and take the lead from emotions that are well grounded."[43]) Gender identity, too, is redefined and honed by romantic relationships in both positive and negative ways.

Like everything else about adolescence, romantic relationships fall into a developmental pattern closely allied to the development of self. Dr. B. Bradford Brown, an expert in adolescent peer groups, has suggested that a series of phases characterize how the adolescent, over time, orients her- or himself toward romantic relationship. Keep in mind that, as Dr. Brown describes them, these "phases" are not set in stone and vary enormously from individual to individual; one girl or boy may stay in a single phase, while another will skip a phase entirely. We think his analysis is particularly useful since it underscores not only the changing nature of romantic involvements during adolescence but the possible areas in which parental supervision, attentiveness, or intervention might be necessary.[44]

### Initiation phase

Precisely because prepubescents socialize in same-sex groups, adolescents have to basically reorient themselves to the opposite sex— this time, as Dr. Brown puts it, "with a markedly different objective:

as potential romantic and sexual partners." This phase actually has less to do with relationship than with the self; the basic objective is to "broaden one's self concept to include being a romantic partner" and to "gain confidence in one's capacity to relate to potential partners in romantic ways." The most socially advanced girls and boys will lead the way in this phase but, according to Brown, "their relationship (with a romantic partner) is not as important as their performance (their public behavior with a partner)." The expansion of self-definition to include romantic partnership will, for girls, likely as not be accompanied by a new "self-consciousness" and a spate of physical redefinitions—hair, diet, and the like—as our daughters begin to assess how attractive they are to the opposite sex.

Relationships in this phase are essentially conducted in a public forum—complete with commentary from the sidelines, not to mention gossip and teasing. From a mother's point of view, this phase will include lot of girl-to-girl discussions as well as communication with boys about potential romantic interests; whispered phone calls and "private" e-mails; that middle school phenomenon, "going together," where girls and boys, often, don't go out or date but are a recognized "couple" within the peer group; and games of truth-or-dare conducted either in person or over the Internet.

This particular phase will strike many mothers as, comparatively speaking, harmless; given the ages of the girls and boys involved, the degree to which the initiation phase includes any kind of sexual activity—including kissing and touching—is a function of parental rules and supervision. (Of course, this does not mean that this stage always precludes sexual activity; it simply means it is easier, from a parental point of view, to monitor.) The cultural scripts pertaining to girls, along with the issues of what constitutes "attractiveness"—which is usually formulated as purely physical—needs to be addressed in an ongoing discussion at this stage.

Dr. Brown notes that while this "metamorphosis" works well for most adolescents in the late elementary and early middle school years, it does not always work well for those who are either early developers or late developers. Early developers who are, in his words, ready for more "involved" relationships may be drawn, dangerously, to relationships with older partners. Late developers, on the other hand, may feel left out and, worse still, become the victims of teasing within their peer group. Mothers whose daughters fall into one of these two groups need to pay particular attention to the degree to which they are affected by their differences.

## Status Phase

Dr. Brown describes this phase as one in which the focus shifts from the self to "the self's connections to others—but not as much toward the prospective partner or relationship as to the broader peer culture in which such relationships will be enacted." According to Dr. Brown, the degree to which the relationship confers status on the adolescent—establishing, improving, or maintaining peer status—will outweigh interest in the relationship itself. In his words, "The critical feature of the status phase is that adolescents pursue dating relationships or make decisions about romantic partners with a cautious eye on the expectations or reactions of their friends and peer group."[45]

This phase offers the potential for many different kinds of problems, some of them serious. One general problem is that because these relationships are scripted with a focus on the peer group, girls may feign romantic interest for the perceived status or, worse, may give up their own sense of self (and their values) for the sake of the relationship and its perceived social benefits, thus taking on a "false" self for a prescribed social role. In Dr. Brown's words, "Dating becomes a game of impression management rather than a mode of identity revelation or self exploration."[46]

It goes without saying that the intersection of sexual behaviors and this phase of romantic relationship has dangerous potential. It is impossible not to connect these observations about the "status" phase of relationship with the statistics pertaining to oral sex and other sexual practices that are not performed in any context of a mutual relationship but have much to do with "pleasing" someone else in every sense of the word or conforming to a set of rules espoused by a peer group. In this context, too, the 55 percent of girls who found themselves in uncomfortable sexual situations in the Kaiser Foundation report takes on special meaning.

This particular phase of relationship—when the girl involved may not have the maturity or enough of a sense of self to withstand the pressures of the peer group—deserves our particular attention and special supervision. To many of us, it may be the phase of adolescent relationship that seems most changed since our own adolescence—sped-up and sexually charged in new ways by the cultural scripts that bombard our youth. As a result, the comparative youth of the girls and boys involved—they are likely to still be in middle school or in the first years of high school—may blind us to the complexity—and possible danger—inherent in these relationships. (This phase may also involve older adolescents but it is the inclusion of the younger adolescents that may come as a startling and unwelcome surprise.)

What can we do? We need, first and foremost, to know where our daughters are, both literally and psychologically, and whom they are with. We need to do what we can to "desexualize" the context in which these relationships take place, emphasizing friendship over "dating," and providing our daughters with safe venues to self-expression. We need to talk to our daughters about the choices they make when they are out of the house and with their friends. We need to talk to them about sex and relationship, and distinguish-ing between healthy needs for approval and companionship and unhealthy ones. We need, as mothers, to help our daughters appreciate their uniqueness and support them when what they want for themselves and what makes them comfortable runs contrary to "popular" wisdom.

And most of all, we need to encourage them to turn to us for help if they need it, and to keep a watchful eye.

### Affection Phase

This phase marks, in Dr. Brown's words, "the shift away from the context in which the relationship exists toward the relationship itself"[47] and is characterized by the adolescent romance idealized, celebrated, and bemoaned in countless songs, books, and movies. This relationship in which "partners in an affection-oriented relationship probe deeper into each other's personalities, express deeper levels of caring for each other, and typically engage in more extensive sexual activity as well," is notably different from those of the first two phases, both for its longer duration and its depth.

These relationships are more mature, particularly insofar as the members of the couple rely on their own assessment of the relationship, relegating peer approval to a much more peripheral role. According to Dr. Brown, what is learned from the affection phase are "important components for identity development," especially for women as "relational thinkers." Expanded or new relationship skills emerge from the affection phase, including patience, empathy, and trust; honest self-disclosure; and conflict management.

The relationships of the affection phase present different challenges for mothers, which will vary from situation to situation, individual to individual. First of all, a daughter's age and maturity will be a factor; apart from the sexual component, a fourteen- or fifteen-year-old runs very different risks from those of a seventeen- or eighteen-year-old in this kind of relationship. In addition, emotional maturity will determine how well a girl manages the pressure and intensity of the relationship. Since such a romantic partner is likely to be a major influence on a girl and her evolution of self (and might be perceived as a challenge to our own influence), our assessment of the boy involved will be part and parcel of how we react to the relationship. One mother of a senior in high school couldn't have been more pleased with her daughter's first "serious" alliance; he was, she recounted, the captain of the debating team and extremely ambitious. His scores on the SATs—in the 700s—and his grades assured his attendance at a prestigious college. If anything, she felt, her daughter was "more on track" than ever. Another mother, though, wrestled with how to "manage" her sixteen-year-old's relationship with "the most irresponsible young man on the planet who hung out with a totally out-of-control crowd." She and her husband fought bitterly over how to handle it—her husband felt they should intercede immediately and simply forbid their daughter to see the boy again. She, on the other hand, counseled that they discuss their worries and objections with their daughter, and then wait it out until their daughter saw him as they did. In their case, the second strategy worked; it doesn't always.

Despite the value of the lessons to be learned from the affection phase, there are also obvious risks, even when our daughters are emotionally ready to handle a more complicated relationship. As Dr. Brown points out, extrapolating from Carol Gilligan's research, "because of their stronger orientation towards relationships than men, women may regard their success or failure in romantic relationships in this phase as a reflection of their *general* self-worth—not just their adeptness at dating or attracting romantic partners."[48] For some of us who have suffered from low self-esteem at one point or another during our lifetimes, these words will have a special resonance; we know what it is like to extrapolate who we are from a romantic relationship. Some girls, more dangerously, will find themselves in abusive relationships that confirm their worst thoughts about themselves. (For more, see page 270 and following.)

How can we make our girls more resilient when they begin to

forge the first romantic relationships of depth in their lives? For one thing, we need to help them see their relationship in the context of the whole self—not as the defining factor of the self. We can do this not only by supporting and complimenting them on the other activities and interests in their lives that make them unique but by actively debunking those myths about love and romance that encourage girls to see themselves as incomplete when they are unattached.

### Bonding Phase

This last phase—the consideration of forming a lasting relationship either within the confines of marriage or not—adds, as Dr. Brown notes, "an important new perspective to romantic relationships," among them practical considerations such as day-to-day compatibility, shared values and interests, and the question of whether the couple would "make an effective team in raising children, working out problems, and serving the community."[49] While the bonding phase now typically takes place in young adulthood or later, Dr. Brown suggests that not everyone graduates to this phase. Clearly, divorce statistics bear out his observation.

The exploration of romantic relationships is clearly an important part of our daughters' exploration of self. But it is vitally important that we do not absent ourselves from this part of the journey; they need our help, our wisdom, our guidance, and, sometimes, our protection.

~ ~

"I'm just holding my breath, hoping she gets from here to there safely and that she'll turn to me if she thinks she's lost her way," one mother of a sixteen-year-old confided to Peg. I think a lot of us find ourselves holding our breath when we survey the complicated societal landscape our daughters need to negotiate during adolescence—a vista filled with all manner of potential mishaps. Many of us will find ourselves playing "catch-up" and feeling absolutely stunned by the changes in our daughters and their social surroundings. Something that happened to me not long ago illustrates the point. Despite what most people think, operating rooms are rarely quiet unless there's a real problem, and during a routine procedure, there was a spirited conversation among us. I was talking about how the adolescent sexual scene had changed since we were young, and the anesthesiologist, who happens also to be the father of a girl going into seventh grade, jokingly commented that it was a pity he'd gone to junior high school then, instead of now. When I answered that he was missing the point—reminding him that his own daughter was about to enter junior high herself—his face fell.

When our daughters are small, we put the knives and household detergents and chemicals in child-proofed cabinets, and have a bottle of ipecac on hand just in case. We strap our girls into car seats and, later, teach them how to cross the street and look both ways, and never to open the door to a stranger. Keeping them safe in early childhood is relatively straightforward in a way that it isn't during the decade of adolescence. Those of us who are, by inclination, authoritarian parents—used to choosing for our children, managing their activities—will find ourselves on what appears to be increasingly hostile ground, with the same battles fought over and over again. "I am simply worn out," said one mother of three. "I have two other children who need my attention and there just doesn't seem to be enough of me to go around. I spend my life dealing with her and the various messes she's gotten into. We set rules and she breaks them. We arrange for her to have help at school, and then I find out she's not doing her homework. She sneaks down in the middle of the night to go online, and I end up having to hide the mouse." Others of us, mistaking the teaching of autonomy with letting go, may discover that our daughters are adrift and in real danger.

As we've discussed, experts distinguish between "authoritative" styles of parenting and "authoritarian" styles, and counsel that the former—in which both affection and parental control are at high levels—facilitates healthy development in both childhood and adolescence. Authoritarian parenting, on the other hand, stresses control over dialogue and affection. With this in mind, we all need to pay attention to how we talk to our daughters—are we lecturing or having a discussion? Are the rules we set for our girls reasonable and do they give them enough room to evolve into mature and responsible human beings? As our daughters' teachers, we need to voice our opinions but we also need to permit our daughters to voice theirs—even when we disagree with them. On the pages that follow, we suggest ways to start the dialogue with our daughters on the important subjects of sexuality and relationship.

In *Reviving Ophelia*, Mary Pipher shares one of the ways she talks to girls in her practice. Both lyrical and inspiring, her words are well worth keeping in mind as we begin one of the more important dialogues we will ever have with our children:

You are in a boat that is being tossed around by the winds of the world. The voices of your parents, your teachers, your friends and the media can blow you east, then west, then back again. To stay on course you must follow your own North Star, your sense of who you truly are. Only by orienting north can you chart a course and maintain it, only by orienting north can you keep from being blown all over the sea.

True freedom has more to do with following the North Star than going whichever way the wind blows. Sometimes it seems like freedom is blowing with the winds of the day, but that kind of freedom is really an illusion. It turns your boat in circles. Freedom is sailing towards your dreams.[50]

By talking and listening, we can help our girls hold a steady course.

There are many different ways to have a conversation—even an important one—with your child. Do make time for it—it is important, after all— and don't try to sandwich it in between television shows or errands. At the same time, don't feel as though you have to sit her down formally for The Big Talk—that pretty much guarantees her eyes will glaze over, expecting a Life Lecture. For an ongoing and open discussion, an informal setting—a ride in the car, a walk in the park, or cleaning up after dinner—may work best. Give her your full attention—use the answering machine to pick up calls, put your other kids and concerns on hold temporarily—and she's more likely to give you hers. Try not to take your daughter's offhand remarks—"Oh, Mom, you don't understand the way things are now" or "Mom, I know all of this already"—personally.

Most of all, remember that listening is every bit as important as talking. The more closely you listen, the more you will learn about her feelings and thoughts. Following are some specific suggestions on how to handle your talks.

### Keep in mind that this is an ongoing discussion, not a single talk.

Discussions about sexuality need to be tailored not just to your daughter's physical stage of development but to her social and emotional maturity. This seems fairly obvious but research data shows that parents usually do not consider talking to their children about sex as a dialogue but as a single talk. While it may be easier to limit your discussion to the physical aspects of puberty, for example, talk to your child about the psychological component as well.

Don't feel as if talking about sex with a certain amount of openness gives your daughter permission to have sex. A recent study conducted by the National Campaign to Prevent Teen Pregnancy found no correlation whatsoever between talking about sex (or, for that matter, about contraception) and the onset of sexual activity.[51] The truth is that your daughter—unless you manage to imprison her in a high tower—will ultimately decide what she will and won't do, and the likelihood is that you won't be present when she does. Your job is to make sure that she makes the best, most informed decision she is capable of, and that she recognizes you as an ally if she needs one.

**Before you talk to your daughter about sex, clarify your own views.**

Particularly as she gets older, your daughter will learn from both what you say and what you don't. Think about your own "comfort" zones—the areas you are fine talking about and those you aren't—because silence on a subject is also a way of communicating. Spend some time reflecting on what you see as age-appropriate explorations of sexual identity in light of your daughter's social and emotional maturity. Keep in mind that, even though parents and educators tend to focus on sexual intercourse, adolescents are typically involved in a broad range of sexual activities. According to the Sexuality Information and Education Council of the United States (SIECUS), by age fourteen, more than 50 percent of all boys have touched a girl's breasts and 25 percent have touched a girl's vulva. By age eighteen, more than 75 percent have engaged in heavy petting.[52] In the last few years, there have been a number of articles in the press describing anecdotal reports of twelve- to fourteen-year-olds engaging in oral sex. These articles prompted a special report published in *Family Planning Perspectives* in December 2000, which noted that "adults do not really know what behaviors teenagers consider to be 'sex,' and, by the same token, what they consider to be its opposite, 'abstinence.' " Even more problematic is the explanation offered as to why a single form of oral sex—fellatio—is a practice among middle-schoolers; according to Deborah Roffman, an author and sexuality educator, "middle-school girls look at oral sex as an absolute bargain—you don't get pregnant, they think you don't get diseases, you're still a virgin and you're in control since it's something that they can do to boys (whereas sex is almost always described as something boys do to girls)." She goes on to say, not surprisingly, that the idea of control is illusory.[53]

It's worth mentioning, too, that while the proportion of adolescents ages fifteen to nineteen having intercourse has declined, the overall proportion of girls having first intercourse by age fifteen has increased significantly—from 11 percent in 1988 to 19 percent in 1995. It is a statistic that holds true across all demographics, including race, family structure, and socioeconomic lines. Close to one out of five, it means that if your own fifteen-year-old daughter isn't having sex, the likelihood is that one of her friends or her classmates is.

Define sexual activity for yourself and then, in your talk, have your daughter define sexual activity as well. Talk to your daughter openly and honestly about the multitude of reasons people engage in sexual activity and be frank about both healthy and unhealthy motivations. As Dr. Lynn Ponton notes in *The Sex Lives of Teenagers*, "All teenagers have sexual lives, whether with others or through fantasies, and an important part of adolescence is thinking about and experimenting with aspects of sexuality."[54] Talk to her about how to handle situations that might make her uncomfortable or nervous, particularly those that involve crossing over from one level of activity—kissing, for example—to another. If there are areas you feel you can't discuss with your daughter, make sure that someone else—an aunt or other relative, or a family friend—does.

Attitudes toward what constitutes healthy sexuality in adolescence vary enormously from individual to individual, family to family. We asked Dr. Pepper Schwartz, Professor of Sociology at the University of Washington in Seattle and the coauthor of *Ten Talks*

*Parents Must Have with Their Children About Sex and Character*, about the nature of the dialogue and she was quick to note, "When we talk to our children about sex, we are in the value transmission business. We need to be really conscious of how we are giving information and how it prepares our child to operate in her own best interests. We are giving her feedback, helping her understand herself, and creating a solid platform for family values and rules."[55]

### Find out what your school's sexual education program includes and leaves out.

Societally, the problem is simple to define: Educators in America look to parents to educate their children about sexuality and, generally speaking, parents look to educators to fulfill the same task. As we've already noted elsewhere, teaching varies enormously from one school district to another, from school to school, from teacher to teacher. Find out what the curriculum includes and try to interview your child's teacher; be proactive and understand that sexual education in school should be seen as an addition to your discussions at home. If your daughter attends a private or parochial school that does not teach sex education, you will need to take full responsibility for what she knows. Talk to your daughter about what she is learning; it will give you an opportunity to expand or criticize points made in class. (Peg was appalled to discover that her daughter's teacher, apparently in an effort to discourage all sexual activity, had announced that "all Latex condoms have holes in them." The teacher had even drawn a picture on the board. Peg thought this was nothing less than a "why bother with condoms then?" lesson for the adolescents in the room.) Even though your daughter may protest that she already knows "everything," don't assume it.

What is left out of the school's curriculum is as much your concern as what is taught in it.

### Remember that "sex" is about lots more than sex.

While it's certainly easier to talk about the nuts and bolts of sex, sex is about more than vaginas and penises. Keep in mind that the outside world already provides our girls with lots of potentially damaging cultural scripts about sex and romance; you have an opportunity to provide alternative ones. Sexual activity raises issues about personal responsibility, commitment, emotion, trust, morality, situational ethics, and values that need to be addressed, in addition to warnings about its dangers.

Pressure to have sex comes from all different quarters, and we need to acknowledge the presence of that pressure openly and directly, and to counter it with alternatives. When we tell our girls to "just say 'no,' " we need to give them a context that they can balance against the pressure brought to bear on them. Do discuss the complexity of sexual relationships, and the need to be emotionally ready and old enough to handle them, in addition to the other risks involved. Discuss the importance of being "true" to oneself—one's own values, thoughts, and emotions—and acknowledge how that is sometimes a difficult task. (You might even want to use Mary Pipher's "North Star" metaphor. See page 188.) Your daughter will benefit from hearing that being different from everyone else—having different standards, one's own thoughts—is much harder than following the herd. Talk about the double standard, and ways in which girls can be hurt by rumors and innuendo. Discuss how first experiences shape us in ways that can hurt us when we are not ready for them or when we do not yet possess the wisdom to choose a partner wisely. When she is old enough, discuss how the physical nature of the sexual act itself—the simple fact that the male enters the female—makes it a very different experience for the two partners involved.

Once again, talking to your daughter about sex and relationship does not give her permission to have sex. There are many different

ways of engaging your daughter in a discussion about sexual relationships between men and women—by watching and critiquing a
television show or movie together, by reading a book together, or
simply talking about a situation that has come up within the family,
your community, or her circle of friends—that can help you better
understand where your daughter finds herself at any given point in
the journey.

### Talk to your daughter about gender roles and how they connect to relationship and sex.

The persistence of cultural gender stereotypes impacts heavily on
how girls (and of course, boys) handle relationships as well as on
the whole area of sexual activity. Don't assume that because you
present what you consider to be a healthy role model your daughter
is "totally clear" about stereotypes; it's really impossible to overestimate the contradictory messages about appropriate roles and
behavior our daughters receive. (On that front, too, it's worth noting that one study, comparing mothers' and daughters' conceptions
of gender roles across generations, discovered that "verbal persua-
sion," rather than "role modeling" influenced a daughter's formulation of gender roles.[56])

Talk to your daughter honestly and openly about the difficulties
girls and women have balancing the cultural messages of "being nice"
and "pleasing others" with speaking their own minds and articulating
their own needs. Ask her about her own experiences and those of her
peers. Discuss the other stereotypes that pertain to romantic love,
relationship, and sex—and find out what she thinks about not only
female gender stereotypes but male ones. Ask her about the kinds of
"name calling" her peers at school engage in—do girls ever get called
"sluts," "prudes," or "bitches"?—and talk to her about power and
intimidation. Find out what makes someone popular at school—and
ask your daughter where she thinks she fits into the social scene.

Last but not least, support your daughter in the healthy ways she expresses how she is different from everyone else in the world, including you. That sense of self will be her greatest ally.

**Keep in mind that you and your daughter's father are also modeling behaviors and attitudes, including sexual ones.**

While the idea may make you uncomfortable, even if you are married to your daughter's father, there's no question that our daughters learn from what we do, as well as what we say. Many aspects of relationship—allocation of duties and responsibilities, resolution of differences, expressions of affection and anger, displays of physical intimacy—are taught in the home without a word being uttered. Who does what in the household—the division of labor—influences your daughter's view of gender roles as strongly as what you say. If you are married, your daughter will take note of and learn from both the arguments you have with your husband and the way you do or don't touch, hug, and kiss. Attitudes toward sex (and men and women) are communicated by tone of voice, jokes, offhand remarks, responses to movies, books, and television shows, and countless other details your adolescent will pay attention to.

More seriously, other patterns of behavior—forms of verbal as well as physical abuse in the home—will shape both your daughter's sense of self and her attitudes toward relationships. If such patterns in your family exist, now is the time to seek help with them—if not for your own sake, then certainly for the sake of your daughter. (For more on this, see the chapter "Troubled Waters," page 230 and following.)

If you are divorced, keep in mind that your daughter will attend to what you do when you socialize with men and what you say about them afterward. The behavior you model—the importance you place on relationships with men, the kinds of relationships you have, the degree to which they define your sense of self—will affect and inform your daughter's behavior. Even if you have been on your own for some time, your daughter's attitudes toward your behavior may change; younger children may fare better with their mother's social life than older ones, for whom it may suddenly become an embarrassment or unwanted complication in their lives. They will become both more knowing about your activities and more critical or judgmental in ways an eight-year-old wouldn't be. As Dr. Pepper Schwartz counsels, "While you can't help your marital status or where you are in life, you can control your behavior. You can decide not to bring home casual boyfriends or, if you do bring someone home, have him sleep in a different room or wake up in one." Single mothers must keep in mind, she says, "that you will model things for them; they will take permission from what you do, and you have to accept responsibility. In the case of girls, research shows that teenage daughters who have mothers who date are sexual earlier." Most single mothers and fathers alike feel as though they deserve both a romantic and a sexual life, and that being single *and* a parent shouldn't preclude them from having one. But if there is a clear disparity between your own behavior and the rules you espouse for your daughter, particularly for an older adolescent, be prepared to need some help along the way.

Divorced fathers should equally be aware that both their behavior and their attitudes toward women will shape their daughter's behavior. Even if it is difficult, try to discuss this aspect of parenting an adolescent girl with your ex-husband in terms that focus on what counts: your daughter's life, not his.

Be attentive to the attitudes you communicate through behavior, and look at them in light of your discussions with your daughter about relationship and sexuality.

**Try to be open and flexible about your daughter's questions.**

For most of us, our own sexuality is a private and closely guarded aspect of self. Your daughter's questions—"How old were you when you had sex?" or, for the single mother, "Are you sleeping with the guys you go out with?"—may take you by surprise, and your first impulse might be to snap, "None of your business." (Depending on how close she is to him, these questions might equally be directed at her father.) The problem is that those words put an end to the discussion; what your daughter hears is, "I really don't want to talk to you about sex except on my terms." Dr. Pepper Schwartz suggests that we try instead to answer in ways that make it clear that while talking about sex is okay, each woman has her own boundaries and the right to be circumspect or keep certain details private. She points out that recasting the discussion to include a lesson in personal boundaries can be equally fruitful. To a fourteen-year-old, you might say instead, "I don't feel comfortable talking to you about that now but I might when you are older," or to a sixteen-year-old, "At the time, I thought the choices I made were right but, in retrospect, I don't think so. I'd rather concentrate on what's right and safe for you now." Another possible answer to an older adolescent, as Dr. Schwartz notes, is, "I don't want to discuss my personal behavior with you for the same reasons I think you have the right to keep some of your behavior to yourself. What I need to know about your behavior I need to know so I can advise and help you."

If you *are* taken by surprise, remember that your off-the-cuff answer can be the beginning of another discussion. As Dr. Schwartz recommends, "If you feel you've given the wrong answer, you can go back and say, 'I was just thinking about what I said about such-and-such, and now that I have thought about it some more, here's what I think really should be the answer.'" Open up the discussion by asking your daughter what she thinks. And, once you've answered the question, ask her if your answer has raised any new questions.

Try not to lecture and remember to listen. Many of your daughter's more abrupt or invasive questions may reflect concerns and worries she can't articulate, real confusion, and some amount of anxiety about specific issues.

### Talk about the connection between relationship, sex, and selfhood.

As your daughter matures, don't limit yourself to discussions about sex as though sexuality and other expressions of intimacy had no emotional context. The culture we live in—and the peer culture she belongs to—teach girls that being desirable is all-important with sometimes devastating results. Talk to your daughter about the ways in which healthy relationships can confirm our best feelings about ourselves as long as our sense of self is grounded in who we are, not what another person thinks of us.

If your daughter is dating, *do* talk to her about destructive relationships as well as violence in dating relationships. While the statistics on dating violence range widely—depending on whether threats or nonsexual physical aggression are included in the definition—the Centers for Disease Control note that "violent behavior that takes place in a context of dating or courtship is not a rare occurrence." If you are shaking your head and thinking that the boys your daughter dates are simply too "nice" and "well-mannered," take a look at the following facts research has yielded:

- A recent study published in August 2001 in the *Journal of the American Medical Association* of girls in ninth through twelfth grade revealed that roughly one in five high school girls reported experiencing physical and/or sexual violence from a dating partner. The researchers note that this percentage correlates to the percentage of adult women who experience violence at the hands of partners. The preponderance of the girls surveyed were white; indeed, the authors note that "black high school students may be at reduced risk relative to their peers

from other racial/ethnic groups for experiencing sexual violence from dating partners."[57]

- A study of eighth- and ninth-graders noted that 25 percent of
male and female students had been the victims of nonsexual
dating violence and 8 percent reported that they were the victims of sexual dating violence.

- The average prevalence for nonsexual dating violence among
male and female high school students is 22 percent and 32 percent among college students.

- In a national survey of college students, 27.5 percent of women
said that they had suffered rape or attempted rape at least once
since age 14.3. Only 5 percent of these incidents were reported
to the police.

- Over half of a representative sample of more than one thousand female students at a large urban university had experienced some form of unwanted sex. Twelve percent was
perpetrated by casual dates and 43 percent by steady dating
partners.[58]

For more, see "Troubled Waters," page 230 and following.

### Examine your attitudes and those of your daughter's father about risk-taking.

The impulse to keep our daughters safe in a high tower runs deep in
many of us, particularly when the statistics pertaining to adolescent
sexual behavior (and drug use) are so alarming. But as we've already
discussed, risk-taking is part and parcel of living—and learning to

distinguish between unhealthy and healthy risks is part of the journey toward adulthood. The various attitudes we may have toward adolescent risk-taking—as an unavoidable part of adolescence, as necessary but needing supervision, or as dangerous and unnecessary—will not only shape our parenting styles but also our daughters' sense of personal responsibility.

In her book *Don't Stop Loving Me: A Reassuring Guide for Mothers of Adolescent Daughters*, Ann F. Caron, Ed.D., coins an extremely useful phrase that describes what every mother, particularly of the older adolescent, needs to practice: She calls it "vigilant trust." In her words:

> Being vigilant doesn't mean trusting less, but it does mean trusting correctly. Mothers have to believe in their daughters, unless there are clear violations of trust, and mothers should recognize those signs.
>
> For instance, do you know what marijuana smells like? Do you know the look of a hangover? Are you alert to signs of sexual activity? Do you know who is calling your daughter? Do you notice a sudden influx of new clothes, cosmetics, or jewelry?
>
> Vigilant parenting is hands-on parenting. It does not mean intrusive parenting, but it means an awareness of a daughter's activities, moods, friends, attitudes, and her well-being. Vigilant trust is caring.[59]

If you think your daughter is taking dangerous risks, seek help.

~ ~ ~

My daughter doesn't usually say much about her adopted status. The last time was quite a while ago, when I read something in her e-mail: She was online with a guy and I guess trying to show off. He asked her what was the craziest thing she'd ever done. She replied that she had taken the bus out of town to go to look for her birth mother. This didn't, in fact, happen but I couldn't talk to her about it because I'd been checking up on how she was acting on the Internet. A few days later, on the way to the mall, I brought up the subject of a search. I told her I'd done some investigating on the Internet and that it wouldn't be hard to find her birth mother, that it was for her to do, though, and usually you have to be eighteen. Told her about the Soundex Registry, where mother and child can find each other, and other options. I emphasized that I would support her, that my feelings wouldn't be hurt, etcetera.

She was somewhat interested but not very. I think she appreciates that I'm open about it, but for the most part doesn't think about it. What she has said is, "The only reason I'd like to meet her is to see what she looks like." I totally understand. Sometimes I'll see her in her room, just looking at herself in the mirror. I don't know what's going through her head—probably she's just thinking how pretty she is (mirror, mirror on the wall). But maybe she's thinking about her genes and the people she's never met. It's been many months since she's said anything.

She is caught up in a lovely social whirl with her friends, both male and female, and I think she's too busy having fun to worry about being "given up at birth." That is, I don't think she has huge abandonment issues. She has a wonderful life with two loving, even adoring, parents.

Maybe the future will bring new issues around this. Sometimes I worry about her following the same karmic path as her birth mother—that is, getting pregnant young. I pray that won't happen anytime soon.

Adoptive mother of a fifteen-year-old girl

Sometimes, the question of identity is complicated by other issues, adoption among them. As the mother of both a biological and an adoptive daughter, I am keenly aware of how being adopted can shape an individual's sense of self. I have always been very upfront with Kate about the fact that she is adopted—she has known since she learned to talk—but the particulars have been given to her over the years on a need-to-know basis and based on what I thought she could handle at any given time. When she was twelve we were in an elevator with a friend, and we ended up discussing Kate's adoption. My friend casually asked how old Kate's mother was when she had Kate and, without thinking about the implications, I replied "fifteen." Kate was taken aback; as it happens, her birth mother's age had never come up as a question and I think she was initially both shocked and embarrassed by how young her birth mother had been. Since then, we've talked about it more than once.

But her birth mother's age took on a different significance as she got older. As her own understanding of sexual activity grew—when she was roughly fourteen—she realized that in order to have a baby at fifteen you must be sexually active at fourteen. Since Kate had just experienced her first kiss, she saw her birth mother's choices with a new perspective. She appreciates the things she gets to do as a teenager—like riding and showing her horse—and has said, more than once, that she couldn't imagine what she would do if she had to take care of a baby instead.

This last year, during Women's History Month, one of her homework assignments was to write an essay about a woman she admired or had influenced her—a true heroine. I called home from New York the evening she began to work on her essay. I could tell by the sound of her voice that she was excited about the project and she asked me to guess who she'd be writing about. Before I could even say a word, she blurted out, "My birth mother. She is my heroine because she was so strong and smart and knew that I would have a better life with you. I can't believe she made the decisions she did all by herself when she was just my age." Her wise perception made me prouder than I would have been had she chosen me as the subject of her essay,

She will soon turn fifteen herself. We haven't yet experienced the yearnings and doubts that I have seen adopted children deal with in other families. I would like to think that some of that is a function of our closeness; for the time being at least, I don't think she has felt the need to search for her biological mother because she knows her real mother lives under the same roof with her. But that doesn't mean that she hasn't had questions, nor does it mean that she won't in the future. She has been concerned about the connection between genetics and health, for example. For my part, I will answer her questions as honestly and openly as I can as she matures.

It is difficult to generalize about the ways in which adoption will complicate or change the process of forming an identity—just as it is to generalize about the ease or difficulty of this passage for girls living with their biological mothers. Each family is unique and there will, inevitably, be other factors that will influence your daughter's development; the issues pertaining to adoption, for example, may be complicated by the number of children you have, by whether your daughter's siblings are your biological children, or by your adoptive daughter's race if it differs from your own. There is a part of the path that is wholly individual—that depends, in large part, on the family dynamic and your daughter's relationship to you, her father, and to her siblings. Some adolescent girls will feel a strong need to search out "why" they are who they are—and they may feel that the answers to that question lie in the gene pool from which they are descended. As they begin to identify who they are—what they enjoy, their talents and weaknesses, their hopes and dreams—many will wonder whether, in that biological family they've never met, there is someone "just like them." Questions that never came up during your daughter's childhood—How old was her mother? Was her mother married to her father? Does she have biological siblings?—will often come up during adolescence—although both the frequency of questioning and the importance attached to the answers will vary from girl to girl. Because identity formation involves thinking about the future and its possibilities, it is, in some sense, inevitable that an adopted child will at least think about who she might have been if her past had been different—that is, if she had been raised by her birth mother or adopted by another family.

Little formal research has been done comparing adoptive and nonadoptive adolescents but one study, conducted by the Search Institute in 1994, concluded that adopted adolescents are at no more risk than other adolescents during the process of identity formation, compare favorably with other peers on an index of self-esteem, and are as likely to "report positive identity as their non-adopted siblings." Only 27 percent of the adopted adolescents in the study reported that adoption "is a big part of how I think about myself." (It should be noted, though, that what distinguished the sample was the stability of marriages—only 11 percent reported a divorce or separation, which is much lower than the national average for adolescents in general. The study also only focused on children adopted in infancy.) Not surpisingly, the study determined that there were six factors that contributed to the well-being of adopted adolescents, which—with the exception of the two points pertaining to adoption—mirror the same factors that pertain to nonadoptive adolescents:

- A strong emotional attachment of child to parent and parent to child

- A goodness-of-fit in which adopted adolescents perceive a good match with parent values, interests, and personalities

- The use of effective parenting styles

- The successful management by parents of factors that can threaten the well-being of adopted youth

- The use of positive approaches to the issues unique to adoptive families

- The affirmation of the fact of adoption without dwelling on it[60]

It's noteworthy that only the last two points differ from what constitutes good parenting for nonadoptive adolescents.

Mothers who have always felt that they love their adopted daughters no differently than they do their biological children may find it hard hearing their daughters talk about another "mother" they have never met. Some mothers will—wrongly—react to their daughters' need to talk about or even find their birth mothers as reflecting on their own inadequacies. Other mothers, more secure of themselves and of their place in their daughters' lives, will have relatively little problem with their children's questions. The testing of boundaries that is part of the mother-daughter dynamic during adolescence may be made more painful when "You don't understand me" becomes, for an adoptive mother, "You're not my real mother anyway." Should that happen, remember the context in which it is said and try hard not to take it literally. Once again, the coincidence of your own life crises with those of your daughter's may complicate—for the moment, at least—both your reaction and hers. It is important to remember that, if she does decide to look for her birth mother, it isn't about you—but about her and her need to define herself.

In the Search Institute's study of adoption, *Growing Up Adopted*, the authors reflect on adoptive families and the health of adolescent children raised in those families. They note that the adoption process is rigorous and challenging for parents—often involving long waits, significant expenditure, and the need to prove their worthiness and suitability. What the researchers have to say is something every adoptive mother should keep in mind:

In an odd way, perhaps the challenges of the adoption process have a positive outcome. Perhaps it is only those parents who are deeply committed to parenting and having a healthy family who have the stamina to navigate the adoption process. Perhaps the hard work it took to build the family redoubles their commitment to making the family strong. As a result, their level of dedication and commitment to their children is higher than is true for some parents who can become parents with little forethought, care, or interest.[61]

• • •

Sexual orientation is a part of sexual identity and, for some daughters, will complicate both the journey toward selfhood and the mother-daughter relationship. Sexual orientation—the pattern of physical behavior and emotional attraction toward others—is separate from gender identity and gender roles. In their book, *Lesbian and Gay Youth*, Caitlin Ryan and Donna Futterman point out that "the struggle to integrate a positive adult identity—a primary developmental task for all adolescents—becomes an even greater challenge for lesbian and gay youth, who learn from earliest childhood the profound stigma of a homosexual identity. Unlike many of their heterosexual peers, lesbians and gay adolescents have no built-in support systems or assurances that their friends and family will not reject them if they share their deepest secret."[62] They write that existing individual vulnerabilities are increased by internalized feelings of stigma and self-hatred.

How do you know if your daughter is struggling with this aspect of her identity? Ryan and Futterman point out that since adolescence "is a time of exploration and experimentation, as such, sexual activity does not necessarily reflect either present or future sexual orientation. Confusion about sexual identity is not unusual in adolescence."[63]

Not long ago, we asked a friend—a brilliant Ph.D. and now a successful businesswoman in her early fifties who has an open and committed relationship with another woman—to reflect on her own adolescence. Even though she is not a mother herself—she's both an aunt and a godmother—she is a daughter. What she wrote us, we think, ultimately applies to all of our daughters—whether they encounter a crisis of sexual identity or not:

I was thirty before I came out to my mother (my father and I never did have a conversation on the subject); even then, my fear of rejection was overwhelming, and it was years before my mother accepted the inevitable. In my small, all-girls high school in the 1960s, it was inconceivable to me that I could tell anyone—not even the two teachers who were a much beloved and fully accepted lesbian couple. The stigma seemed too great, ostracism too likely, and—most important—the almost certain turmoil at home too much to contemplate. Among other issues of which I was well aware, the psychotherapeutic community in those days believed firmly that homosexuality was a disorder—arrested development, narcissism, pick your category—and my firmly atheistic family placed all its faith in therapy. I didn't know much, but I knew I didn't want to be "cured."

If you think your daughter is a lesbian, or if you are fortunate enough in your relationship with her that she confides in you, the single most valuable thing you can do is embrace her, literally and emotionally. Don't assume she knows that you love her no matter what—say so, emphatically and often. Don't let her confuse your fear for her happiness with rejection of her emerging identity. And most important, don't belittle what for her is deeply serious: "Oh, you're just going through a phase." "You'll feel different when you get older." "Why don't you go out with that nice John Smith? He likes you so much."

On the other hand, you're still her mother. Expressing your concerns is not only legitimate but can be helpful. Life is harder for young lesbians than for other adolescents (and adulthood has its own trials); your daughter needs your help in learning how to cope: who to tell, and how, and when; what behaviors are appropriate; how to handle both ecstasy and heartbreak. And, yes, you need to talk to her about sexual activity. The emotional impact of the first sexual encounter between two girls is as enormous as for heterosexual adolescents, and there are good arguments to be made for waiting.

However unhappy, and for whatever reason, you may be to learn that your daughter is a lesbian, she's still the child you raised and love. It isn't the end of the world. And if you handle the revelation

with calm, patience, good humor, and affection, it won't be the end
of your relationship either.

Much has changed since this woman, now in her 50s, confronted
the issue, although in their book, Ryan and Futterman write that a
"critical aspect of identity management for all lesbian and gay youth
is learning to assess when and with whom they can safely disclose
their lesbian or gay identity."[64]

In an interview with Caitlin Ryan for this book, she pointed out
that many more young people are "coming out" in adolescence than
ever before, which has been a tremendous catalyst for change. But
she notes, "This is the most highly charged disclosure that a young
person will ever make, and it's no accident that the first people they
come out to are their close friends, not their parents. More of them
will come out to mothers than fathers but it is oftentimes put off
for years." Mothers who find themselves confronting this situation
will have a myriad of reactions—and even the most supportive of
parents, as Ryan and Futterman put it, "will need time, access to
accurate information, and an opportunity to process what for most
will be a distressing and guilt-provoking experience."[65] We asked
Caitlin Ryan what, in her experience, was the reaction of most parents and she responded: "Most people getting this news will be
really upset by it. For most parents—even some lesbian parents—
it's not exactly what they think they want to hear. It has so much to
do with their own dreams and aspirations—for a mother, some of
the first things she imagines for her daughter are her wedding day,
grandchildren, possibly a successsful career but definitely a successful relationship. The myths and stereotypes of homosexuality
belie those dreams—the myths that a lesbian girl will never be
accepted, will never have a stable relationship. One of the things
that parents talk about is their worry that their child will be alone."
Ryan believes that a critical step for mothers (and fathers) is positive exposure to models of gay and lesbian lives, so that they can

"reframe" their expectations. Parents also need support in what Ryan calls the "grieving" process—grieving for the loss of social acceptance that comes with being nonheterosexual. Organizations such as Parents, Families, and Friends of Lesbians and Gays (PFLAG) can provide not just support but guidance. Finally, though, she says, "It's a struggle to adjust but, in general, love wins out. Most parents will, out of love for their children, come to some accommodation, and very few will reject their children. At the other end of the spectrum, there are also those parents who celebrate their daughters and who they are."

In his book based on studies he conducted, *Mom, Dad. I'm Gay.: How Families Negotiate Coming Out*, Ritch C. Savin-Williams notes that "parental reactions to the disclosure appear to be individualized, diverse, and complex." In his interviews with young women, he found that "over 60% reported that the mother-daughter relationship has essentially stayed the same from the initial disclosure to the present time. This stability most often characterized those relationships in which the mother's initial response was positive or neutral (80% of all such reactions)." Only one third of the most negative reponses, in his words, "remained very bad."[66]

Dr. Savin-Williams notes that the mother-daughter relationships most resistant to improvement are those "in which the mother initially denies her daughter's same-sex attractions or suggests that she is only passing through an adolescent or women's studies phase (20% got better). Although many of the young women report progress in their relationship with their mother, far more desire or expect it." Although, as Dr. Savin-Williams notes, there is no single factor responsible for improving the mother-daughter relationship, "the aspiration of both dyadic members to maintain a close bond is a powerful motivator."

Although Dr. Savin-Williams did not interview mothers, what daughters reported about the "makeover" of the mother-daughter relationship is illuminating and valuable:

Daughters often believe it is the consequence of time and love. Indeed, several daughters note that it simply took time for their mother to move beyond her initial shock and disappointment to discover that she, the daughter, has remained essentially the same person. Mothers remind themselves that their daughter is still their daughter, and they do not want to lose her.[67]

For more, see the Resources section, page 355.

~ ~ ~

My divorce was devastating to me—and it affected my daughter in many ways. She is very cautious with people, and with men in particular, and I know it has to do with her father's betrayal and my reaction to it. I have had no reason to trust men after all that I have been through. My ex-husband was a liar during our marriage—he had many affairs I didn't know about and some I did—and during the divorce. We separated when my daughter was five but I took him back after three months. He left when she was seven, and moved in with his lover. My daughter was aware of much too much. I am not the best role model for trust issues and, even at twelve, she is smart enough to know it. Her father has let her down many times but she always finds an excuse for him and tries to protect him—which is just what I did during our marriage.

When she is an adult, I hope that she will be able to balance these issues when it comes to relationships with men. For the moment, she often says she doesn't want to get married or have children. Maybe this will change later but I really can't blame her for these feelings. I do know, though, that she trusts *me*.

"Victoria," divorced, thirty-eight, event planner and mother to "Christina," twelve

Finally, something needs to be said about divorce and how it affects our daughters' formation of identity. Nearly half of all American children born in the late 1970s through the 1990s will spend part of their lives in a single-parent household. It's worth pointing out that I was a single mother of two until my girls were, respectively, ages four and six and a half. Although they didn't experience divorce (Kate was a toddler when my second marriage broke up and has no memory of it, and Rachel wasn't born), they did live with a harried single mother. They also experienced a new "blended" family—complete with a new father (who since has adopted both of them) and a new younger brother. My coauthor Peg is now divorced, after five years of relatively amicable separation, and has been a single mother since her daughter was eight. It is a subject with which we have some familiarity, both through our own experiences and, anecdotally, those of friends and acquaintances—as most women reading these pages will. Despite how common the fact of divorce has become, culturally we tend to see an intact family—no matter what the dynamics within that family are—as always better for children and preferable to a single-parent household. As a result, the words "She's from a broken home" or "Her mom's divorced" are often used as a shorthand description of and explanation for an adolescent's behavior—much the same way as "raging hormones" or "teenage rebellion" are—not just by the popular press and media but by guidance counselors, teachers, and next-door neighbors alike. "Divorce" is yet another label that carries its own stigmas and associations, despite its prevalence in our society. This is not to say that divorce does not complicate the journey that is adolescence; it is simply that the research paints a more complicated and nuanced picture than the popular comparison of the mythical "Ozzie and Harriet" family and the "broken" one. There are, of course, unhappy and troubled children in both families with two married parents and single-parent households and, equally, well-adjusted and happy children in both.

"All unhappy families are unhappy in different ways" is how Leo Tolstoy put it in *Anna Karenina*, and the differences among divorces are no less real. The "why" of your divorce, the extent of hostility between you and your daughter's father, the duration and complication of the divorce process itself, the age of your child and the num-

ber of children in the family, and finally, the economic circumstances of postdivorce life of the custodial parent (still almost always
the mother) will all affect the degree to which your daughter's sense
of self is modified by divorce. Negatively changed economic circumstances—the one sweeping generalization that can be made
about the outcome of divorce for women—are estimated to be the
cause of as much as half of the adjustment problems seen in children
of divorce. Each divorce is, in the details, different from every
other—as is the degree to which any mother involves her child in
the process. (For example, research shows that, post-divorce, adolescents who are "caught in the middle" are more poorly adjusted
than those whose "parents have conflicts but do not use their children to express disputes." Even when parents have "substantial conflict, but avoid placing their youngsters in the middle, their children
are not significantly different from youngsters in families with low
conflict.")

In a review of a decade of research, Dr. Joan B. Kelly summarized
that "marital conflict is a more important predictor of child adjustment than is divorce itself or post-divorce conflict." As it happens,
conflict alone isn't predictive of a child's adjustment; rather "the
intensity and frequency of parent conflict, the style of conflict, its
manner of resolution, and the presence of buffers to ameliorate the
effects of high conflict are the most important predictors of child
adjustment."[68] Research has shown that, in the presence of conflict,
many different buffers—a good relationship with one parent or
close sibling relationships, for example—can offset the effect of a
high marital conflict.

There is no question that divorce causes pain and distress for all
involved. But overall, to quote Dr. Kelly, "This decade of research
supports the view that the long-term outcome of divorce for the
majority of children is resiliency rather than dysfunction."[69]

What can we learn from the research? For one thing, the fact of being divorced should not make you feel as though you have "no control" over how divorce affects your child's development. While it may be true that some areas are beyond your control—such as your ex-husband's behavior, his possible remarriage, and its effect on your child—there is, in fact, much you can do to make sure that your divorce isn't the defining factor during your child's adolescence:

**If you are still reeling from the effects of your divorce, get help for yourself.**

Often, single mothers are harried, overworked, and stressed; raising a child or children is never easy and is even harder to do without a partner. If you have not fully recovered from the emotional effects of your divorce, it is likely that how you feel will affect how you parent. Some women will have familial and community support after divorce; others will not. Anger, grief, and feeling depressed are all "normal" responses to a life-changing event—but they need to be managed. In her study of adult children of divorce, *The Unexpected Legacy of Divorce*, Judith Wallerstein describes how children may become "caregivers" in the aftermath of divorce, when parents are unable to function. They may take on adult responsibilities or feel as though they are responsible for their mother's or father's well-being. While becoming a caregiver temporarily is an act of devotion, becoming a permanent caregiver to a troubled, depressed parent has, according to Wallerstein, serious and damaging consequences for the adult lives of divorced children.[70]

Make sure that the roles your daughter takes on in your household—particularly if she is an older adolescent—are ones she can manage, both literally and psychologically. If you are struggling, *do* seek help for yourself—getting help is a sign of strength, not of weakness. .

### Focus on how you parent.

No matter what your other circumstances are, this is an area very much within your control. A study reported by Shelli Avenevoli, Frances M. Sessa, and Laurence Steinberg confirmed that different parenting styles generally distinguish two-parent from single-parent homes—that single parents "exhibit diminished parenting, particularly with respect to behavioral control and limit setting (i.e., more permissive and less involved parenting)." How this happens needs little explanation—single mothers who have to work and parent may find it hard to fill the demands of both at once. But the study's second finding is one every single mother needs to absorb and appreciate: "Authoritative parenting is related to adaptive adjustment *virtually regardless of family structure, ethnicity, or social class* [emphasis added]."[71] In other words, authoritative parenting—characterized as warm, firm, and democratic—supports emotional adjustment, school performance, and healthy self-esteem, and lowers the risk of deviant behavior regardless of whether the household is intact or not.

Whether we are married or alone, we can pay attention to how we parent during the years of adolescence. Make raising your daughter a priority and, once again, don't buy into those wrongheaded notions about adolescence that encourage us to let our daughters raise themselves.

### Make every effort not to involve your daughter in your disputes.

While in most divorced families hostilities between the two parents will eventually cease, some 8 to 12 percent of parents will remain in high conflict, even as long as three or more years after divorce. There will almost always be some disagreement between divorced mothers and fathers on issues related to child-rearing, as there are in stable, two-parent families—and adolescence will raise new issues about appropriate behavior and rules. Some amount of fractiousness—even in the "best" of divorces—is inevitable, as it is in the "best" of marriages.

Do not involve your daughter in your disputes with your ex-husband. For some of us, this will be easier said than done, but the research is absolutely unequivocal on this point. Do not use your child as a "messenger" or a "spy" and above all, do not ask your daughter to take sides. Do not tell your daughter "secrets" that she is required to keep from her father. If you think your ex-husband is using your daughter as a go-between, talk to him about it.

Be honest with yourself. If you are involving your daughter in your disputes in either small ways or large ones, confront it as a problem you need to deal with for her well-being. Old patterns of behavior can be broken, and it is never too late to change. If you and her father are unable to reach an agreement on important issues, try to seek help. Mediation has been shown to be a powerful and useful tool in negotiating between divorced mothers and fathers. If you can, avail yourself of it.

### Give your daughter room.

Yes, your ex-husband and her father are, indeed, the same person but your relationships to him are different. Reformulating relationships to parents and exploring degrees of relatedness are key developmental tasks of adolescence, and your daughter needs room to do both with *both* of her parents. Do not impose your feelings about your ex-husband on your daughter; she needs to be able to explore her own thoughts and feelings, and the ways in which she relates and connects to him. Unless being with him presents a real danger to her health and well-being—which should be dealt with as a legal, not an emotional, issue—she needs to make up her own mind.

Because in most cases—though not all—the divorced father will end up financially better off, it may seem to both you and your daughter that it is patently unfair that he is living an easier life, at precisely the moment material goods are likely to be more important to her. Try, if you can, to put that in context—and read about "boundaries," below. As painful as it might be, if your ex-husband has remarried, your child also needs the room—and your permission—to explore her relationship to her stepmother and other members of her newly extended family.

### Recognize boundaries when you engage your daughter in discussion.

In the wake of divorce, mothers (and fathers) face the challenge of renegotiating family boundaries—among them, the nature of the mother-daughter dialogue, which is likely to include different disclosures than in an intact family and will sometimes resemble a "confidante" model. The difficulty here is separating what constitutes a close and healthy relational tie between mothers and daughters—an open sharing of information—from one that burdens adolescent girls with concerns and problems they cannot handle. To put it plainly: How open should the dialogue between mother and daughter be on issues pertaining to divorce and life post-divorce?

A study conducted by Drs. Susan Silverberg Koerner, Stephanie L. Jacobs, and Meghan Raymond specifically examined the effect of divorced mothers' disclosures to their adolescent daughters in two sensitive and important areas—financial concerns and complaints or anger toward the daughters' fathers. The adolescent girls were ages eleven to seventeen; the divorces in the sample were comparatively recent, with a mean of a little over a year; and all the mothers were custodial parents. The study examined the mother's motivation in discussing these issues, the frequency of the discussions, and the effect on the daughters. A majority of mothers talked about financial concerns to their daughters—with more than three quarters of them talking in detail—but appeared to have different motives. Some did it to expose their daughters to adult issues (that is, money management) while others raised the topic "in the context of complaints about the ex-husband." The daughters' responses were either to feel frustrated by the fact that they could not help their mothers (because they were too young to work) or to offer emotional support. Some 84 percent of mothers did voice negative complaints or comments about their daughters' fathers for two purposes, according to the researchers: either to have the daughter "relinquish her idealized view of her father" or so that she would "realize that her mother is not completely to blame for the break-up of the family." The researchers found a direct correlation among the *depth* and *intensity* of disclosure on financial issues, negative comments toward the ex-spouse, and daughters' psychological distress.[72]

In an interview conducted for this book, we asked Dr. Susan Silverberg Koerner of the University of Arizona about what constituted "healthy" boundaries for the mother-daughter dialogue. In her view, "It's a difficult question, and it's not easily answered. The idea is *not* 'never bring up these topics'—it's *how* you bring them up. Bringing them up every once in a while in a reassuring context is different from having a very emotionally intense conversation or blowing up about something and giving every last detail—about how the father didn't do this or how we're going to lose the house. That's what distresses a child." Although the findings were not included in the original report, Dr. Silverberg Koerner and her colleagues also looked into how much detail mothers went into on other topics—such as job ups and downs, personal concerns (things the mothers might regret or feel ashamed of), and parenting concerns. Once again, the study showed that when these topics were brought up emotionally, in detail, and with frequency, the daughters' psychological distress increased.

What should mothers do? As Dr. Silverberg Koerner puts it, "In a nutshell, be a parent first—and that takes effort. Take a moment to think about what you are going to say, be brief and to the point, and don't use your child as a sounding board." This sound advice is often, in the day-to-day of postdivorce life, hard to follow but, keeping your daughter's welfare in mind, try your hardest.

Dr. Silverberg Koerner's conclusions are interesting in light of the findings of E. Mavis Hetherington, Ph.D., since they confirm an important point we have made before: The "best friend" or "sister" model isn't the right one for the mother-daughter relationship at this time of your child's life, particularly in a single-parent household. In an article entitled "Should We Stay Togther?" Dr. Hetherington examines "parentification," which is described as "a type of role reversal where the child assumes roles usually considered to be parental roles." Parentification has two forms; in "instrumental parentification," the child takes on household tasks and care of siblings normally allocated to the parent, while in "emotional parentification" the child acts as the emotional support or confidant of a "needy" parent. Not surprisingly, girls encounter more emotional parentification from *both* mothers and fathers than do sons, particularly in high-conflict divorced families. Moreover, high levels of both instrumental and emotional parentification were associated with depressed or anxious internalizing behaviors in daughters, but not sons.[73]

While it is true that "some responsibility and nurturing of others may enhance development," according to Dr. Hetherington, "excessively high demands may lead to competence and responsibility accompanied by feelings of self-doubt, depression, low self-esteem, a lurking sense of failure, and apprehension about performance and personal adequacy." Dr. Hetherington calls this "competency at a cost"—and daughters of divorced mothers are much more likely to fall into this category than other girls.[74]

These findings—which make it clear that while an adolescent girl may appear to be growing with and capable of the tasks given to her, her psychological health may be jeopardized—should be a wake-up call to all single mothers. Respect the boundaries of parent and child in discussions, no matter how capable, caring, or "mature" your daughter seems, and do make sure that your daughter isn't overburdened by other work. She already has "work" to do—the work of adolescence. If you need emotional or other support, look outside of your household for it.

### Pay attention to the behaviors you are modeling.

We have mentioned this before but it is worth repeating. Your adolescent daughter will take cues from your "performing self"— everything from how you deal with stress or resolve conflicts with your ex-husband (or anyone else) to how you act when you are with other men who are not her father. Divorce is a life-changing event and some women will find themselves struggling with issues of identity similar to those their daughters are wrestling with. If you are dating, be aware that you are modeling behavior on a whole range of issues, including sexuality and male-female relationships, and teaching your daughter—even if you are not conscious of it— about self-esteem, self-reliance, and dependence. If your social life has become your central concern—and that concern is changing the way you parent—your daughter will learn from that as well. In the same study quoted earlier, Dr. E. Mavis Hetherington notes, too, that "disclosures about intimate and sexual relationships are associated with earlier initiation of sexual relationships and increased externalizing behaviors in girls."[75] Similarly, keep in mind that even an older, more mature adolescent daughter will react to your dating (and the men you date) not as a peer or girlfriend but as your child—and that if your house rules for her and your own behavior are contradictory both in kind and spirit, she will pay attention.

## And if you remarry. . . .

Here are the facts: Sixty-six percent of women and 75 percent of men will remarry. But because the rate of divorce is even higher in remarriages than it is in first marriages, one out of ten children will experience at least two divorces of their residential parents before they reach age sixteen. Even though the "stepfamily" has existed since ancient times (then, usually because of the death of a parent) and is commonplace today, its connotation is still negative. (Think Cinderella and her stepmother—and countless other fairy tales and stories.) In addition, while there are plenty of cultural models—some useful, others not—of what constitutes a "good" mother or father, the appropriate role of a stepparent is much less clear. What makes a "good" stepmother or stepfather? What, precisely, is the right or healthy amount of involvement for a stepparent in a child's life? Research has only recently begun to explore the answers.

Remarriage is a difficult and thorny issue, particularly because, in some cases, what may be "best" for you may not be "best" for your daughter—at least from her point of view. There's evidence, too, that remarriage may become specifically problematic during the years of adolescence. According to a paper written by Dr. James H. Bray, earlier divorce research indicated that it takes about two years for a family to adjust after a divorce, and roughly two to four years after remarriage for a stepfamily to stabilize. But in a study conducted by Dr. Bray and others that looked at stepfamilies after remarriage at six months, two and half years, and five to seven years, contrary to the researchers' expectations, difficulties with adolescents took place long after the formation of the stepfamily:

> We were surprised by these findings. We expected children in stepfamilies to have more behavior problems than children in nuclear families during the early transitional phase of stepfamily formation.

However, children suddenly erupted after several years of seemingly healthy adjustment to stepfamily life.[76]

The researchers concluded that adolescents were "again struggling with their parents' divorces." They surmised their findings were similar to what has been called "the sleeper effect of divorce," in which children who experience divorce at the ages of four to six come to terms with it only when they reach adolescence.

The researchers concluded that the timing of the disruption was directly tied to the developmental tasks of adolescence. As they put it:

Part of the individuation process is to interact with parents as a means of finding out who one is and who one is not. However, in stepfamilies, an important person is often not present—the nonresidential parent, who is usually the father. Thus, the individuation process is transferred to the stepfather and may become problematic because adolescents need their other parents to complete this process.[77]

As a result, they note that it is common for adolescents in stepfamilies to develop "an increased interest in the nonresidential parent" and that some 20 percent of the adolescents in their study actually went to live with their fathers during this period. Girls, not surpisingly, reported more stress than boys.

Obviously, not all girls—or, for that matter, all boys—from divorced and remarried families will have emotional and behavioral problems; it's simply that they are at greater risk. The researchers note, too, that younger children are more accepting of stepparents than adolescents and that boys are more accepting of stepfathers than girls.

Combining the developmental tasks of adolescence with other

major adjustments—living with a new stepfather, relating to step-brothers or -sisters, moving to a new home, or starting at a different school—will complicate the process of self-formation and, likely as not, your daughter's relationship to you. In some blended families, the mother's energies will be directed away from her daughter (and perhaps from her other children as well) as she negotiates the boundaries of a "new life." These are relatively uncharted waters—more families than ever before are "blended" and reconfigured by divorce and remarriage—and it is hard to generalize about them. Remember, though, that while you, as an adult, may experience these changes in one way, your daughter will experience them in another.

It's particularly important that you set aside whatever ideas you have about "necessary separation" and "letting her work it out" during adolescence, and make sure that you are not only paying attention to your daughter but paying the right kind of attention. Once again, do not feel as though bullying your way through a difficult situation is a mark of character or endurance. If the stress level in the household becomes unmanageable, do seek professional help.

Just a few days ago—it's summer as these words are being written—Peg and I took our two daughters, Alexandra and Kate, up to an enrichment program held at a women's college where the two of them will be roommates. The girls had never met—they live on opposite sides of the country—but had spoken on the telephone and had e-mailed. We, the two mothers, watched as these adolescent girls talked nonstop and strode through the airport—a respectable distance behind their moms—like seasoned and confident travelers, their laden backpacks slung over their shoulders. They giggled and whispered, pulled out photos they'd brought of the people and pets they loved, and allowed as how they couldn't be more excited by the prospect of the next three weeks.

We got up to the college and all around us there were adolescent girls of every size and shape—dressed in every style imaginable. There were girls who looked as if they had been born with a tennis racket in hand and girls in tank tops and tiny shorts, with green or pink streaks in ash or brown hair and rings on every toe. There were clean-scrubbed faces, bright-blue eyelids, and kohl-ringed eyes; high-glossed mouths and braces in every color of the rainbow; wrists and ankles bedecked with beads, bracelets, and baubles. The hallways to the dorm rooms were piled high with the accoutrements of American adolescence—CD players and boom boxes, sports equipment, stuffed animals, books, sketch books and paints, mirrors and makeup, flip-flops and fuzzy slippers. Whatever else one may say, adolescent girls do not travel light.

As we waited for our daughters as they stood in line to register, the energy around us was palpable. We watched the girls—all breasts and braces—hug old friends and smile at strangers. The din was extraordinary—girls laughing and shrieking with excitement, eager to say good-bye to parents and be off on their own. Their body language was as vivid as their clothes: They struck poses, jumped up and down, and clapped. They seemed to expand outward into every available space, crowding out their sweating parents, who were tired from lugging bags and fans out of car trunks and up flights of stairs.

This chapter is called "Blossoming" and that's what we saw, not just in our own girls but in the daughters of strangers. If you could capture the process of adolescence—that long ten years—on film in slow motion, the way they shoot the opening of a cactus flower in the cool twilight of the desert, we think you would see the extraordinary unfurling of layer upon layer of self, opening up piece by piece, to new potential and possibilities. These are the women of tomorrow, we thought as we stood there watching. These are our daughters and our successors.

That's what we all need to remember as we make our way on this part of the journey. There is, as Dr. Silverberg Koerner noted in our

interview with her, "a lot more continuity in adolescence than people usually ascribe to the period. It's fairly rare to have an adolescent
who is a completely different person than she was as a child." There
are changes and challenges, to be sure, but our girls are still the
babies and children we loved. We all need to keep that in mind as
we move on to explore what we call "troubled waters."

## CHAPTER FIVE

# Troubled Waters

Expectations are the most perilous form of dream, and when dreams do realize themselves it is in the waking world: the difference is often subtly but painfully felt.

Elizabeth Bowen, *The Death of the Heart*

OUR HOPES AND DREAMS are inextricably bound to our girls from the first time we hold them in our arms. It is a defining moment that sweeps away every worry and fear we've entertained during pregnancy, every difficulty we've encountered in the months that preceded birth, every hesitation we've had late at night. In their place is the miracle of life, and the awesome sense of possibility new life brings with it. If our child is adopted, the moment is modified only by the nature of the journey we have taken to get there. Looking into her face is like nothing else in the world—except, perhaps, what we feel when we see the sun rise on a brand-new day. That radiant sense of possibility permeates the years of mothering, even when it is tempered by difficulties; she is living proof of high hopes and new beginnings.

But sometimes the problems our daughters encounter during the years of adolescence, as they do the work of forging the self, threaten the very basis of those hopes and dreams. The formation of self is hard work for everyone—and sometimes losing the way becomes the defining part of the journey. When and if this moment of challenge comes—and during adolescence, it can take many different forms—we, as mothers, will face challenges of our own. The ties that bind us to our daughters are not single, easily separable threads but are woven more like the densest of tapestries. Some of us will have the things we worried about late at night—the common and the not-so-common pitfalls and dangers we know can be part of the adolescent's landscape—become uninvited visitors in our lives. Statistics about eating disorders, depression and other mental health illnesses, promiscuity, sexually transmitted diseases, dating violence and rape, and substance abuse take on a wholly other shape and form when it is your child who is among their number. And these experiences will change us, just as surely as they change our daughters.

Navigating troubled waters takes special skills and endurance, and very few of us, if any, will be able to go it alone. The myth of the Perfect Mother has its corollary—the All-Responsible Mother—and all things good, bad, and indifferent are culturally attributed to her. She is considered responsible equally for raising a girl who will graduate college as a Phi Beta Kappa and go on to Harvard law school, and for the daughter who is promiscuous or becomes addicted to drugs. I don't think a single one of us is immune to the enormous sense of guilt we feel when our daughters are troubled—or the way in which, culturally, we are likely to be blamed for what has happened to our children. Some of us will feel enormous pressure to prove that *it*—no matter what *it* is—is not our fault. Many of us, raised in a culture that sees a successful and healthy child as proof-positive of parental accomplishment, will react to our daughters' problems as personal admissions of failure—or worse, will find ourselves blaming our children for their "imperfections." When our daughters' problems become public knowledge, what we know intellectually may be at odds with what we feel. We may feel embarrassed or jealous of others whose lives seem comparatively easy—whose daughters' growth into adulthood is seemingly effortless. If our daughters suffer from mental illness, both they and we will feel the burden of social stigma in addition to everything else we are feeling. (How influential the stigmas attached to mental illnesses and their treatment are cannot and should not be underestimated. A very large percentage of the mental illness experienced by Americans goes untreated as a result of stigma.) The myth of the All-Responsible Mother may encourage us to overlook warning signs in our daughters' behavior or actively involve us in denial—to the equal detriment of mother *and* daughter. The mythology may make it hard or impossible for us to take more limited but true responsibility for our own actions and behaviors that have contributed to the crisis at hand. Alternatively, it may make us take on inappropriate feelings of guilt and responsibility, triggering depressive or other symptoms in us. The myth of the All-Responsible Mother may also complicate our relationships with people in our lives, both those who are intimates and those who are more peripheral. Wives and husbands may find themselves divided by feelings of guilt and blame. "How could you not know?" says the grandmother of an anorexic girl to her own daughter. "Don't you cook for her?"

Most important, the myth of the All-Responsible Mother ignores the complex interaction between our child's development and a whole nexus of factors, only some of which are in our control. As *Mental Health: A Report of the Surgeon General* notes:

> There is now good evidence that *both* biological and adverse psychosocial experiences during childhood influence—but not necessarily "cause"—the mental disorders of childhood. Adverse experiences may occur at home, at school, or in the community. A stressor or risk factor may have no, little, or a profound impact, depending on individual differences among children and the age at which the child is exposed to it, as well as whether it occurs alone or in association with other risk factors. Although children are influenced by their psychosocial environment, most are inherently resilient and can deal with some degree of diversity.[1]

More to the point, the myth of the All-Responsible Mother may get in the way of our getting the help our daughters and we need, and from learning from what we and our daughters experience.

Mental disorders—despite the social stigmas attached to them—are neither rare nor unusual. Just as one in five adults will, in the course of a year, experience some form of mental illness, so too almost 21 percent of children and adolescents—boys and girls—will experience a diagnosable mental or addictive disorder associated with at least minimum impairment. Roughly 13 percent will suffer from anxiety disorders; 6.2 percent from mood disorders; 10.3 percent from disruptive disorders; 2 percent from substance abuse disorders.[2] Research indicates that depression onset is occurring earlier than in past decades, meaning that we cannot assume that a child is "too young" to be clinically depressed. Adolescent girls, as we've already noted, are not only twice as likely as boys to suffer from depression but make up the preponderance of those afflicted by anxiety disorders (the most common of mental illness) and eating disorders.

While research has confirmed that adolescent girls are, indeed, more vulnerable than adolescent boys, a full answer to "why" still eludes us. For the mothers of daughters, this is obviously a subject of great concern. Girls' vulnerability to depression, for example, has been partly explained by reference to the greater value they place on social relationships; it has been suggested therefore that they are more negatively affected by the interpersonal stresses that are common in adolescence. The coincidence of pubertal changes and the entry into middle school has been put forth as a possible factor, as have, among Caucasian girls, heightened concerns and worries about looks during puberty. How girls cope with stress—as opposed to how boys cope—may also be a factor. We've already mentioned that girls' "ruminative" style—their tendency to mull over and reanalyze details and scenarios—may also both be detrimental to emotional health and constitute a risk factor for depression. Family dynamics and how families socialize girls may, inadvertently, normalize depressive behavior by emphasizing emotionally as "feminine" in nature. Research also reports that the higher level of conflict between the mother-daughter dyad—compared with mother-son, father-son, or father-daughter relationships—may be a risk factor. The different ways in which girls and boys react to external stresses—such as parents' arguing or fighting—may be different in kind, and contributory to girls' being more at risk for depression. Even "how" parents fight may, for girls, be a risk factor.[3]

Studies conducted by Drs. Betsy Davis, Lisa Sheeber, Hyman Hops, and Elizabeth Tildesley of the Oregon Research Institute examined the different ways in which adolescent girls and boys responded to parents' depressive and aggressive behaviors in conflict situations, and found significant differences between the two.[4] "Aggressive" behaviors were categorized by angry or irritated behaviors (both in voice and gesture) as well as criticisms and threats—which is what most of us associate with marital conflict. But the researchers noted that there is another, more subtle, kind of conflict that also directly affects adolescents—depressive behaviors. "Depressive" behaviors included not just sad behaviors such as a depressed tone or crying but self-derogatory statements such as "I guess I'm a bad person" or "It must be hard to love someone like me" and the like. The girls most likely to experience depression were those who, observing their father acting depressively toward their mother, acted as "caretakers"—assuaging their mothers' feelings—or as "peacemakers." The researchers note that "this caretaking role may place girls in a position of tackling problems that are not within their direct control and for which they may not be cognitively or emotionally equipped." In addition, when confronted by the situation of a mother acting depressively toward a father, girls most at risk for depression were those who suppressed their own aggressive response toward their mother. (Boys tended to react aggressively to aversive behavior by either parent.)

We turned to the Oregon Research Institute team to ask them what mothers (and fathers) could learn and use from their research. Here's what they said:

### Be attentive to your daughter's involvement in your conflicts.

According to Drs. Betsy Davis and Lisa Sheeber, when parents try to resolve issues or problems, they should be intensely aware that if their children are present, the form that the parent's behavior takes *could* have an impact on their child's functioning, particularly if the child has a response to the parent behavior. We stress "could" because not every child who responds to, or becomes involved in, her parents' conflict will develop later problems.

Common sense would say that aggressive behavior displayed by parents in the presence of a child is not a good thing. But aggressive behavior is not the only parental conflict behavior that children find distressful and to which they respond. Our results indicate that children also respond to depressive behavior displayed between parents.

### Just because your daughter doesn't seem to be reacting doesn't mean she isn't.

Parents should know that children's responses to their conflict behavior might not be directly observable. Our research indicates that, particularly for adolescent girls, the inhibition of child behavior in response to marital conflict behavior is strongly related to the girls' depressive functioning.

If parents find themselves in the unavoidable position of discussing and trying to resolve important issues in the presence of the child, they should certainly be aware of the behaviors they are displaying, but also they should be on the lookout for if, and how, the child is responding to their conflict. Unfortunately, knowing if the child is responding is made particularly difficult if the child response involves the inhibition of behavior.

### If my daughter gets involved in an argument between me and my husband, what should I do?

Drs. Davis's and Sheeber's studies indicate that within families where the mother acts aggressively toward the father (e.g., "You can't handle our finances because you're incompetent!"), girls who suppress their feelings toward the mother are at risk for increased levels of depressive functioning.

The question then becomes "Why are these girls at risk?" Though our examination did not directly seek an explanation, we conjectured that perhaps these parents might be intolerant of adolescent emotional expression during stressful situations, which can take the form of parents directly punishing the adolescent's emotional displays or simply ignoring their child's feelings. In fact, if parents do not allow the child to express the emotion she is feeling in stressful situations, they may implicitly encourage her to suppress her feelings and cope with stressful situations by avoidance. Such avoidant coping has been linked to depressive functioning. Clearly, within these intolerant families adolescent girls do not have the opportunity to learn the skills necessary for handling difficult situations that elicit negative emotional reactions. Rather than encouraging children to avoid their negative feelings, parents should help them understand and control their emotions during stressful situations.

### Pay attention to the family dynamic during conflict.

In families where parents display depressive behavior toward each other, we saw a completely different set of adolescent girl responses that were linked to their depressive functioning. Our results indicated that adolescent girls who are at risk for increases in depressive symptoms are those who: 1) Display positive behavior toward their mother immediately after their father has directed depressive behavior toward the mother (father to mother: "Based on what you're saying, I must be a terrible man"; adolescent girl immediately interjects: "Oh, Mom, what you said wasn't that bad"); and 2) inhibit their aggressive behavior toward the mother immediately after the mother has made a depressive statement to the father. For example, adolescent girls are less likely to be aggressive toward the mother when the mother says to the father, "I know it's difficult to love someone like me."

Why are these patterns of response related to increases in depressive symptoms in girls? They may be indicative of the adolescent girl's attempt at caretaking. The first response—"Oh, Mom, what you said wasn't so bad"—may reflect caretaking by trying to lessen the mother's feelings of guilt or to minimize her involvement. The second response—not commenting negatively on the mother's statement—may reflect the adolescent girl's attempt to nurture the mother in response to her sadness. Adolescent girls who take on these caretaking roles may place themselves in a position of trying to handle a stressful situation that is not in their direct control or which they are not equipped to handle. If these girls are unsuccessful in resolving the situation by caretaking, such failure may bring about feelings of hopelessness and self-blame that have been shown to be predictive of depression.

There's more: The inhibition of the adolescent girl's aggressive behavior toward her mother may have the unintended effect of exacerbating the mother's display of sadness. Supporting the mother's use of depressive or sad behavior may have two potential repercussions for the adolescent girl: 1) the female adolescent then has a stronger role model for depressive behavior; and 2) given that depressive behaviors are associated with ineffective problem-solving, the mother's use of depressive behavior may result in sustaining the conflictual behavior with the father, thereby producing an on-going stressor for the adolescent girl.[5]

Each of us needs to pay attention to how we involve our daughters in our familial conflicts and, more important, what behaviors we—and their fathers—are modeling for them.

In the pages that follow, we will be looking at what *can* happen to our girls, and what we can do to help them. The advice and suggestions we offer are not intended to encourage you to be the primary diagnostician, nor are they a substitute for the counsel of a trained professional. Rather, they are offered to increase your awareness and to encourage you to seek professional advice if you believe your daughter needs help.

As you read these pages, there is something we would like you to keep in mind—an image of a beautifully woven carpet. For over twenty-five hundred years, the weavers of the Orient have created the most exquisite of tapestries, hand-loomed rugs that, in their ornate designs, testified to the multiplicity of the universe. Since ancient times, these rugs—made of thousands upon thousands of hand-tied knots—have been fashioned by teams of weavers, each working on a small section of the whole, under the watchful eye of a master weaver. Even so, a carpet takes years to finish. The rug is woven from the underside and, from time to time, a mistake—in color or pattern or knotting—is discovered. These mistakes are not ripped out, as they might be in the West, but are, instead, accommodated into the overall design—testifying that, in the universe, nothing created by human hands is ever perfect and that true beauty cannot be marred by imperfection.

Most of us have very different visions of what constitutes "perfection" and less humility then the weavers of the Orient. But should we find ourselves negotiating troubled waters, there is much that the weavers can teach us—particularly when it comes to definitions of "wholeness," "beauty," and "perfection" as they relate not just to ourselves, but to our daughters. Try to keep the image of the carpet—in all of its intricate, hard-won beauty—in mind.

And remember that, in many cases, this will just be a passage in your daughter's life—just a single strand in the tapestry of life.

Not long ago, I received a phone call from a young woman, now nineteen, whom I've known since she was ten or so. A sweet and unassuming youngster with strawberry-blond hair, she'd done well in junior high and then in high school, and was now a freshman in college. By any standard, her family was supportive and loving, if comparatively strict; she grew up in a relatively structured and protective environment, partly informed by the family's strong commitment to faith. She was—as far as her parents and I knew—a girl who was very much on top of things with a good and stable sense of self, and there was no reason to expect anything other than that she would continue to thrive and develop in this next stage of her life. On the phone, though, she was crying and her voice was filled with pain. She was in terrible trouble, she said; even now, under medical treatment for depression, she still felt as if her life was spiraling out of control, and she didn't know what to do next or how to be happier or more comfortable within herself. Some months before, she had discovered that her boyfriend, her first real lover and the first boy she'd ever loved, had been with another girl. She was devastated and disconsolate when he refused to see her again. Desperately lonely, she started drinking too much and partying indiscriminately, doing anything she could to attract boys. It turned out that while this young man was, in fact, the first one she'd actually had intercourse with, the pattern of getting attention from boys was not a new one. She had, she admitted, engaged in numerous acts of fellatio with different boys in high school but, she was quick to add, so did lots of her classmates.

She continued to drink and party until, one morning, her life just unraveled; she quite literally could not get herself out of bed. She knew enough to seek help, and the doctor on campus prescribed antidepressants. But he had not prescribed therapy and, even though the medication lessened some of her symptoms, she remained deeply depressed and listless. She was, she said, calling me for help—she just couldn't see her way clear to feeling better. Listening to her, I realized more than anything else that she needed to talk about where she'd been and where she might go next, and she couldn't do it alone; she needed help and support. Her family rallied around her quickly and without judgment, and she is now on the way to rebuilding both her sense of self and her future.

The formula she arrived at—equating pleasing with validation, sexual favors with relationship, self-worth with being desired—is not nearly as unusual as any of us would like it to be. What surprised me most was the degree to which she had managed—even in a household with attentive parents—to keep so much of her life completely private and hidden from both her parents and the world at large. In retrospect, it was clear that she had been floundering alone for some years, without anyone being the wiser. The story troubled me profoundly and I wondered whether there was anything her parents—her mother, in particular—should have done differently. Was the environment she'd been raised in too structured? Had she had enough room to learn how to take reasonable risks? I thought about what I knew about the family and it seemed, on the surface at least, that they had done just about everything right. They had been involved, concerned, and connected to their daughter; they had a solid framework of faith and consistent values that should have, according to every study ever published about adolescent girls, provided their daughter some measure of protection against being at risk.

And yet it hadn't worked. This was a young girl who found herself under siege in high school—unable to negotiate the waters of popularity—and like so many other girls, had embraced the values of the culture, despite everything her mother and father had tried to teach her. It seemed more than likely that she was already depressed in high school, but that her symptoms had probably, wrongly, been attributed to the "normal" mood swings of an adolescent girl. In all of these details, unfortunately, she is not unusual.

Estimates of depression in adolescence vary slightly, but none of the news is good. According to the National Institute of Mental Health, almost one in ten adolescents will suffer from depression, a preponderance of them girls.[6] *Mental Health: A Report of the Surgeon General*, issued in 1999, somberly reflected that ten to fifteen percent of children and adolescents will exhibit *some* symptoms of major depression; among nine- to seventeen-year-olds, 8.3 percent will exhibit depressive symptoms that last one year. (In contrast, only 5 percent of adults will exhibit depressive symptoms for that long a period of time.[7]) While girls and boys in childhood are equally at risk for depression, by the age of fifteen the ratio of depressed girls actually *doubles*. Twenty to forty percent of adolescents who suffer a period of depression will relapse within two years; 70 percent will relapse during adulthood.[8] There are links between depression and substance abuse, as well as other disorders.

These statistics may well not fully reflect the true incidence of depressive disorders—which include major depressive disorders, chronic mild depression, and bipolar disorder, or manic depression—because they are often undiagnosed or misdiagnosed. According to the National Institute of Mental Health, there are probably two contributing factors. First, as we've already mentioned, is the widespread belief—among both families and physicians—that mood swings are part and parcel of the normal adolescent experience. Second is the reluctance on the part of health-care professionals to "prematurely 'label' a young person with a mental illness diagnosis." Many parents certainly will share that same reluctance; in fact, research reveals that parents are "even less likely to identify major depression in their adolescents than are the adolescents themselves."[9]

While recent research has helped to demystify depression, there is still much work to be done. For example, while the risk factors that contribute to depression are known, the precise cause of depression isn't. Popular literature, too, often oversimplifies what science knows. For example, while research notes a correlation between adolescent depression and a family history of depression, the studies in question—which, according to *Mental Health: A Report of the Surgeon General*, were conducted with patients at mental health clinics who tended to have the more severe and recurrent forms of depression—may not accurately reflect the whole population of adolescents with depression.[10] It's also unclear whether genetic factors are responsible for the connection between parental and adolescent depression—or whether just the environment of living with a depressed parent increases the likelihood of childhood or adolescent depression. The findings of a recent study suggest that the relationship between maternal depression and adolescent depression is, in many ways, complicated. The authors, Drs. Constance Hammen and Patricia Brennan, studied the depressed fifteen-year-old children (both boys and girls) of depressed and nondepressed mothers.[11] They hypothesized that the depressed adolescents with depressed mothers would show more interpersonal dysfunction than those of nondepressed mothers; they assumed that both the way in which a depressed mother interacted with her children and the child's observation of a depressed mother's interpersonal skills would make him or her more vulnerable to both depression and impaired interpersonal skills. As expected, a higher percentage of children of depressed mothers experienced depression themselves (18.4 percent) than children of nondepressed mothers (9.8 percent). In addition, the children of depressed mothers were more likely to have more problems with relationships, particularly within the family. But interestingly enough, while the sons of depressed mothers were much more likely to suffer from depression than the sons of nondepressed mothers (13 percent as opposed to 3.9 percent), girls were equally likely to come from either group. Moreover, the children of depressed mothers did not have an earlier age of onset nor did they have more episodes of discernable depression. And as the authors note, the really intriguing question that was not studied is why "many of the offspring of depressed mothers did not display depression or other disorders." In other words, while research has delineated the factors that put an adolescent at risk, we do not know what makes one individual vulnerable to those risks and what makes another resilient to them. There is no A + B = C equation. If your daughter finds herself in troubled waters, this point is an important one to remember.

If you suspect your daughter might be suffering from depression, we offer you the following suggestions:

### Understand the difference between depression and sadness.

Every one of us feels "depressed" or "blue" from time to time and, in conversation, we usually use the word "depressed" to refer to an intense feeling of discouragement or sadness tied to a specific event in our lives. Bad days, unexpected outcomes, and even failures are facts of life, as is feeling bad or "down" about them. So is sadness triggered by a painful or life-changing event or loss—a divorce in the family, death, or even moving to a new house or new town. Feeling sad—now and then or, after a major loss, for a longer period of time—is part and parcel of the human condition, both as an adolescent and an adult. Depression in the clinical sense is quite different—untied to any specific event or condition, diffuse in the sense of affecting every aspect of life, and persistent. Even when depression is triggered by a major loss, it is still distinguishable from the emotional states that normally accompany loss. Unlike the process of grieving, which lessens or heals over time, depression shows no signs of abatement. Depression affects every part of a person—how she thinks, feels, and acts, both physically and emotionally.

Despite the persistence of stigmas associated with depression and other illness, depression is *not* a character flaw or a sign of moral, emotional, or intellectual weakness. While there are factors that increase the risk of depression, as we've said, there is no single "cause" for depression; depression in a child or adolescent is never simply a function of bad parenting. Depression is not a phase that a daughter will outgrow or a condition that can be ameliorated by thinking "positive thoughts" or by "getting ahold of oneself." Clinical depression will *not* go away on its own.

It is worth noting that, according to the Substance Abuse and Mental Health Services Administration, two thirds of children with mental health problems do not get the help they need. Suicide is the third leading cause of death in ten- to twenty-four-year-olds, and it is estimated that among adolescents who develop a major depressive disorder, as many of 7 percent commit suicide.[12] In addition, according to the National Institute of Mental Health, 20 to 40 percent of adolescents who suffer from major depression will, within five years, develop bipolar disorder (manic depression).[13]

### Familarize yourself with the risk factors for depression.

Remember that the symptoms of depression in adolescents are often masked; what appears to be hostility may, in fact, be a symptom of depression. Knowing these risk factors, taken from the National Institute of Mental Health, may aid you and your health care professional assess whether your daughter needs help:

• A family history of depression

• Stress

- Smoking

- A loss of a parent or loved one

- Breakup of a romantic relationship

- Attentional, conduct, or learning disorders

- Chronic illnesses such as diabetes

- Abuse or neglect

- Other trauma, including natural disasters

While it's clear that divorce or a death in the family can and will be a major source of stress for an adolescent, it is easy—particularly in the case of a younger adolescent—for a parent to underestimate the amount of stress a child is under. Even though adolescents are not subject to the same stresses as adults—such as earning a living or taking responsibility for others—nonetheless they can and do experience significant stress. Remember that no child is "too young" to be at risk. Similarly, the breakup of an adolescent romantic relationship—a clear source of stress and, sometimes, depression in adults—may wrongly be discounted by parents since "it was only puppy love" or "it wasn't really serious anyway." Pay attention to the amount of stress in your daughter's life, and focus on how she is coping with it.

The connection between smoking and depression is noteworthy in part because more and more adolescent girls are smoking than ever before; while the risks of smoking are well known to the general public, the connection between smoking and depression is not. Fifteen percent of adolescents between the ages of twelve and seventeen smoke; by eighteen and older, 40 percent do. Unfortunately, the gender gap between girls and boys who smoke has, since the mid-1990s, closed. Research has consistently demonstrated a relationship between smoking and depression; a recent study additionally suggests that while smoking was a predictor of depressive symptoms, depressive symptoms equally predicted increased cigarette use.[14]

If you think or know your daughter smokes, you need to pay attention.

**Don't assume that changes in your daughter's behavior or sleep or eating patterns are "teenage stuff"—particularly if they are prolonged.**

According to the National Institute of Mental Health, while some of the defining features of a major depressive disorder are the same in adolescents as in adults, they may be expressed differently. Among the symptoms common to adults and adolescents are persistent sad or irritable moods, loss of interest in activities, significant changes in appetite or body weight, sleep problems, difficulty concentrating, feelings of worthlessness, and recurrent thoughts of death or suicide. The following signs may also be associated with depression in children and adolescence:

- frequent absences from school or poor performance in school

- outbursts of shouting, unexplained irritability, or crying

- boredom

- alcohol or substance abuse

- extreme sensitivity to rejection or failure

- increased irritability, anger, or hostility

- reckless behavior

- difficulty with relationships

If you just glance down this list, you'll note that many of these symptoms are popularly associated with stereotypical "teenage" behavior, making it clear why their seriousness is so easily and often overlooked. Pay attention to significant changes in your daughter's behavior, and remember that you are looking for clusters of symptoms that persist for several weeks or even longer without apparent cause. Talk to your daughter, remembering that she may not be able to fully articulate what she is feeling.

Examine your own thoughts (and those of your daughter's father) about seeking help; make sure that the common stigmas and prejudices about mental illness don't get in the way of getting the help your daughter needs. Depression is a mental illness and your child is no more responsible for her depression than she would be if she had diabetes. (And if she did have diabetes, you would not hesitate to treat it.) If you had a negative experience in therapy, have never been in therapy, or have hesitations about therapy, inform yourself about the therapeutic process by doing research.

If you do think your daughter is suffering from depression, discuss it with her primary care physician to get a referral to a psychotherapist. Inform yourself about depression and its effect on adolescent girls. (For Resources, see page 352.) Do *not* feel as though you are solely responsible for what is happening to her and, equally, do not try to assign blame elsewhere. Although there are some risk factors that *are* under our control, depression is no one's "fault."

**Be proactive on your daughter's behalf and your own.**

There are different types of psychotherapeutic approaches, all of which—with the exception of family systemic—were developed for adults and then tailored for children. Be aware that deciding which therapies are best for which conditions is still an evolving art, as *Mental Health: A Report of the Surgeon General* notes. Learn as much as you can about both your therapist and his or her approach to your daughter's condition, including the possible use of medications. According the Surgeon General, psychotherapy can be a valuable tool for children:

> Psychotherapists are especially important alternatives for those children who are unable to tolerate, or whose parents prefer them not to take, medications. They are also important for conditions for which there are no medications with well-documented efficacy. They are also pivotal for families under stress from a child's mental disorder. Therapies can serve to reduce stress in parents and siblings and teach parents strategies for managing symptoms of the mental disorder in their child.[15]

*Do* monitor your daughter's progress. Remember that your daughter's therapist is providing you with a service for which he or she is being compensated, and that you have every right—even if you don't have an M.D. or Ph.D.—to ask questions or even to challenge him or her. If you are unsure about the quality of care your daughter is receiving, seek other opinions. There are also help lines on the Internet (see page 351) you can contact. You—and your daughter's father—are her best advocates.

Don't ignore or hide your own feelings—even if they are not the feelings you are "supposed" to have, such as anger or frustration. Coping with your child's mental disorder will create new kinds of stress in your life and the lives of other family members. For some families—because of the vagaries of health insurance coverage—there will be economic consequences. If you have other children, be aware that your daughter's disorder will inevitably change certain aspects of the family dynamic, and siblings will be affected in large ways and small. For example, they may resent the amount of time and attention the disorder appears to garner her; your other children may be upset or alarmed by the changes in their sister and in you. In some families, one parent (or another influential family member) may resist either a daughter's diagnosis ("There's nothing wrong with her expect she's hanging out with the wrong kids," said one father) or disagree about the course of treatment. Many, many people are hesitant to make a mental disorder part of a child's "permanent record," and some will feel that having a child in therapy is tantamount to putting out a banner that reads "I failed as a parent." If you and your husband (or ex-husband) disagree about important issues concerning your daughter, get help resolving those differences. In many cases, family counseling is rightly recommended.

Remember, too, that helping your child through this passage—and any of the others discussed in these pages—will require another evolution in your parenting skills. There are many groups that provide support for families; be sure to seek professional help if you feel overwhelmed. For more, see "Resources," page 352.

Depression is not all we need to watch for: Some 13 percent of adolescents will suffer from anxiety disorders (and all of these disorders are more common in girls than boys). Once again, we offer the following symptoms and warning signs for these conditions so that you can better assess your daughter's behavior and make sure that what you are seeing doesn't interfere with her healthy functioning. If you are concerned, do consult your health care provider and seek treatment promptly.

*Separation anxiety*: Anxieties about separation, usually from a parent or regular caretaker, are normal in young children and are familiar to many of us. In children ages nine or older, however, separation anxiety is a disorder. Signs of separation anxiety may include your daughter's inability to spend the night elsewhere or to go to camp or school. To be diagnosed, separation anxieties must be shown to interfere with social and academic functioning, and must last at least one month. Adolescents with separation anxiety worry that their parents will die, get sick, or "disappear" from their lives. *Mental Health: A Report of the Surgeon General* notes that this disorder may be overdiagnosed when adolescents live in dangerous neighborhoods and don't want to leave the house for other, legitimate reasons.

*Generalized Anxiety Disorder*: This is just what it sounds like: a pervasive and generalized anxiety about everything in everyday life. Roughly 3 percent of adolescents suffer from it. Girls who suffer from it tend to be extreme perfectionists and need constant reassurance about their performance, even if they aren't under pressure to succeed and even if they tend, in fact, to be largely successful in their efforts. The physical symptoms of this disorder may include headaches, insomnia, and nausea.

*Social Phobia*: While it's perfectly normal for an adolescent girl to be anxious in new or challenging situations—going to a different school, giving a speech, or taking a test, for example—some girls will experience extreme responses, such as panic attacks or crying. According to the *New York University Child Study Center Letter*, there is a continuum of shyness that sets the social phobic apart. For example, a normally shy person would be "jittery" in a new situation but would eventually relax. An extremely shy person clams up and avoids starting conversations. But a person with severe social anxiety is "most comfortable alone, leads a life restricted by fear, may have panic attacks and worries constantly about being embarrassed or humiliated." The letter reports, as well, that "health professionals fail to recognize children and adolescents with worrisome levels of social anxiety"—even though it is highly treatable.[16]

**Obsessive-Compulsive Disorder (OCD):** This disorder is characterized by repetitive actions that impede normal functioning—such as checking and rechecking a backpack to make sure everything is in it, or washing one's hands compulsively. These ritualistic gestures mirror overly obsessive trains of thought.

For a number of daughters and mothers, the road will not simply take a turn but will, frighteningly, seem to stop or entirely disappear from view as they confront chronic conditions—among them bipolar disease and eating disorders such as anorexia nervosa and bulimia—which can seriously threaten their daughters' very survival. These crises will not only affect your daughter's definition of self and her future, but will change your relationship to her in meaningful and significant ways. How you mother your daughter may be challenged in ways that you never imagined; it is hard to parent successfully when you are scared out of your wits. Your own sense of self may feel as if it is under siege as you confront the reality of your daughter's condition; you may be filled with equal amounts of pain and anger, hopefulness and hopelessness. Precisely because the mother-daughter relationship is dyadic, the effects on both of you will be profound. There are lessons, though, for each of us to learn from a woman whose daughter's journey took an unpredicted and sometimes frightening turn.

"Barbara" 's daughter had always been a bouncy and extremely bright girl. Even at the age of six or seven, the little redhead had verve—strapping on her roller skates when her mother had to work on Saturdays and zooming through the otherwise staid halls of a publishing company. Both academically and artistically gifted, "Lisa" had talents—and a penchant for drama—that were immediately recognized by everyone who came into contact with her. Despite her parents' fractious divorce and a joint custody arrangement that had Lisa shuttling between two New York City apartments, she truly blossomed—both physically and intellectually—during adolescence.

In an effort to minimize the scars left by the divorce, Barbara made sure that Lisa had regular psychotherapy sessions—just to give her a place to talk and blow off steam.

There were areas of contention between mother and daughter, of course: In the last years of high school, Barbara worried about her being out on the city streets late at night, and they fought over the condition of her room, which was, according to her mother, unbelievable chaos—a jumble of clothes, books, and what-have-you. There were other things, too, that got under Barbara's skin—Lisa's quicksilver mood changes, the way she'd forget to run an errand or complete the few chores Barbara assigned to her. But for the most part, she seemed to be flourishing, bound for a prestigious college where she would, as she had in high school, perform brilliantly. She was beautiful, smart, and talented—and in the context of adolescent turmoil and the pressures all people feel in college to prove themselves—the ways in which her behavior wasn't always what Barbara expected were easily discounted. Of course, she was rightly furious when she returned from a trip to find her apartment in chaos—reeking of cigarettes, unwashed dishes in the sink—and dismayed when Lisa somehow managed, time and again, to lose or misplace the check or the cash she'd given her. The time Lisa came home with her glorious red hair dyed pitch-black threw her mother for a loop (and it turned out not to be too easy to fix) but then again, there were so many worse things she could have done.

Four years of college passed without incident, leaving Lisa only an independent study project to fulfill the requirements for graduation. For her mother, Lisa's graduation would be a turning point, both financially and psychologically. With Lisa away at school, the balancing act of day-to-day single mothering and work had ended, but paying tuition for a private college had been a terrific economic burden. Barbara had gotten into the habit of benchmarking Lisa's finishing college as both a time to launch Lisa independently and to restructure her own life. As she neared her fiftieth birthday, she looked forward to a lessening of financial responsibility and thought, perhaps, that she could cut back just a bit on work and spend some time doing the things she really loved—sculpting and gardening. It was, she thought, an exciting time in her life—one that would start her and her daughter on new paths.

In January, Lisa went back to school to complete her senior project. She was, understandably, feeling pressured but Barbara had every confidence that Lisa would manage. The following month, late on a Saturday night, her mother got an urgent phone call from the school; Lisa had been hospitalized. She had suffered a psychotic break.

For mother and daughter alike, the journey took an entirely different form. Barbara reeled under what she had to take in; as she puts it, "There is nothing that really prepares you for seeing your daughter hallucinate. There is a terrible moment of fear and confusion when you realize that your child's reality—of hearing voices in the computer and television—is another country, another universe than the one you are used to. Realizing that, on some level, you quite literally can't understand or picture what she's going through adds another emotional dimension to the whole experience." Amid the fear, there was the work of first finding a diagnosis and then a successful course of treatment. In Barbara's case, the entire process was made all the more difficult because, from a legal point of view, her daughter was no longer a minor, and the doctors involved were bound to respect patient-doctor confidentiality. Even the course of treatment—which included adjusting the dosages of medication to allow Lisa full functioning—was a process that stretched out over time. (Because bipolar disorder has both manic and depressive aspects to it, the right balance of medication is often difficult to achieve.) Both Barbara and Lisa learned there were no simple solutions.

With the diagnosis of bipolar disorder, both mother and daughter, each in her own way, had to make an enormous adjustment; accepting a chronic medical condition as a fact of life is hard work for all involved. A chronic illness modifies, in small and large ways, almost every aspect of the present and the future, including the mother-daughter relationship. Not surprisingly, each of them struggled with acceptance, though in different ways. Lisa went through stages of both denying the disorder—letting her prescription run out or drinking alcohol—*and* taking responsibility for managing it. Barbara needed to define what "normal" was in terms of the illness, and to redefine and renegotiate issues of independence and dependence between mother and daughter. In her case, it was made more difficult by her ex-husband's response; he flatly refused to accept the diagnosis. As Barbara puts it, "People who have bipolar disorder need different kinds of support that have nothing to do with chronological age. In some ways, I had to revert to a different kind of mothering—being watchful and protective—which felt at times, to both of us, like a step back in time. At precisely the moment we both assumed Lisa would be able to do more on her own, it turned out that, for the time being at least, she couldn't. It was very, very hard. Each of us had ambivalences about it."

Barbara's voice becomes quiet when she talks about the particular stigmas associated with manic depression: "Dealing with the feelings of shame that bubble up despite yourself is very difficult. This is a disorder which people associate with terrible things and frightening behaviors—crazy people and psycho wards. Acknowledging it first to yourself and then to others is harder than anyone might imagine." Amid her concerns for Lisa's well-being were the questions Barbara asked herself: Was she, somehow, responsible for her daughter's emotional fragility? Should she have known that what Lisa was going through wasn't normal? Were there signs that another, different, mother might have picked up on but that Barbara missed? Like so many other parents who find themselves in unfamiliar and frightening territory, she turned a critical eye inward. Had she been supportive enough? Granted, she'd worked hard—she had to do without alimony and with only marginal child support from her ex-husband—and there had been, inevitably, conflicts between work and her daughter's needs. Sometimes—maybe too often?—work won. Had she somehow missed important signals that Lisa was in trouble? Was it the divorce? Even though science confirms that bipolar disorder has strong genetic links, there are environmental factors that help shape the disease as well. Had she somehow failed her child?

These are questions every mother of a daughter who suffers from a chronic disorder will, at some point, ask herself—whether she is looking into the face of a girl with anorexia or one diagnosed with bipolar disorder. It has now been almost a decade since Barbara got that late-night phone call. Lisa has long since finished college and her condition is managed by a combination of drug therapy, nutrition, and psychotherapy. Lisa's career is branching out in different directions and she's about to move into a lovely, sunny co-op apartment, which her mother has helped her finance. More than anything, Barbara emphasizes that living with a chronic condition is a process, a journey that sometimes involves taking one step forward and one step back. Mother and daughter remain close and their relationship continues to evolve. It is a journey, Barbara remarks, that has taken them to places they never expected to go. Reflecting on that journey, she says, "In a way, there have been some odd, unpredicted results. Because of what she has gone through, has suffered, her humanity is deeper, richer in empathy, than I might ever otherwise have expected. I, too, have changed. There are moments—precisely because of the challenges Lisa has faced and somehow managed—that I love and admire her in ways more profound than if she had lived a more ordinary life, with the usual smattering of challenges and successes."

It is not known how many adolescents are affected by bipolar disorder; the disorder affects an estimated one to two percent of adults worldwide.[17] In addition to the link to depression, bipolar disorder is often linked to attention deficit hyperactivity disorder, with which its symptoms are sometimes confused, as well as to conduct disorder.

In addition to depressive symptoms (such as those listed on page 241), according to the National Institute of Mental Health, the following manic symptoms may also signal bipolar disorder:

- Severe changes in mood—either extreme irritability or exaggerated silliness and elation

- Overly inflated self-esteem, grandiosity

- Decreased need for sleep

- Increased talking—too much, too fast, moving from topic to topic

- Distractibility

- Hypersexuality

- Hyperactivity

- Excessive involvement in risky behaviors

Bipolar disorder can be managed with a combination of drug and other therapies. For Resources, see page 352.

While bipolar disorder has not gotten very much media attention, other chronic disorders such as anorexia nervosa, bulimia nervosa, and more recently, binge eating have—partly because of the connection between these disorders and the cultural attitudes toward female beauty and thinness. Both anorexia nervosa and bulimia nervosa are mental disorders that manifest in physical symptoms; while it is not known precisely what causes them, they appear to involve genetic, psychological, and sociocultural factors. Binge eating, which has only recently been recognized as a distinct condition, is the most common eating disorder; unlike sufferers of bulimia and anorexia, most binge eaters are obese. Research has shown that the incidence of eating disorders has steadily increased over the decades, as has the prevalence of eating disorders among college-age women.[18] Most importantly, the statistics only include those with *diagnosed* eating disorders, and do not include girls and young women who suffer from borderline disordered eating, whose number is estimated at 15 percent.[19] It's worth remembering that a young woman with anorexia is twelve times more likely to die prematurely than nonanorexic women her age. Finally, there are the sobering facts about recovery: While about half of those with anorexia or bulimia will have a full recovery, 30 percent will have only a partial recovery and 20 percent will have no substantial improvement.[20]

Because each of these disorders begins as a volitional act—by restricting food intake or by deliberately purging the body of food through one means or another—but ends beyond the individual's control, attitudes toward them are considerably more complicated than those associated with other disorders save substance abuse, which also begins with a deliberate choice. The volitional element—despite the loss of subsequent control—increases the feeling of shame associated with these disorders for both the victim and her mother, and for the rest of the family. For the anorexic or bulimic girl, the disorder will inevitably involve some form of hiding or separating from the world, including her mother, so that her behavior goes undetected. It's not uncommon for an anorexic girl to become a skilled cook, serving gourmet feasts that she will never taste; bulimics will incorporate any number of subterfuges into their daily routine so that their purging goes unnoticed. Guilt will become an issue for many mothers who see distorted but still recognizable reflections of their own attitudes and preoccupations with weight and beauty. Girls with eating disorders tend to be part of an elite cadre: They are usually high achievers with good grades, popular, involved in all manner of activities from editing the school newspaper to captaining the cheerleading team and, from the outside at least, seem to be "perfect" and problem-free girls. In fact, what they have done is internalize the impossible "perfection" and the control attaining that "perfection" requires to the nth degree. There is, according to Dr. Anne Becker of Harvard Medical School, no single "cause" of disordered eating. In some cases, eating disorders are linked to rebellion; girls use control over their eating as a "voice" to express resistance or disconnection. For others, particularly those who are bulimic, purging is a way of controlling or coping with what Dr. Becker calls "intolerable affect"[21]: While bulimia may start as a behavior meant to control weight, it becomes a way of modulating affect and emotion, or of not "feeling"; as hard as it may be for us to understand, it becomes a way of "self-soothing." (Other self-destructive behaviors, such as cutting and mutilation, are also "self-soothing" in the same way.) For still other girls, disordered eating may constitute a form of control at a time when an adolescent girl perceives much in her life—including growing up—as "beyond her control." The fact that anorexia nervosa effectively "undoes" puberty—decreasing breasts, suppressing menstruation, reducing the body back to its childish proportions—testifies to the potency of all of these explanations. Discovery of the disorder will, inevitably, involve an absolutely enormous adjustment on the part of parents—an adjustment not just of their image of the child they raised and love but also of the measure of their own parenting skills.

Treating disordered eating is neither simple nor straightforward and requires patience and support for everyone involved.

It isn't the existence of eating disorders alone that is so disturbing but their steady rise, despite public awareness. In 1969, when Peg and I were, respectively, finishing and beginning college, we both knew anorexic and bulimic girls although, at the time, these disorders weren't commonly named. (In fact, bulimia nervosa was not clinically identified as a disorder until 1979.) Neither we nor the doctors who tended to these girls understood these behaviors as disordered or pathological; our adolescent contemporaries saw them as weird and slightly desperate extensions of dieting and weight control, which we accepted as part of "normal" girl behavior.

Of course, the late twentieth century didn't "invent" eating disorders. Because we must eat to survive, food—its provision, preparation, consumption—has a complex and laden symbolism the world over. Eating is not only necessary but pleasurable and, thus, both the consumption and the renunciation of food have enormous symbolic and psychological resonance. It's no accident, then, that all religious and spiritual practices incorporate eating as a celebratory act and fasting as an act of piety or renunciation. The deliberate and continued renunciation of food has a long history, most notably chronicled in the lives of the female saints and medieval religious women. In her book *Holy Feast and Holy Fast*, Professor Caroline Walker Bynum examined the ways in which medieval women, particularly religious women, used their food intake (or lack of it) to remove themselves from controlling familial and religious structures and to control their destinies at a time when women had no political or economic control at all. Dr. Bynum argues that the medieval context is very separate from the modern one—in part because the medieval vision of food was much more complex than the modern one and in part because the application of "modern" labels to behavior in the Middle Ages denies important distinctions. But it is hard to avoid how the renunciation of food—for women in particular—has always been a way of asserting control in the absence of power:

> The traditional association of women with food preparation *rather than* food consumption helps us understand certain aspects of the religious significance of food. To prepare food is to control food. Moreover, food is not merely *a* resource that women control; it is *the* resource that women control—both for themselves and for others. In the long course of Western history, economic resources were controlled by husbands, fathers, uncles, or brothers. Yet human beings can renounce, or deny themselves, only that which they control. . . . It was far more difficult to flee one's family, to deny a father's plan for one's betrothal, or to refuse sexual relations to a husband than it was to stop eating.[22]

Reading this particularly in the context of the minor adolescent girl who, after all, has relatively little "real" control over anything in her life—including economics, where and with whom she lives, major choices, and the like—the renunciation of food takes on a different aspect that goes beyond appearance and dieting.

The social, cultural, and political backdrop to disordered eating in girls has informed most of the discussion about its frequency during the last twenty-five years. (It's worth noting, though, that boys and men are not immune to disordered eating. In fact, to borrow Dr. Joan Jacobs Brumberg's phrase, our cultural vision of the body as a "project"—with perfect pecs and washboard stomach—has also increased the numbers of boys and men who suffer from these disorders.) In the mid-1980s, in her influential and important book *The Hungry Self*, Kim Chernin suggested that "the onset of an eating disorder coincides with an underlying developmental crisis, regardless of a woman's age." Chernin associated the rise in eating orders to the mother-daughter dynamic, an "anguished concern about the mother [which] is hidden just beneath the surface of the eating problem." She noted:

At a moment when serious political gains have been won and women are able to take up the opportunity for further development, there is a marked tendency among women to retreat, to experience a failure of nerve, a debilitating inner conflict about accepting advantages and opportunities denied to their mothers. The "Cinderella Complex," the fear of independence from which we are supposedly suffering, is in reality a pervasive worry about our mothers' lives.[23]

Understanding what she called "the contemporary struggle for female identity" requires seeing it "in relation to this fateful encounter between a mother whose life has not been fulfilled and a daughter now presented with the opportunity for fulfillment." Writing at the beginning of the 1990s, feminist Naomi Wolf—who was herself anorexic by the age of thirteen and was the beautiful daughter of a beautiful and dieting mother—also understood anorexia and bulimia in terms of power and powerlessness; in her terms, the "cultural fixation on female thinness is not an obsession about female beauty but an obsession about female obedience." As she writes:

The youngest victims, from earliest childhood, learn to starve and vomit from the overwhelmingly powerful message of our culture, which I found no amount of parental love and support strong enough to override. I knew my parents wanted me not to starve because they loved me; but their love contradicted the message of the larger world, which wanted me to starve in order to love me. It is the larger world's messages, young women know, to which they will have to listen if they leave their parents' protection. I kept a wetted finger up to the winds of that larger world: Too thin yet? I was asking it. What about now? No? Now?[24]

Toward the end of the 1990s, Dr. Joan Jacobs Brumberg—who also wrote an important book on anorexia called *Fasting Girls: The His-*

*tory of Anorexia Nervosa*—dispiritedly noted the confusion among the young women in her Cornell University seminar:

> On the one hand, their parents and teachers told them that being female was no bar to accomplishment. Yet girls of their generation learned from a very early age that the power of their gender was tied to what they looked like—and how "sexy" they were—rather than to character and achievement. Because of the visual images they had absorbed since they were toddlers, they invariably wanted to be thinner, a desire that motivated them to expend an enormous amount of time and energy controlling the appetite and working on their bodies, all the while thinking about food. Although they were aware that diet and exercise regimens could become obsessive and lead to eating disorders, in their own lives they walked a narrow line between the normal and the pathological. Almost all of them admitted that they did battle, on a daily basis, with what therapists in the eating disorders world call "bad body fever," a continuous internal commentary that constitutes a powerful form of self-punishment.[25]

Mind you, these were girls at Cornell University—some of America's brightest stars—who walked that line between the "normal" and the "pathological," suffering from "bad body fever."

In an interview, we asked Dr. Anne Becker if she foresaw the continued presence of eating disorders in our society. "Yes," she replied slowly. "They will be a continuing problem, supported by both cultural underpinnings and market forces."

In girls who develop anorexia, their internalization of what the culture associates with physical perfection is usually mirrored by body image distortions in which they see themselves as overweight, regardless of what the scale or mirror actually show. Identifying disordered eating is not always easy for a number of reasons. First, many families only eat one meal together—dinner—and even then, not always. Second, idiosyncratic eating habits as well as weight consciousness among girls—eating on the run, skipping a meal, counting calories—tend to be accepted as "normal" adolescent behavior, particularly by mothers who themselves have been skipping meals and getting on the scale twice a week for years. So does excessive or compulsive exercising. Third, your daughter is likely to try to hide her patterns of disordered eating from you and, for that matter, from everyone else. This, too, will be made easier for her to accomplish because of the cultural assumptions we make about the adolescent's need to be "fully independent" and responsible for herself. And, finally, because dieting and concern with weight is so pervasive among girls, unless a daughter's weight loss is pronounced or she stops functioning in other areas, it is entirely possible that no one will notice unless you do. In *The Beauty Myth*, Naomi Wolf recounts an absolutely terrifying story about the self-starving girls, herself among them, in her junior high school and how "every one was a teacher's paragon." In her words, "We were allowed to come and go, racking up gold stars, as our hair fell out in fistfuls and the pads flattened behind the sockets of our eyes."[26]

While little research has been done to pinpoint factors that make a girl resilient to eating disorders, certain risk factors have been identified. Involvement in activities that require a specific body type—among them gymnastics, modeling, cheerleading, and ballet—puts a girl at possible risk. Familial emphasis on looks, weight, and diet increase the risk, as does being bullied, teased or criticized about being overweight as a child. Similarly, the experience of early menarche and difficulty coping with physical maturation increase the risk, as do sexual and other forms of abuse.[27] Be aware that since an effort to establish "control" is often part of disordered eating, family dynamics or parenting styles that are authoritarian or inflexible may also be factors.

Be responsive to your daughter's concerns about weight; do not accept her self-criticism about her body ("I hate my thighs and stomach," "I can't stand my butt") as "normal" or "inevitable" for a girl. Pay attention to "bad body fever." Try not to reinforce cultural stereotypes either by your words or your behavior. *Do* pay attention to your daughter's eating habits; no one is "too young" (or, for that matter, "too old") to develop an eating disorder. If your child's weight fluctuates dramatically or if both what she eats and how she eats change, consult your physician. (Cutting food into smaller and smaller pieces and eating fewer of them or hoarding and hiding food are often telltale signs.) If you think your daughter's patterns of dieting and eating could lead to an eating disorder, do not wait "to see if she outgrows it" or "if it stops."

Possible warning signs of anorexia include: deliberate self-starvation; intense fear of weight gain; refusal to eat and denial of hunger; constant exercising; greater amounts of hair on the face or body; absent or irregular menstrual periods; and loss of scalp hair. Possible signs of bulimia include: evidence of binge eating; evidence of purging behaviors; an excessively rigid exercise regimen—despite weather, fatigue, illness, or injury; unusual swelling of the cheeks or jaw area; calluses on the back of hands and knuckles from self-induced vomiting; discoloration or staining of the teeth; complicated schedules or rituals to make time for binge-and-purge sessions; and withdrawal from friends or activities.

Discovering that your daughter has an eating disorder may initially throw you into a panic, fill you with despair, or even make you angry. Many mothers reel with shock and disbelief; others are filled with terror. The Harvard Eating Disorders Center makes the following recommendation for parents who find themselves dealing with these problems: Keep in mind that disordered eating is your daughter's "desperate way of trying to cope with underlying problems. Even though you can see how unhealthy and unproductive her disordered eating is, your child may feel it is her only way of dealing with life." Remain calm in your daughter's presence; do not let her see you distraught or panicked. Try to discuss your worries with your husband, her doctor, and other advisors out of earshot. Before you talk to your daughter, do your homework first so that you have a strategy.[28] Talk to your pediatrician or internist about information and therapeutic referrals.

The Harvard Eating Disorders Center also recommends that you meet with the referred therapist without your child for the initial visit. You need to find out about the therapeutic approach and should seek advice as well about how and when to talk to your daughter. Do not be confrontational and keep in mind that your daughter may be afraid that you are going to take away her only coping mechanism. As the Harvard Eating Disorders Center notes, denial and anger are common, and it is important that you "raise your concerns, then give your child time and space to think about them." Be aware that your daughter may perceive the efforts to help her as threatening and it may take many approaches before she agrees to get help.

There are many support groups that can help mothers and their daughters cope with eating disorders. For more, see "Resources," page 353.

~ ~ ~

From the time I was twelve until well after I'd graduated college, become self-supporting, and moved into my own apartment, I routinely engaged in behaviors that my parents would have strenuously objected to, and which I successfully hid from them. I experimented with drugs, sex, and alcohol, cut myself, went on bizarre diets (and subsequently binged). My parents never even suspected.

I'm the eldest of five children. I kept up a straight-A average throughout my scholastic career. I had lots of friends and was never without a steady boyfriend. I worked part time. I helped out at home. To all appearances, I was an extraordinarily mature, together teenager, the very last person whom anyone would suspect of being troubled or depressed.

My parents were involved, caring, devoted parents; but, as devoted as parents are and want to be, they are not equipped to break the laws of physics by being in more than one place at one time. There were four other kids. My father worked full time, my mother, part time in the evenings. As I was the eldest, and extremely self-reliant, no one thought that I wasn't okay—not even me.

Believe me, I wasn't doing what I was doing to get their attention. That was the last thing I wanted. So why did I do this stuff? Because I wanted to; because I was interested in things beyond the day-to-day life I saw at home; because I could, I guess.

As an adult, I wonder how anyone could have missed what was going on with me. Was I really that good at hiding my true self? Apparently so. I don't know what the answer is. If my parents had been very easy to talk to, I don't think I'd have confided in them anyway. I never told any of my siblings until I was in my thirties.

I don't know why some kids don't make it out, even when they have the help of an interested and committed adult. I think the answer must be in how one is made, almost at the cellular level; I also think now that God's grace has a lot to do with it.

"Nicole," forty-six, married and a lawyer, no children

Nowhere are the consequences of treating adolescents as a tribe apart more evident than in the ubiquity of drugs in the contemporary American landscape. Despite the hopefulness of the signs that dot our streets, there is, alas, no "Drug-Free Zone." The mythology of adolescence—as a rite of passage that, by its nature, includes experimentation—has included alcohol for decades and, since the 1970s, illegal drugs as well. The statistics on adolescent drug use—including cigarettes and alcohol—are alarming. Again, while research shows that talking to our children about drugs— openly and frequently—makes a difference, parents don't talk—as they don't about sex and sexual activity. Why is it that? Our own adolescent experimentation with alcohol and drugs—which for many had no long-term consequences—may blind us to the consequences of a new generation trying what experts agree is a new generation of drugs. We were okay and so we think they will be too. Others among us may choose to believe that, somehow, our own children will be miraculously immune to the culture around them without our active intervention—after all, kids know drugs are dangerous, right? Because drug activity surrounded us when we were growing up, we may feel that there's not much we can do except pray that we have brought our girls up right. There may be a feeling, too, that this is somehow beyond our control—nothing can be done. The research, however, says otherwise.

For mothers, substance abuse raises issues different in kind from the other crises described in this chapter. For one thing, the correlation between parenting practices and negative or positive outcomes for our daughters is extremely high. In a report issued by the National Center on Addiction and Substance Abuse at Columbia University (CASA) in February 2001, researchers noted that the extent to which parenting is "hands-on" significantly lowers risk, regardless of family structure. As they put it, "a teen living with a single mother who is 'hands-on' is at lower risk of substance abuse than the average teen living in a two-parent household." The twelve indicators used to define "hands-on," as opposed to "half-hearted" and "hands-off," parenting, are:

- Parents expect to be told where teen is going in the evening or on the weekend and are told the truth by teen

- Parents have made it clear that they would be "extremely upset" to find teen using marijuana

- There are not periods of time of an hour or more after school or on the weekend when parents do not know where teen is

- Parents monitor what teen is watching on TV

- Parents impose restrictions on the kind of music CDs teen is allowed to buy

- Parents are very aware of how teen is doing in school

- Parents monitor teen's Internet usage

- Family typically has dinner together six or seven nights a week

- Teen has a weekend curfew

- An adult is always home when teen returns from school

- Teen is responsible for completing regular chores

- The TV is not on during dinner[29]

Ask yourself whether these behaviors—or ones that are similar and characterize involvement—are part of how you parent. How many times can you answer "yes" or "always"? Be aware of the fact that many of the statistics quoted throughout this book make it abundantly clear that most parents—regardless of their socioeconomic status—don't do many of these things or things like them on a regular basis, particularly as the daughters get older. Note that, according to CASA, in a "hands-on" household, teens said that their parents perform ten out of the twelve actions; in what the researchers called "half-hearted" households, parents performed six to nine; in a "hands-off" household, teens said parents performed five or fewer of these tasks.

Although only 27 percent of the households surveyed qualified as "hands-on," adolescents living in them were at *half* the average risk of substance abuse. In comparison, teens living in "hands-off" households were at *four times* the risk of those living in "hands-on" households. The risk for teens in "half-hearted" households was *twice* that of teens in "hands-on" households. Looking at the degree of monitoring involved, it would be easy to assume that exerting that amount of influence might strain relationships between parents and adolescents, but researchers found that not only does the exercise of parental authority directly lower substance abuse risk but it also appears to have a positive effect on the teen-parent relationship. Fifty-seven percent of teens living in "hands-on" households reported having an "excellent" relationship with their mothers, compared with 24 percent in "hands-off" households. It should be said that age increases the risk of substance abuse dramatically: At age twelve, 20 percent are at moderate risk, compared to 47 percent at age seventeen. (High risk goes from 3 percent at age twelve to 37 percent at age seventeen.) It goes without saying that as adolescents get older, parents are less likely to be "hands-on" in the way the study described. Once again, the message is clear: Don't confuse giving your daughter "monitored freedom" with "letting go."

While the CASA study is unique in that it isolated discreet family practices, other studies confirm the direct relationship between active parenting and risk reduction. Robert William Blum, M.D., Ph.D., and Peggy Mann Rinehart, the authors of *Reducing the Risk*, a monograph based on a survey of eighteen thousand adolescents, stressed that adolescents' "sense of connectedness"—both to the family and to school—is paramount in reducing risks.[30] They confirm that when parents are "present in the home at key times," the likelihood of smoking, drinking, and use of marijauna declines. They note that there doesn't appear to be what they call "a magical time of the day" when parents need to be present; they conclude, instead, that "it is having access to a parent and perhaps parental supervision in general that matters most." It's worth remarking on the fact that they report that since the 1960s, because of work pressures on parents, teenagers have lost ten to twelve hours a week of parental time. Perhaps it is time for all of us to rethink our priorities and to realize that when our girls get older, they don't necessarily need us "less."

Unfortunately, substance abuse is rarely a behavior that exists in isolation; it usually links to other self-destructive behaviors, as the following story demonstrates.

Dark-haired and vivacious, Kelly, the youngest of two children, was the one her parents didn't worry about—that position was already filled by her older brother, a highly intelligent boy whose learning disabilities made him the focus of his mother's attention. Kelly was everything a parent would hope for—a good student, level-headed, committed. She was active in sports during high school—lacrosse and sailing—and had nice friends from nice families. To her parents' relief, Kelly didn't belong to any of the groups or cliques that got into trouble in the small Northeastern city they live in. Kelly was above all responsible—she saved her babysitting money, and bought her own car at the age of seventeen—and while her relationship to her mother was extremely contentious and difficult, she seemed to be on track. During her senior year, her parents' marriage finally split wide open and her dad moved out. That was the same year she made plans to attend a college "as far away from home as possible"—on the West Coast, in fact—and had her first serious boyfriend. Her parents didn't approve of the boy—he seemed, in their words, "spectacularly unmotivated"—but each was confident that the relationship, which would soon become a long-distance one, would end in due course. Summer came and went. What Kelly's parents didn't know was how involved she—and her boyfriend—had become with drugs.

She put off packing for college until the very last moment but said nothing that might have alerted her parents to what was coming next. Her dad was flying her out, and planned to stay for the orientation to help her acclimate. On the plane with her father, Kelly dissolved into hysterical sobs; she did not want to go, after all. They drove to the college and, after meeting with the school psychologist, withdrew Kelly from school. Kelly first moved into her mother's house and then moved in with her boyfriend. Now, almost a year later, Kelly is still adrift—talking about "maybe" going back to school and then "maybe not." Drugs are still an integral part of her life—even though she denies it. Her father thinks that drugs are an important part of Kelly's loss of direction. Her boyfriend lives a hand-to-mouth existence—doing the odd job here and there, scrambling to pay the rent—and doesn't seem to have any plans for his own future. What Kelly earns isn't enough to pay the rent or maintain the car so she still depends on her mother for handouts. Somehow, this bright young girl has lost sight of the horizon that rightly ought to be hers. Even more important, she is actively unhappy, even though she doesn't seem to recognize it herself.

Her father continues to struggle with understanding what happened to Kelly, why it did, and how he and her mother contributed to it. Having come of age in the late 1960s, he is no stranger to experimentation with drugs but, as he says, "marijuana today is a whole different ballgame." Sometimes he thinks what she is doing with her life represents her effort to separate herself from her parents, but he notes that she remains dependent—her separation is incomplete, a failure in important ways. The degree to which she is dependent makes her angry and hostile to both of her parents. He is profoundly worried, and unsure what he should do next. The concerns he has raised with her—about her boyfriend, her drug use, her circle of friends— have only seemed to toughen her resolve to stay the course—if it can be called a course—she seems to have chosen for herself. He worries that the combination of both the boyfriend's influence and power over Kelly and her drug use have a kind of synergy that will make it hard for her to change directions unless, as he puts it, she manages to see through both at once.

For both of her parents, figuring out what to do next is harder still. Kelly is steadfast in her unwillingness to listen to either of them. Her father hears of the struggles one family had with a daughter addicted to heroin; in the end, he says somberly, they had no choice but to cut her off. It is a frightening, draconian thought.

He is both angry and heartbroken, wounded and worried. "There is," he says, "a terrible sense of rejection when a child says 'no' to everything you've worked for, everything you have valued in your life." In a quiet voice, he adds, "It's one thing to understand what is going on intellectually. It takes a lot of work to embrace it emotionally." In his wallet, there is a photograph of a smiling fourteen-year-old with a bright future. It is hard to find that young girl in the angry young woman of almost twenty who won't speak to him.

He hopes that that future is still recoverable.

Once again, the research confirms that we need to be proactive on our daughters' behalf. Do not assume—as your daughter is likely to tell you—that her school has already told her "everything" about drugs or drug use. Make a point, as you should about sex education, to find out what the school's curriculum does and does not include. Talk to your daughter openly and honestly about peer pressure, the desire to fit in, and how they connect to substance abuse. If she is old enough to go out on dates or to parties, talk to her about the high corollary between intoxication and both unwanted and high-risk sex. Do not assume that your daughter is too "smart" to try drugs, either the illicit varieties or the ones that are legal for adult use—cigarettes and alcohol. Face up to the fact that your own behaviors—whether you smoke and how much you and other adults in her life drink—will be observed and learned from. Make it your business to know what the drug scene is like in your town—what's happening will vary from place to place. (Suburban mothers, for example, should know that, according to *Reducing the Risk*, one in five suburban kids uses alcohol.) Doing the laundry, one mother found a pill in the pocket of her daughter's jeans and discovered that it was Ecstasy, which her daughter—not yet fifteen—had been handed but didn't take at a party. She used the pill as a starting point for a discussion. What follows are observations and suggestions which can help you be a proactive parent.

**One talk is not enough.**

We all need to talk to our girls about drugs throughout the adolescent years, tailoring the talk as they grow up and get out into the world. According to the Partnership for a Drug-Free America, these talks should take a different form at different stages. The partnership reminds us all to keep the following facts in mind:

- Teens are twice as likely to use marijuana as parents think they are, and they are getting high in places parents consider "safe"—around school, at home, or at a friend's house.

- Two thirds of eighth-graders report using alcohol in the past year.

- More than 20 percent of eighth-graders have reported trying an inhalant.

- More than 50 percent of eighth-graders have tried smoking cigarettes.[31]

Set rules for your daughter's behavior and make sure she understands you will enforce the consequences. Talk to her about the damage drugs do—to the body and mind. Familiarize yourself with the drugs that are part of the adolescent's contemporary world—and talk to your daughter about them. The statistics bear out the fact that "just saying no" will not happen without your involvement.

**Experimentation is not "inevitable."**

Don't buy into this idea or the corollary one that there is "nothing" you can do to influence your daughter's behaviors. Many parents appear to avoid talking about drugs in order to avoid the inevitable question "Did you ever try drugs when you were young?" Unless you are able to answer "no" truthfully, you may feel trapped into lying or holding up your own history as a possible bad example for your child to follow. If your child finds out that you are lying, though, you risk a loss of credibility. The Partnership for a Drug-Free America suggests that you tell the truth—but without giving details. (This is similar to the strategy for talking about sexual activity.) Ask your daughter why she wants to know about your history, and keep your answers limited to her questions; remember that the discussion isn't about your past but her future. Put giving her this information into a meaningful context; your ability to talk openly about why you tried drugs, why they're dangerous, and why you don't want her to do what you did will have resonance for your daughter.

**Be watchful about signs and warnings.**

The signals of drug use are, unfortunately, similar to symptoms of physical illness or psychological distress or even to what can be the temporary "ups and downs" of adolescent life. The Partnership for a Drug-Free America suggests that you pay attention to the following indicators and discuss them with your daughter's physician (and, if necessary, schedule a physical exam) to rule out illness:

- Your daughter is withdrawn, depressed or suddenly careless about her physical grooming.

- She is hostile and uncooperative and frequently breaks curfew.

- Her relationships with family members have deteriorated.

- There is a marked change in her school record or attendance.

- She shows loss of interest in what were her favorite activities.

- She evidences a change in eating and sleeping patterns.

- She has difficulty concentrating.

- She has red-rimmed eyes and a runny nose—when she doesn't have a cold or allergies.

- Household money has been disappearing.

- You have found any of the following in your home: pipes, rolling papers, small medicine bottles, eyedrops, and any other drug paraphernalia.

For more, see "Resources," page 354.

And, finally, as the mothers of daughters, we have to look at violence, particularly violence directed at girls and young women—by both strangers and people they (and, often, we) know. Rape and physical abuse are the most underreported crimes in the United States and we need not only to make the world a safer place for our daughters but, if something happens to them, to make it safe for them to talk about it—with us and the world at large, without fear or stigma. I write these words as someone who was raped at knifepoint by a stranger in my college dorm when I was nineteen. Like so many victims of rape, I told no one—and by locking the experience inside of me, I made what happened to me a larger part of myself than it might otherwise have been. For two years, I struggled alone, and denied both my mother and father the opportunity to help me. I felt guilty for something I could not prevent and felt responsible for something I didn't choose; I became afraid. Even after I told my parents, I did not seek out therapy, still denying the rape's profound effect. Looking back, I see that, like a stone thrown in a pond, many things—some that I recognized and others I didn't—rippled out from that event in my life. The experience validated my own insecurities and sense of unworthiness which, in turn, propelled me into a number of relationships and even marriages that were based in the wrong reasons and choices. Only years later, when my life really fell apart, did I fully confront what had happened to me. Not surprisingly, only a small circle of intimates knew that I had been raped—and it stayed that way until, several years ago, I told the story both in the book *Necessary Journeys* and on television. Women all over the country responded to me, many of them with their own stories. The point was eminently clear: The prevalence of violence against women—and the social shame associated with its different forms—need, in the twenty-first century, to come out of the closet for all of our sakes.

While rape by an armed stranger remains one of a mother's worst nightmares, the truth is that our daughters are much likely to be raped or assaulted by someone they know. The statistics pertaining to dating violence as reported by the Centers for Disease Control are alarming (see page 199)—and require each and every one of us to address these issues openly and directly. And the findings of the study reported in the *Journal of the American Medical Association* (see page 198) were disheartening, the authors noting that "violence against adolescent girls from dating partners is extremely prevalent." The time to initiate a discussion with your daughter about abuse and violence in relationships should coincide with her readiness to go out on dates. Realize that if violent or abusive behaviors—both the verbal and physical kind—are tolerated in your household, your daughter already has formed an opinion about them—and will perhaps tolerate them in others; the same goes for the behaviors tolerated or even accepted in her peer group. Among the factors the CDC cites as contributing to male-female dating violence are: a male who has sexually aggressive peers; a male's assumption of key roles in the dating relationship such as initiating the contact, making the decisions about the date, paying for it, doing the driving); previous sexual intimacy; adversarial attitudes about the relationship; belief in traditional sex roles; and a history of either observance of violence or violent behavior.[32] Not surprisingly, studies show that alcohol consumption—by either the perpetrator or the victim—is an important component of dating violence.

Abusive relationships are another subject we must address—and be on the lookout for. In her book *But I Love Him: Protecting Your Teen Daughter from Controlling, Abusive Dating Relationships*, Dr. Jill Murray cites a definition of dating violence offered by the University of Michigan Sexual Assault Prevention and Awareness Center: "the intentional use of abusive tactics and physical force in order to obtain power and control over an intimate partner." She points out that the key words are "intentional," "power," and "control." All violent behavior is, as she writes, "intentional." And while many of us who have no firsthand knowledge of abuse—save from the script of a made-for-television movie or magazine article—are likely to associate abuse with telltale signs such as bruises or black eyes, physical abuse is, according to Dr. Murray, usually the last phase in an abusive dating relationship. As she puts it, "Where physical abuse is present, in almost all cases there has been a long history of verbal and emotional abuse and often some kind of sexual abuse as well."[33]

Much of abusive behavior is about control and some of these behaviors, given an adolescent girl's inexperience, may be readily confused with what passes for "normal" fooling around or, for that matter, "love." We need to educate our girls about verbal and emotional abuse—name-calling, threats, intimidation, and humiliation—which constitute the first phase of abuse. We need to keep in mind that the constraints on abusive language—calling a girl a "bitch," for example—have disappeared in many quarters of the world our girls inhabit. They hear these words in songs, in movies, and even on television—and likely as not, they are more insensitive to or accepting of them than you or I were at the same age. Some abusive behaviors—such as monopolizing a girl's time, isolating her from her friends, even making a phone date with her and then never calling—may be too easily confused with signs of "love" or "attention" instead of what they are, manipulation and control.

How can you talk to your daughter if you think she is involved with a boy who is abusing her? Dr. Murray points out that "love is a behavior":

> Love is not what a person says but how he acts. This applies not to romantic relationships exclusively but to every interpersonal relationship in your life and your daughter's: parent/child, teacher/student, employer/employee, siblings, female friends, male friends, and so on.
>
> After your daughter's boyfriend treats her cruelly, he undoubtedly tells her later on that he's sorry, he loves her, and he'll never do it again.
>
> He tells whatever has worked in the past. As you speak with your daughter about the tangible actions her boyfriend has taken against her, you can ask her, "Is that loving behavior?"[34]

Raising our girls with a clear vision of what constitutes "loving behavior" and what does not is an important part of mothering—as is intervening if we believe our daughters are in over their heads.

~ ~ ~

Throughout my childhood, I assumed that everything that was wrong with my relationship to my mother was my fault. She always said it was—that I was difficult, impossible to love, and the like—and after my father died, there was no one around to correct that impression. While she was abusive, even physically abusive to me in private, in public she was charming and nice—and most of my schoolmates from that time remember her as a pretty, well-dressed woman made all the more charming by her pronounced foreign accent. No one quite believed the stories I told. The physical abuse

stopped when I was eleven or twelve and taller than she. I hit her
back once and that was that. My adolescence was marked by periods when my mother picked on me unmercifully—screamed at and
punished me for no reason—and then ignored me for long
stretches. Nothing I ever did for her or accomplished on my own
made the slightest difference.

By ninth grade I started a calendar that marked the exact number of days until I left for college and, once I left, I never lived with
her again. It wasn't until I was in my twenties and a therapist suggested that, perhaps, there were very real ways in which my mother
was profoundly disturbed that the light began to dawn—and, partly
freed of the tremendous need I had for a mother, any mother, I
could begin to see her for who she was.

Peg, fifty-two, my coauthor and mother to Alexandra, age thirteen-and-a-half

Sometimes the source of the troubled waters isn't the daughter.
Precisely because the mother-daughter relationship is so central to
a woman's formation of self and involves a great deal of "mirroring"
for both the parent and the child, the mother will sometimes
become the "boulder" that blocks the path during the years of adolescence. Mothering is not instinctual but an act of invention—
which draws both on those conscious parts of ourselves and those
forged from experience that are often less fully realized. Becoming
aware of who we are when we mother our adolescent daughters is a
step each of us must take, and will require that we look at how the
ways we were mothered affect us now. Our past can affect our present in a myriad of ways. One mother of a fifteen-year-old—whose
own mother was distracted at best and neglectful at worst—made a
conscious decision to be a stay-at-home mother, precisely because
her own mother hadn't been. She now finds herself enormously
threatened by her daughter's efforts to define herself as independent: "I know it's not rational but every word she utters sounds as
though it is a criticism of me, my choices, and my values. The fighting sometimes gets so bad that my husband literally has to peel us
apart." The constant validation she needs from her daughter may,

in fact, be a legacy from her own mother. Similarly, another mother who was brought up to always put work first—whether it was the work of high school or college, or the work she does as a lawyer—simply cannot understand why her daughter is content to earn Bs and Cs in school and puts her busy social life first. "The problem is that I simply don't understand her," she says. "It's as though I'm talking to someone who speaks a foreign language and doesn't understand a word of English. I end up getting enormously frustrated and angry with her when she allows as how her grades are 'good enough.' Nothing I do can motivate her." Accepting the ways in which our daughters are different from us may be harder if our own mothers refused to acknowledge the ways in which we were and are different from them. If our own "individuation" remains incomplete, it is unlikely that we will be able to give our daughters the room they need. The fifty-year-old mother of a seventeen-year-old girl says, on the one hand, that her own mother, who died last year, was "constantly disappointed in me because her unyielding and exacting standards of behavior and achievement were simply impossible to meet." A few minutes later, though, she describes her mother as the "perfect role model." "She was good at everything," her daughter remarks wistfully. "She worked part time, raised two kids, had a house that was beautifully decorated and always pristine, yet always managed to spend hours volunteering for her church groups and charities. She was a master gardener, could design and sew clothes, and was a fantastic cook and baker. She was always immaculately groomed and my parents entertained constantly. The problem for me is that I never quite measured up. Even now that she's gone, I seem to be playing catch-up with her memory." Not surprisingly, high standards and achievement are the issues that also dominate her relationship to her own daughter.

Midlife crises—either physical or psychological—may also alter the mother-daughter relationship if they are not tended to. One mother confessed that "menopause and all the other physical changes in my body totally overwhelmed me. During my daughter's junior and senior years in high school, I became preoccupied with myself and felt physically lousy a lot of the time. My daughter reacted by totally shutting me out of her life—which only made everything worse. But I didn't realize how angry she was with me until she came home from college during Christmas break of her freshman year. She felt completely abandoned by me at a time when so much in her life was changing."

In their book *Mending the Broken Bough: Restoring the Promise of the Mother-Daughter Relationship*, therapists Barbara Zax, Ph.D., and Stephan Poulter, Ph.D., describe six common "styles" of mothering drawn from their experiences with their own patients, mothers and adult daughters who are trying to mend or revitalize their relationships with each other.[35] These styles of mothering are useful for us to reflect on as we try to become the mothers we want to be and the mothers our daughters need. Try to locate your own mother within these styles—and think about how the way you were mothered affects you now:

**The "Me First" style**: This is just what it sounds like—the mother is the centerpiece, and everything her daughter does is, inevitably, about her. No matter where a conversation begins, it will end up being about the mother. Since she is unable to brook any criticism, this relationship is often openly fractious. (The authors note, by the way, that "Me First" mothers usually had "Me First" mothers themselves.) From the daughter's point of view, this style of mothering may create a situation in which she's constantly seeking her mother's approval—all the way from childhood through adolescence and into adulthood. The problem here is that, since the mother is the reference point, the daughter has little support or validation in her own right. Every choice the daughter makes or doesn't make is seen from the mother's point of view.

*The "Super Mom" style*: While on the surface, this kind of mother may look like a role model—the "Super Mom" is likely to be highly involved in the PTA, the Girl Scout troop, and other areas she thinks are "safe" and "healthy"—this style of mothering masks a view of the world as essentially unsafe and dangerous. Overprotective and unduly cautious, this style of mothering is about control—and effectively prevents the daughter from taking the necessary risks to grow. Daughters of "Super Moms" often avoid taking on challenges and tend to stay close to home, ceding their choices—even as adults—to their mothers.

*The "Always Look Good" style*: This style of mothering is the hallmark of a woman who is very concerned with outside appearances—looking good and acting appropriately in the eyes of others. With this type of mothering, the inner self tends to be neglected—and girls who grow up with "Always Look Good" mothers will continue to rely on others—lovers and husbands, bosses or supervisors—to supply them with a sense of their worth. Girls raised in the "Look Good" style often lack a healthy sense of self-acceptance, despite what they achieve in the outside world.

*The "Distracted" style*: She's the mother who forgets to pack her daughter's lunch or schedule her dentist appointment on a regular basis. Busy with her life—she may be involved with her work or have a large, unwieldly household to run—while she's physically on-premises, she's really not paying attention to her daughter in a consistent or supportive way. What the daughter learns from the "distracted" style of parenting is that she's not very important—and she is likely, according to Drs. Zax and Poulter, to seek out other people such as girlfriends to give her the consistent emotional support she needs. While daughters of "distracted" mothers often are high achievers, they nonetheless remain deeply unsure of themselves.

*The "Empathetic" style*: This positive style of mothering focuses on understanding the girl in front of you—and emotional connection is its cornerstone. Drs. Zax and Poulter are quick to say that the empathetic mother is not perfect—she has the occasional flare of temper and sometimes she will miss her daughter's cues altogether—but "the daughter knows she has her mother's love and support to carry her through periods of great difficulty." Empathetic mothering supports a daughter in her growth—giving her the confidence she needs to take healthy risks and take on challenges. It's worth pointing out that, according to the authors, it is never too late to incorporate an empathetic attitude into parenting.

*The "Responsive" style*: This last style goes beyond "empathetic" mothering, and endows the daughter with the tools to develop into a healthy and productive individual. According to Drs. Zax and Poulter, the mother with a "responsive" style was probably raised by a "responsive" mother herself—who gave her permission to "separate and make a life for herself." The daughter raised by a responsive mother has healthy role models on which she can base her behaviors. In "responsive" parenting, mother and daughter have the freedom to talk and to disagree, to be both separate and connected at once. As the authors put it, "The daughter does not feel the pull of her mother's unfulfilled dreams or unresolved fears, so her own struggle for independence, beginning at about five years and continuing through her life, is not fueled by her mother's unresolved issues from the past."

No matter where you locate yourself within these descriptions, it is important to remember that each of us has the capacity to change how we act and how we mother our daughters. If there are aspects of your personality or history that get in the way of what you want not just for your daughter but for yourself, it is within your power to change them. Get help if you feel as if you are floundering; being in over your head doesn't teach you anything useful.

Not one of us is perfect, and parenting—like living—is an ongoing process of learning and unlearning. The decade that comprises your daughter's adolescence is a long enough period of time for you to grow and change if you want—both as a person and a mother. Substitute the mythology of the All-Responsible Mother with a commitment to being as conscious of and responsible for your own behavior as you can be. And no matter what, keep the image of the Oriental rug in mind and learn from its weavers. It is the flaws woven into the carpet, after all, that testify to the beauty and power of human endeavor.

## CHAPTER SIX

# Reflections

I long to put the experience of fifty years at once into your young lives, to give you at once the key to that treasure chamber every gem of which has cost me tears, struggles, and prayers, but you must work for these inward treasures yourselves.

Harriet Beecher Stowe, in a letter to her twin daughters

More than once, my father—the senior and wiser Dr. Snyderman, as he would be quick to remind me—has accused me of living vicariously through my daughters. He's talking about our horses—both my girls and I ride—and my father has some pretty definite ideas about them. I wanted to ride as a girl and then as an adolescent but he wouldn't let me; the girls who rode horses in Fort Wayne, Indiana, were altogether too snooty for his taste and he thought that parents who bought their kids horses were over-indulgent. So that was that, and he's never changed his mind. Of course, what I did after I finished my residency, divorced my first husband, and got my first real job as a doctor in Little Rock, Arkansas, was to buy myself a horse. It was a small act of rebellion during my otherwise obedient coming-of-age. Horses have been a part of Kate and Rachel's life since they were small.

I have always told my girls that I want them to ride and compete for themselves, not for me. The day they no longer find the sport fun or challenging is the day they can quit—with my blessings—and I've made sure that each of them does something different that suits her own talents and personality, without increasing the competition between them. Rachel is a natural athlete and a born competitor, and jumping is her specialty; she has the fearlessness and drive this particular sport demands. Kate, on the other hand, has an intuitive understanding of and rapport with her horse; she is gifted at managing the "oneness" of horse and rider that dressage requires. Both girls are better riders than their mother, which makes me undeniably proud. The horses have taught the girls about responsibility and love; taking care of them has been a good discipline. I hope, too, that during their adolescent years, their horses and their riding will provide them with a safe haven—an activity to retreat to when life gets a little too fast, when there's pressure to conform in terms of sex or drugs, or to hang out with the wrong people, or even when the outside world has wounded them to the core.

But none of this—not even the evident pride and increase in self-esteem in both girls—will convince my father. He wonders, I am sure, whether I would be quite so sanguine as I say if either of my daughters gave up riding entirely. Sometimes I wonder too. So far, at least, neither of my daughters has quite said "no" to me on important issues. What will happen, I wonder, if or when one of them does? Not about horses, of course, but something infinitely more important. What would happen if my vision of what was needed for one of them was totally contradicted by what she wanted for herself? How would I handle that, I wonder? Would I able to listen? Would she?

Of course, in some sense, my father is right about my "living through my girls." Having high hopes and expectations for our children, after all, is the vision that inspires committed parenting; we encourage our girls to be the best that they can be precisely because we want them to live not just fulfilled and happy lives but, in some sense, "better" lives than we've lived. Each of us—whether it's true or not—tends to see each succeeding generation as arcing in an upward progression. Where we've been and where we never got to go, who we are and those aspects of self that remain ever-elusive even in adulthood inevitably inform our vision of what we want for our girls. The inchoate dreams we have when we peer over our daughters' crib rails take on new shape when, in adolescence, our children begin to come into their own. Often, our dreams for them are closely bound to our own lives and experiences. The thirty-nine-year-old mother of an almost-thirteen-year-old who grew up feeling that her parents never supported her dreams wants nothing more than for her daughter to go to college and then on to graduate school—things she thought were beyond her reach. "She'll end up living the life I wanted, with all the opportunities I could only dream of," the mother says. "Her life is going to be bigger, more important, than mine ever was or will be." She is proud of her daughter's inquisitive mind—"She writes poetry! Imagine that: poetry!"—and her high grades and academic achievements. Another woman, the single mother of twelve- and fifteen-year-old girls, is more blunt and practical: "My girls need education and training. They need to be able to do things in the world and take care of themselves. I want to make sure that they never have to scramble the way I have these last five years. I don't want either of them to spend Sunday nights the way I have—staring at stacks of bills I can't pay on time, wondering if their father will get 'around' to sending me the child support he owes me, worrying that I will get laid off from my job because the company isn't doing too well."

Sometimes, our dreams have less to do with where our daughters will go than who they'll be when they get there. A freelance writer, mother to a ten-year-old, who, in her words, "spent more than half of my life trying to be self-confident enough to take risks and to do what I want" dreams for her daughter to grow into "a resilient person who is able to be independent in a good way, to be able to negotiate life with confidence, in the way I couldn't for years and years." For this mother, the signs of material success—money and possessions—play a smaller part in her dreams for her daughter than the deeper, more intangible gifts: "I want her to be happy within herself, with whatever work she chooses to do, and to be happy with friends and those she loves." My coauthor, Peg, confides, "I want Alexandra to be able to look in the mirror and like the person she sees, without needing someone else to validate that vision for her. I would like her to live a life without ever feeling that she needs to tailor who she is to suit someone's vision of whom she ought to be, as I did during all of my adolescence and a large part of my adulthood. I want her to be as happy for other people's successes as she is for her own—without feeling that someone else's achievement has somehow detracted from hers."

Back to my father, and his criticism of the horses: I know he's not just talking about the horses but is worrying aloud about the more privileged environment my daughters—and, for that matter, my son—are growing up in. Even though neither I nor my husband, Doug, wanted for much during our childhood and adolescence, our children do live in a different world. And my father is talking about staying grounded, about caring about the right things in life, not just those on the material surface. The things I want for my girls can get lost in a landscape of abundance, which sometimes emphasizes the fruits of winning over the efforts of competition, and my father is right to make me pay attention. I worry, too, that some things come too easily, too quickly for them; they need to know that, sometimes, there is a direct connection between the value of an experience and how hard-won it is. I want my daughters to live a life that gives them pride and satisfaction, whether it is in the workplace or in the home. I want them not to be scared by opportunity when it offers the possibility of failure, as invariably things of true worth do. I want them to be kind and aware of those around them—not just the familiar faces of their next-door neighbors or their colleagues at work. I hope they face enough adversity to gain strength, though not enough that they feel bitter or hopeless. I hope they realize that there is always someone out there who has seen worse times.

We all want our girls to be happy and successful. But what precisely do we mean by that? And what, as mothers, do we need to give our girls so that they can accomplish both? In his book *When All You've Ever Wanted Isn't Enough: The Search for a Life that Matters*, Harold Kushner explored why so many of us—both "those people who get what they want in life and those who don't"—don't feel, deep down, that we are happy. He tells a story—it's a parable, really, which isn't altogether surprising since Harold Kushner is a rabbi—which illustrates some of the definitions of winning and success that seem, for many Americans, to get in the way of true happiness. It's a story worth keeping in mind as we explore what we need to give our girls to take with them on the journey:

An American tourist found himself in India on the day of the pilgrimage to the top of a sacred mountain. Thousands of people would climb the steep path to the mountaintop. The tourist, who had been jogging and doing vigorous exercise and thought he was in good shape, decided to join in and share the experience. After twenty minutes, he was out of breath and could hardly climb another step, while women carrying babies, and frail old men with canes, moved easily past him. "I don't understand it," he said to an Indian companion. "How can those people do it when I can't?" His friend answered, "It is because you have the typical American habit of seeing everything as a test. You see the mountain as your enemy and you set out to defeat it. So, naturally, the mountain fights back and it is stronger than you are. We do not see the mountain as our enemy to be conquered. The purpose of our climb is to become one with the mountain and so it lifts us up and carries us along."[1]

In order to know what our girls need to take with them, we first have to define the nature of the journey—and, to use Rabbi Kushner's words—the "purpose of the climb."

~ ~ ~

I think the pressure on girls to have a fulfilled life on all levels has become nearly unbearable in one generation. These days, many women feel that they need to have a full-time job and a reasonably satisfying family life and, hey, how about enough time to spend with my husband, and who the hell is going to keep the house clean, and the net result is that most women have the equivalent of at least two full-time jobs, and so they end up feeling like they're failing at all of their obligations. I don't see any easy answers.

In terms of how having a "a high-achieving and professional mother" has affected the girls, I think it's generally had a very positive effect. The girls see that their mother is a very good lawyer, one who can win high-profile cases, and this seems to have given them the confidence that they, too, can become professional women, if they so choose. But where her parents went to school affects Mary, my eldest, more than what either of us does for a living. Mary is painfully aware that her mother went to Radcliffe and I went to Harvard, and for all that she enjoys that connection (and dotes on the movie Love Story), what it really has done is to make her feel a tad demoralized. She worries out loud: "Gee, Mom, both you and Daddy went to Harvard, and what if I don't get in? I would feel awful." It doesn't seem to help when I point out that my going to Harvard was very little about merit, much more a combination of the fact that my Dad went there and I was a bit of a preppie jock; and that her mother had double 800 SATs. Talk about pressure! Mary is a very smart girl herself and does very well in school and is having a ball on the track team and I think she would be much better off if she attended a smaller school where she could excel across the board as a scholar and an actress and an athlete, but for the moment she has this tough standard of Harvard hanging over her head.

"Tim," age fifty-three, media executive and father to "Mary," age fifteen and "Jane," age twelve

Pressure to succeed begins early in American society. Park yourself alongside a sandbox just about anywhere in the country and you'll become an eyewitness to what Peg laughingly calls "competitive baby"—the exchanges between new mothers about developmental landmarks reached or, in their terms, "achieved" by their children. "Competitive baby"—wherein the winner holds a cup, walks, talks, and toilet-trains first in her class—ultimately gives way to similar competitions in elementary school, although the focus shifts from the more homely tasks of early childhood to those supposedly predictive of long-term success and intellectual development, and then continues into middle and high school. Childhood, as most of us experienced it, has undergone a sea change of its own—the wobbly clay ashtrays and finger paints of our kindergartens, the afternoons spent tossing a ball around in the neighborhood or just hanging out under the shade of a tree, have long since given way to exercises in numbers and reading and "enrichment" programs tailored to every age group, from baby gym to French lessons for four-year-olds. Type in the keyword "parenting" on Amazon.com and close to twelve thousand titles will come up on the screen—a cornucopia of information on how to make your child do just about everything faster and better, so that you can get a leg up on that college application, no matter how many years your child has to go before the fat or the thin envelope arrives. Neither we nor our children are immune to the pressure—it's hard, despite what your brain tells you, to stay above the fray—and even the ordinarily sane parent rips open the envelope that contains her child's standardized test scores—the Iowas, the Terra Novas, the Whatevers, and ultimately the SATs—with a quick intake of breath, looking for confirmation of a bright and rosy future.

It's been suggested that, somehow, as a group, we have indeed lost sight of the forest for the trees. "Hyper-parenting," as Alvin Rosenfeld, M.D., and Nicole Wise called it, is easy to satirize—and who among us doesn't know a "hyper-parent"? But the truth is that while easy to make fun of—the micromanager mother who has every single moment of her daughter's "free" time booked to the

max with the private soccer clinic, the Spanish tutor, ballet and skat-
ing lessons—"hyper-parenting" is also hard to escape, precisely
because it is, as Rosenfeld and Wise point out, rooted in the best
intentions. Because we think parenting is important, we load our
shelves up with books—including this one, no doubt—to make sure
we've got it right. But this kind of thinking has serious consequences, which Rosenfeld and Wise point out:

> American parents have been persuaded that average, typical or even
> "normal" is no longer good enough. To prepare children for the
> impossibly competitive millennium, parents are exhorted to give
> them an edge over the competition. The media uses strong, active
> verbs to convince parents that they not only can but should work
> hard at helping a child excel: "Make Your Baby Smarter," *Parenting*
> magazine urges. "Build a Better Boy" advises *Newsweek*. It is as
> though children were born mediocre and by tinkering with their
> valves and fine-tuning their design to help them function at the opti-
> mal level, parents could engineer them into superachievers.[2]

Think back to the story Rabbi Kushner told about the American,
the holy mountain, and "winning" and it becomes clear that, some
of the time at least, we may find ourselves shepherding our daughters onto a fast track of a race in which, somehow, we've lost sight of
why we started in the first place. Just listen to what Rosenfeld and
Wise have to say:

> It says a lot about our priorities that many parents today put more
> energy into teaching children how to serve a tennis ball than to serve
> humanity. They work harder at making sure children are skilled at
> public speaking than teaching them to communicate openly and
> honestly with one another. Should our goal be preparing our kids to
> get into the college of their choice or to live the *life* of their choice?
> They are not necessarily one and the same.[3]

What is it that we want for girls to learn, to achieve, to become? It is less demanding, for some of us, to write a check for soccer camp or to drive them to swim meets so that they can get into a better college than it is to make the time to reflect on what we think it is important that they learn—to live happier, more productive, more fulfilled lives as mothers, daughters, partners, lovers, wives, coworkers, and denizens of the planet, as well as doctors, lawyers, money-market managers, writers, teachers, television producers, and the like. It is easier to set getting her into a good four-year college as the goal than it is to tackle the complexity of what makes a fine specimen of Homo sapiens. This is not to say that learning and education aren't important—no one in her right mind is going to argue that our experience of the world and people isn't enriched by what education gives us—but that isn't *all* we need. It's one thing to be able to walk into a museum and properly identify Claude Monet's painting of Rouen Cathedral; it's another to learn how to look at the evening sky through Monet's eyes. I graduated from college and from medical school but I didn't become a good doctor—which involves more than just skill and technique—until I became a frightened patient myself, dependent on other doctors. Peg swears it took her twenty years to grow and unlearn the style of writing favored by English professors—writing aimed at "impressing people with how smart you are."

We dare you to ask anyone you know who is good at what they do—"successful," as it were—and we bet that each one of them will tell you about an aspect of their expertise that has nothing to do with their formal training. All of us need to reflect on what the journey that is life will demand of our girls—and what they will need to pack for that journey.

At the same time, we have to make sure that our dreams for our daughters don't get in the way of their own. As we've already noted, one reason the mother-daughter relationship sometimes feels uncomfortable in the years of adolescence is that different things are required of us as mothers. Becoming a better listener is one of them. As the authors of *Mother-Daughter Revolution* put it:

> By listening, we don't mean the basic function of hearing, although that is usually involved. Mothers who are deaf can be extraordinary listeners. Listening means an awareness, an openness to learning something new about another person. In ordinary conversation, people often speak in shorthand with each other, assuming an understanding to make the conversation flow. Interruption, even for clarification, can seem to be rude or a breach of some unwritten code of sympathy. But listening with the intent to learn is both an approach to conversation and a different type of conversation.[4]

While it is true that our experiences of the world are richer than those of our daughters who are still fledglings in these matters, the conclusions we have drawn from our experiences are not always those our daughters will, in time, draw from similar experiences. Put in a more homely fashion, we need to make sure that our older, louder voices don't drown out theirs. Dr. Sharon Frith, a psychologist in private practice who treats adolescent girls and their mothers, reminds us that it is "important for mothers to tolerate their daughters' differences." She stresses the importance of empathy—the ability to understand someone else's feelings and thoughts—and is quick to say that "not all mothers do empathy very well." The very closeness of the mother-daughter dyad—our shared biology and femaleness, the vividness of mothers' dreams for their daughters—sometimes gets in the way of appreciating those meaningful ways in which our children are not always like us.

There is no question that parenting an adolescent is more challenging, more rigorous than mothering a five-year-old, for which the energy expended is more physical than emotional or intellectual. Mothering our daughters authoritatively in these years requires self-

examination—and given the likely coincidence of a child's adolescence and one's own midlife, self-examination may feel most unwelcome. At the very time that our girls graduate from the mini–life
lessons taught during the elementary years and begin to take on the
larger ones, we may find that our own answers to the questions first
posed in adolescence and young adulthood are no longer working.
We need to be able to see this not as an inevitable conflict between
our own needs and those of our daughters that requires us to pull
back from motherhood but as a possible window of opportunity for
us to become better guides to our children at this stage of life.

   In her book *Secret Paths: Women in the New Midlife*, based on a
study of women in their forties and fifties, Terri Apter writes that
when she studied mothers and adolescent daughters (for the book
that ultimately became *Altered Loves*), she "was puzzled by the ways
in which mothers were often knocking over the psychological
blocks that their daughters were putting in place. As adolescent girls
were becoming more controlled, more circumspect, their mothers
were often growing more impulsive, wickedly relishing a new spon-
taneity. Many mothers, too, were fired by anxiety about their own
lives, and were taking apart the assumptions on which they were
built."[5] But Apter discovered it wasn't about just the mother–adolescent daughter dynamic—women in their forties, whether or not
they had adolescent children, demonstrated the same behavior.
Apter calls this moment the "third crossroads" in women's development—the first two being puberty and the passage into adulthood—wherein women confront the pulls they have felt between
twenty-five and forty, the "clashes between affiliative needs—to be
closely, carefully involved in the emotional needs of others—and
expansive needs—to achieve, to meet challenges, to gain social recognition for skill and competence."[6] Women in their fifties who
successfully negotiate what Apter calls the "midlife reconstruction"
"devote the energy they once directed towards meeting idealized
expectations to managing their own needs and desires."[7] It's worth

pointing out the Joan Borysenko, Ph.D., in her book *A Woman's Book of Life: Biology, Psychology, and Spirituality of the Feminine Life Cycle*, also examines what she calls the "Midlife Metamorphosis." She notes that the term "midlife crisis"—which has passed into the vernacular of the culture—isn't a "crisis" at all but a period of transition in the life cycle. In her words, "One of these periods occurs between the ages of forty and forty-five, when we reflect back upon the culminating life structure of early adulthood and set about constructing an entry life structure for middle adulthood."[8] Dr. Borysenko calls this transition the "Midlife Metamorphosis," which has both physiological (perimenopause/menopause) and psychological bases. She, too, notes what she calls "a fiery new directness during the midlife metapamorphosis" (as Terri Apter does), though she is quick to say that it "can cut in two directions": "When a woman is emotionally mature and psychologically healthy this new boldness is channeled into personal, family, and social causes that further the feminine values of relationality and independence. When a woman is emotionally immature, however, her fierceness may express itself instead as increased self-hatred, fear of aging, or an unfortunate need to control other people."[9] The coincidence of our midlife— our own crossroads of development—with the crossroads of our daughters' adolescence requires us to take stock of our emotional maturity, so that we pay attention to where that "fiery new directness is channeled." If we can see the midlife reassessment as a time of positive change, of new energy, it may yield unexpected riches. Our own self-examination may actually empower us to become better, more effective mothers to our daughters—provided we can accept the possibilities this life transition offers us.

In *Secret Paths*, Terri Apter notes that women in midlife often reformulate their relationships to their own mothers—and as a result, find new things of value even in mother-daughter relationships that, over the decades, have not always been sustaining. As Apter writes:

Forty was often cited as the magic age whereby a woman no longer cared in the same way about what her mother thought. Forty was the time, finally, to grow up. This age was a marker both because women observed change within themselves, and because forty had symbolic impact. Though a few women said they still "heard a mother's running commentary" as a "companion reel to their own responses," they were now able either to confront it and stop it at will, or "let it go on running, without really caring about it." This "lack of care" was often linked to a different kind of care: As a woman no longer tried to please her mother she often felt a new concern not to hurt her.[10]

This is not to minimize the degree to which the issues of midlife will, for some of us, cause either physical or emotional discomfort. It is simply that the growth of consciousness, of self-awareness, that results from this particular sea change can help us better help our daughters grow into happier, more fulfilled women themselves.

We need to know consciously what we think is important to help set the standards of academic, emotional, moral, and spiritual behavior our daughters need to guide them. The balancing act authoritative parenting requires—of listening hard to learn what our daughters are thinking and feeling while sketching out meaningful and safe boundaries for their exploration of self—may be hard for some of us who are, by nature, temperamentally unsuited to this kind of exchange. The introspection that is a hallmark of authoritative parenting at its best may feel foreign to us or make us uncomfortable. We may feel caught in turmoil as our relationships and our own definitions of success and self-worth suddenly seem to be built on shifting sands. But as the closest thing to a mirror our daughters have, we each have to look within and discover what we think is of value and importance in our own lives, so that the lessons we teach are the lessons our daughters need to learn to go out into the world and live the lives they choose. We need to let both our successes and our failures guide us.

In her book *My Mother, My Self*—published over twenty-five years ago, but ultimately enormously influential in persuading Americans that the mother-daughter relationship was, by definition, strained and difficult, and that "overcoming" the mother within and without was a necessary part of growth—Nancy Friday relates a funny but telling story about mothers and daughters.[11] A newly married young woman named Peggy is making her very first meal at her new home with her parents as guests. She's prepared a Virginia ham. When her husband gets up to carve it, he asks her why she's sliced four inches off the shank end. Her answer? "Mother always does it that way." Her mother is, of course, at the table and, when asked why she does it, she replies "That's how my mother did it too. Doesn't everyone?" The next day, Peggy calls her grandmother to ask why she cuts off the shank end. The grandmother answers by saying "I've always done it that way because that's how my mother did it." As Friday tells it, the great-grandmother just happens to be alive so Peggy can go right back to the source and find out why three generations of women have been throwing out four inches of perfectly good meat. It turns out that once, when Peggy's grandmother was little and learning how to cook, her mother had a ham that was too large for the roasting pan at hand—so her mother cut the shank to make it fit.

It's an amusing story, of course, but it illustrates—as Nancy Friday intended it to—"how we incorporate those parts of mother we choose to imitate—like her skill in cooking—but right along with them, we also take in less rational and unexamined aspects all unaware." It's true of all of us as daughters—just as it will be true for our daughters in turn. It is our job to make sure that the lessons they learn are the ones that will serve them well.

Once again, we offer you some suggestions to get you thinking about what it is that you need to teach your daughter and how that teaching might take place:

**Ask yourself: What do I mean when I use the word "success"?**

The culture tends to equate success with money and, bombarded by literally thousands and thousands of commercials in every shape and form, at first blush most adolescent girls might give the same answer. Talk to your daughter about more than just material success; expand your definitions of success to other areas of life, particularly those that emphasize our humanity, including the ability to form and nurture emotional connections, make commitments, and learn new ways of understanding life. Make a list of the women you love and admire—and discuss why each of them is, in her own way, unique and "successful." Try to help your daughter look past the importance of the belonging and fitting in with the herd by exploring creativity—the meaningful and interesting ways people are different from one another. Talk to her about choices—making decisions about motherhood and work, for example—and examine the solutions you and other women in her life have discovered for themselves at different stages of life. Adolescent girls enjoy exploring philosophical questions, and talking to your daughter not just about your views but hers opens new doors for each of you.

In Marian Wright Edelman's *Lanterns: A Memoir of Mentors*, she includes twenty-five lessons for living life. Lesson 21 is one worth remembering:

> *Be a good ancestor. Stand for something bigger than yourself. Add value to the Earth during your sojourn.* Give something back. Every minute you drink from wells you did not dig, are sheltered by builders you will never know, are protected by police and soldiers and neighbors and caretakers whose names are in no record books, are tended by healing hands of every hue and heritage, and are fed and clothed by the labors of countless others.[12]

Opening up the definition of "success"—girl by girl, woman by woman—is a step we can all take. For more on this, please look at the section on spirituality, page 313.

### Ask: Which is more important: effort or achievement?

Imagine the following scenario—a true one, as it happens. Your daughter in middle school has a group science assignment on technology and the future. The teacher tells the girls that each student will be graded separately, even though the presentation will be made by all three of them. Two of the girls do all the work—researching and writing on the subject—while the third coasts. The day of the presentation, though, the three get up to present their findings and, despite what the teacher had said earlier, all three are given the same grade: A. Your daughter comes home angry and upset at the inequity of the situation. Should she be? Alternatively, your daughter finds herself the only motivated party in the group of three. She decides that, since both the experience and the grade are important to her, she will do the work independently and share the credit and the grade. Should she? Or should you intervene by speaking to her teacher?

Examine your attitudes—and those of your daughter's father—toward effort and achievement. Do you see them as necessarily linked—or are they sometimes separate and discrete? Which is more important—taking on a task for which you have a "natural" ability or trying one that tests your ability to adapt? Are you able to enjoy activities at which you don't excel? Is your daughter?

Research shows that children who believe that intelligence is a "fixed trait"—a quantifiable trait you are born with—tend to pursue avenues of learning which yield positive evaluations of their abilities and avoid negative ones. These children are more vulnerable, more liable to be discouraged in the wake of failure because they understand failure as proof-positive that they are not "intelligent" enough to achieve whatever they set out to do. In contrast, children who believe that intelligence is "malleable"—a trait that can be developed through learning—pursue the goal of increasing their abilities. They tend to weather failure better than those who see intelligence as a fixed trait because they perceive obstacles as a normal part of the learning process.[13]

Research confirms that bright girls are twice as likely as bright boys to see intelligence as a fixed trait, a finding that may explain why girls' achievements in science and math drop precipitously after elementary school. (In an article entitled "Motivation and Achievement," Valanne L. Henderson and Carol S. Dweck point out that the requirements of mathematics, unlike those of verbal subjects, "repeatedly [require] the student to master new skills and new conceptual frameworks." Verbal subjects tend to build on a set of skills already acquired and apply them "to increasingly difficult material." As they put it, "bright girls may view ordinary difficulties in math and related subjects as indicating that they lack ability and may come to doubt that they can do well in these subject areas."[14])

Do talk to your daughter about what constitutes intelligence (and see the last question, "What constitutes being 'smart'?" on page 307), and encourage her to see intelligence as a trait that can be enlarged and expanded on through the course of a lifetime, not just this marking period or next. Encourage her to explore new areas of competence—without requiring her necessarily to succeed at every single one. Don't reward her for "achievement" alone, but motivate her by praising her for effort.[15] Remember, too, that our intelligence is broadened by many different things, most of which are not academic in nature, but which ultimately contribute heavily to our achievement.

## Examine your own attitudes toward failure.

Our sense of what constitutes failure connects not only to achievement and resilience, as we've just discussed, but ultimately to motivation. While the easy, off-the-cuff answer for most of us will be "Failure? I don't like it one bit," our attitudes toward failure go to the heart of how we see life. Do you see life as a race to be run (or, to use Rabbi Kushner's example, a mountain to be climbed) or do you view it as a process? Think about how you respond when your daughter brings home a less than perfect grade or, despite everything you've done to help her, she's still unable to master something you think she ought to be able to do with no problem. How do you react when your daughter loses a tennis match, or fluffs a play in a soccer game? Pay attention to the lessons you communicate when she brings home a grade or a test score: Do you always ask, "How did you miss those points?" or "How did everyone else do?" Sometimes—but not always—these questions are useful. Discovering that your daughter invariably does better at essay questions than at multiple choice opens the way to help her evolve different strategies to succeed; finding out that everyone in the class did poorly on a test might give you valuable information about the teacher's competence and her or his teaching methods. But not always. If you ask these questions out of habit—because your mother did or because you think they will motivate your daughter—you need to look again.

Resilience is an important component of achievement, and few of us will have gotten to this stage of life without experiencing one variety of failure or another. Having our girls learn that life isn't always an upward trajectory but sometimes feels more like a meandering trail is an important lesson that teaches them something about the nature of the climb. Among the findings of *See Jane Win: The Rimm Report on How 1,000 Girls Became Successful Women* was that 62 percent of the successful women described "times in their education when they experienced great difficulty or 'hit a wall.' "[16] Experienc-

ing difficulty can teach us and our daughters to regroup and to refo-
cus, and to seize the opportunity to develop new skills. This is true
not just in the academic realm but in the social one as well. In an
interview, we asked educator Arlene Gibson, head of the Spence
School in New York, about the pressures girls are under and what
parents should do. She commented, "Students get confused messages when we reward them only for their achievements. We also
need to praise them for hard work and for taking risks. Practicing
'benign neglect'—standing back and letting our girls sort through
things rather than rushing in and fixing them—is extremely important. We have to let our children find their own paths."

### Examine your attitudes toward confrontation and conflict.

While research denies the existence of necessary and inevitable
"storm and stress" in adolescence, some amount of conflict in the
mother-daughter dyad—about small things and sometimes large
ones—is probably inevitable, not just in the years of adolescence
but even later in life. It's worth repeating that your own reactions to
conflict and argument will be a part of the dynamic. According to
Dr. Laurence Steinberg, while "mother-daughter relations are the
most effectively charged, characterized by high levels of both discord and closeness, and a high level of shared activities"—please
note the combination of "discord" *and* "closeness" for your files—
he goes on to say that "most parents and children who enter adolescence with a sturdy foundation of trust and a strong bond in all
likelihood negotiate the transition with relatively little cost (albeit
with some increase in daily hassling) and youngsters may actually
benefit from the interchange and dialogue that accompany disagreement." Mind you, this obviously does not mean escalating
fights, day and night. What Dr. Steinberg calls "low-level quarreling," "bickering," or "daily hassling" may, in fact, serve a developmental purpose during puberty.[17]

Some of us—raised in traditional households where expressing anger or "quarreling" was considered an unattractive trait in anyone, but especially in a female—may have trouble negotiating the degree to which disagreement between mother and daughter is not only normal but necessary. As one mother admitted, "Anger wasn't expressed in my household when I was growing up, and I am uncomfortable with it. My husband's anger is loud and frightening to me, even though they are just summer storms—over quickly and forgotten about by him. My anger doesn't get out of control—it gets turned inward and ends up as depression or self-criticism." We've already mentioned how "peacemaker" roles within families can sometimes lead to depression in girls and women—roles we may, following our own mothers' examples, take on without even being conscious of them. Other research has suggested that girls are, from a young age, socialized to learn that sadness is a more acceptable emotion than anger. (Obversely, boys are actually discouraged from displaying sadness.)

In the best of all possible worlds, a daughter's learning to find her voice wouldn't necessarily involve her raising it—but who among us lives in the best of all possible worlds? Similarly, a mother striving to make the boundaries clear to her daughter shouldn't have to find herself screaming from the rooftops. Again, keep in mind that some of this "daily hassling"—about her messy room, her sometimes inconsiderate behavior, the undeniably annoying "mouthy-ness" of her responses—is par for the course, and it is up to you not to over-react to it.

Remember that "authoritative parenting"—shown in study after study to be the style of parenting most beneficial to adolescent development—combines high levels of emotional warmth with clear expectations and boundaries and "tolerance of disagreement and the discord that may ensue." Disagreement and discord are different from rudeness or outright anger.

**Ask yourself: Is her success your success, her failure your failure?**

Our cultural mythologies of motherhood clearly equate how "well" our daughters turn out with how "well" we've parented; how and what our daughters achieve becomes, from this point of view, yet another one of life's report cards. Seeing motherhood in this way has a number of different consequences. In her book *Flux*, Peggy Orenstein, writing about women who combine motherhood with full-time careers, notes that "micromanaging their childrens' lives—retaining a sense of authority over packing lunches, choosing clothes, and coordinating activity schedules—is what makes them feel that they are Good Mothers"[18]—but how long can anyone micromanage? By the time your daughter reaches adolescence, being "micromanaged" will run counter to every impulse she has toward self-definition; on the other hand, the burnout factor on "micromanagement" is high and may encourage you to absent yourself from your daughter's life in important ways sooner than you should.

Seeing our children as "works in progress" testifying to our abilities as mothers is not only bad for us but bad for them. This is, of course, not to say that you shouldn't hire a math tutor if your daughter is struggling or sign her up for an enrichment program at the local Y or elsewhere. Certainly you should. It's *why* you do these things that deserves attention. In our effort to produce perfectly well-rounded and highly successful human beings—as if there were such a thing to begin with—we may overlook the very qualities that make our child truly outstanding in significant ways.

In *The Over-Scheduled Child*, Dr. Alvin Rosenfeld and Nicole Wise delineate what, in their words, "our how-to, can-do" culture encourages us to see as parents:

> While today's parents understand abilities to be part of our genetic endowment, we also firmly believe they reflect good parenting. We very definitely consider virtually every one of a child's deficiencies

to be something we need to work on. We rarely see "problems" as an opportunity for a child to strengthen his or her character. Increasingly, we are defining anything short of excellence as a "deficiency"—and treating them as though they must be some sort of diagnosable deficit disorder.[19]

Moreover, as Rosenfeld and Wise assert, from the child's point of view the cost of this type of parenting may be very high indeed since, "by urging our children to fulfill every iota of their potential, as viewed from where we stand, we parents end up devoting an inordinate amount of attention to all the things that are wrong with them. Despite mechanically repeating how terrific they are—after all, we know that praise builds their self-esteem—our behavior shows that we take for granted all those things that are right with them."[20]

This is not to say that we should not work to better educate our daughters or, given the parameters of time and finances, expose them to learning experiences of every variety. It is more a question of examining *why* we do what we do for our children. Educator Arlene Gibson makes a point of talking to the parents of the students at Spence School about what she calls "unconditional positive regard," which she regards as a "birthright, something you get just for being." She notes that "unconditional positive regard takes you through the good times and the bad. It's different from saying 'I love you' every time your child gets a good grade or making her feel as though she should be rewarded for every good thing. We need to love our children regardless of their failures or achievements."

In addition to adjusting our parenting skills, adolescence may also be a time when we need to adjust both our dreams for our children and our vision of them, as who they are comes more clearly into view. As one mother of a now twenty-year-old put it: "When my daughter was young, everything about her was exciting potential. I overlooked the characteristics I found disappointing because I was sure she would grow out of them. I had trouble accepting the fact that, as she grew up and became herself, there would be things about her I wouldn't entirely like. When she was in high school, it was hard for me to accept what I saw as the narrowing of potential in some areas and equally hard for me to remember to notice that there were also areas of potential that were expanding. Now that she's in college, I must trust her to make choices that are right for her own life. As a young adult, I could not understand why my parents could not see the wisdom of my life choices—and it never crossed my mind that those choices did not, in fact, express a whole lot of wisdom. Those choices I made seemed to be things I absolutely had to do. Unfortunately my parents gave up on me long before my choices began to make sense. So, when I deal with my own daughter, I try to remember to just be there and to be positive and supportive. I will only jump in if I see danger signs or opportunities that she cannot see. At the same time, I also have to accept that she may reject my suggestions. We will both be better off if I can wait out her twenties before I pass judgment on my child as an adult. She is a kind, decent and intelligent human, whose parents love her; she will reflect those things no matter what."

Seeing our daughters whole will yield, at times, a mixed bag of emotions. Remember that growth doesn't end in adolescence or even in young adulthood; it is a lifelong process. Keep in mind that your dreams for her are, finally, *yours*, not hers.

In nature, the chrysalis provides the protection and space the caterpillar needs to transform itself into a butterfly. The butterfly stays within the chrysalis until its adult wings are fully developed and, when it is ready, breaks free from the chrysalis's confines. So, too, our daughters will inevitably break free from the shelter our hopes, attention, and love have given them to test their own wings. Emerging from it will be their first true act of young adulthood.

## Nurture your daughter's "moral" intelligence and spirit.

In his book *The Moral Intelligence of Children*, Dr. Robert Coles makes an important distinction between "following the rules" and what he calls "moral intelligence":

> "Moral intelligence" isn't acquired only by memorization of rules and regulations, by dint of abstract classroom discussion or kitchen compliance. We grow morally as a consequence of learning how to be with others, how to behave in this world, a learning prompted by taking to heart what we have seen and heard. The child is a witness; the child is an ever-attentive witness of grown-up morality—or lack thereof; the child looks and looks for cues as to how one ought to behave, and finds them galore as we parents and teachers go about our lives, making choices, addressing people, showing in action our rock-bottom assumptions, desires, and values, and thereby telling those young observers much more than we may realize.[21]

Think about yourself as a "moral communicator" and the values you and your daughter's father display in daily life. What lessons does she learn about ethical behavior—both in word and deed?

In his book, Dr. Coles tells a wonderfully instructive story, which is worth retelling here because it contains so many lessons.[22] Elaine, a nine-year-old fifth-grader, is, from the outside at least, an extraordinary child—from a well-to-do and admired family, popular, ambitious, and high-achieving. Her ability in math distinguishes her as well—a fact which, you might imagine, heartens her teacher and does her proud. One day, though, another student—a boy, as it happens, who is not proficient in math—sees Elaine cheating from a crib sheet on a test. The crib sheet flutters to the floor, and the boy brings it to the teacher, who rebukes him. The boy does badly on the test and does nothing further, except to tell his parents. His parents decide he should let the matter drop.

Meanwhile, Elaine wages warfare on the boy—taunting and teasing him—and enjoying every moment of "her triumph." The teacher, too, appears to be cold to him—the more so because he has failed the test. The boy gets increasingly upset and, finally, with great reluctance, the mother decides to confront the teacher. As Coles tells it, in Elaine's defense, the teacher "summons up psychology" explaining the girl's behavior by reference to her beloved grandfather's being stricken by cancer and her mother's losing an important law case. The boy's parents back off, feeling, in Coles's words, "properly rebuked." Several days later, though, the boy catches Elaine cheating again, this time on a spelling test. He happens to be an ace speller and the unfairness of her cheating really bothers him. But afraid of angering the teacher, he says nothing until he gets home.

Dr. Coles is summoned in since everyone, including the school's principal, treats what is happening as "a psychological crisis." Coles hears about Elaine's family's "good standing," about the family's "medical and psychological crisis" and the girl's "academic achievement." The boy's "problem" is also discussed in psychological terms—he is described as "distressed" and "timid" in class, and, moreover, his work isn't up to "par." As it happens, though, other students come forward to testify to Elaine's cheating, which started at the beginning of the year, long before any familial crisis. Elaine herself has a ready answer for her accusers—the boy is "jealous" of her and the others are his "friends"—as do her parents. While they acknowledge that, occasionally, Elaine "exaggerated things" and "told white lies" they understand it because "she was very ambitious" and "she hated to lose—ever." Wisely, Dr. Coles comes to see this not as a psychological crisis but as a moral crossroads Elaine's parents did not confront. As Coles writes, "This evasive, protective talk, grounded in psychology, told me a lot. A *family's* moral life was really at stake here: a mother and a father had signaled to a child how she ought to behave, what she ought to accomplish."

Ask yourself how you would react to a similar set of circumstances. As it happens, the issues raised by Dr. Coles are not exactly theoretical. Consider, for a moment, what has been called an "epidemic" of plagiarism in America, facilitated by the Internet. Plagiarism is not new, of course, nor is cheating—but educators agree that both are on the rise. In a study of forty-five hundred ninth- through twelfth-grade students at twenty-five schools across the country, both public and private, Professor Don McCabe of Rutgers University discovered cheating to be widespread: Seventy-four percent of students reported serious cheating at least once or more on a serious test, while 72 percent admitted serious cheating on written work. Moreover, 97 percent admitted to engaging in a questionable activity—anything from copying someone's homework to copying a paper. Thirty percent reported repetitive serious cheating on tests and exams.[23]

Dr. McCabe discovered that the reasons students cheat are various: Some 32 percent say they didn't prepare; some 29 percent cheated to pass or to get a grade; and 12 percent said that they cheated because of the pressure on them to succeed. Often this pressure comes from parents or teachers who want to see their children or students get into a good college. According to Professor McCabe, while boys generally report more cheating than girls, at both the high school and college level, these differences are eroding and are, in any case, what he calls "modest." He notes, too, that, while "generally girls have a greater tendency to follow the rules and fear the consequences if caught, at least at the college level these tendencies may be falling victim to a growing sense among women that they may have to cheat in order to compete effectively with male students they observe cheating in class. This seems to be especially true in such historically male-dominated majors as business and engineering."

We asked Dr. McCabe what his findings suggested about parents and moral education, and his answer was, to say the least, sobering:

"It certainly appears that a large number of parents have neglected at least some aspects of moral education. The most important issue may not be what they say or don't say to their children, but rather the behaviors they model. Students responding to my surveys often talk about how trivial cheating is in school compared to what they see going on in adult society—in their homes, in politics, in society at large. In this environment, they don't understand what the big deal is over a little bit of cheating." When we asked him whether he thought the results reflected how young people view integrity or character, what he said was something every parent should keep in mind: "I think that young people feel that these are traits they'll worry about later in life—after they have achieved the successes to which they feel they are entitled. In short, for many of them, when it's 'get a good grade' or 'act with integrity,' integrity comes in second. But that probably paints a pessimistically unfair picture. There are also many students who truly worry about their own integrity and the lack of integrity they see among others. I think it's this group of students, which seems to have been slowly increasing over the last few years, that holds the best hope for change."[24]

College campuses—as the headlines attest—have faced similar and mounting problems with both cheating and plagiarism. As parents— regardless of where our daughters fit into the picture—we should all find these statistics an upsetting commentary on the goal of "success at any cost" that appears to have been set for a new generation. Talk to your daughter directly about issues pertaining to moral behavior— and discuss how our moral choices shape us as people. Separate the punishments for cheating and plagiarism from their other "real-life" consequences—such as feeling fraudulent and being dishonest about what you do and don't know. Pay attention to the behavior you model, and set standards for what constitutes personal integrity; initiate a dialogue about character and choices. For example, can a person who cheats in one area of life be relied upon to be honest in others? Is "success" achieved through morally dubious, if not dishonest, means still "success?" This discussion can, of course, dovetail with others—about effort and achievement, for example.

**Ask yourself what constitutes "being smart."**

While American parents tend to focus on and generally set store by standardized tests, there is no question that what constitutes intelligence includes more than just the skills those tests measure. In his brilliant and thought-provoking book, *Emotional Intelligence: Why it can matter more than IQ*—which should be one of those books that are required reading for every mother and father in the country—Daniel Goleman writes:

> One of psychology's open secrets is the relative inability of grades, IQ, or SAT scores, despite their popular mystique, to predict unerringly who will succeed in life. To be sure, there is a relationship between IQ and life circumstances for large groups as a whole; many people with low IQs end up in menial jobs, and those with high IQs tend to become well-paid—but by no means always.
>
> There are widespread exceptions to the rule that IQ predicts success— many (or more) exceptions than cases that fit the rule. At best, IQ contributes about 20 percent to the factors that determine life success, which leaves 80 percent to other forces. As one observers notes, "The vast majority of one's ultimate niche in society is determined by non-IQ factors, ranging from social class to luck."[25]

How can we explain why some people with a high IQ flounder while those of modest IQ do surprisingly well? The difference, Goleman argues, often lies in emotional intelligence, which includes self-control, zeal, and persistence, and the ability to motivate oneself. Goleman argues convincingly that "we leave the emotional education of our children to chance, with ever more disastrous results." And, there is another, important ramification, as we—as parents—continue to focus on grades as a measure of what our daughters are learning:

> . . . academic intelligence offers virtually no preparation for the tur-
> moil—or opportunity—life's vicissitudes bring. Yet even though a
> high IQ is no guarantee of prosperity, prestige, or happiness in life,
> our schools and our culture fixate on academic abilities, ignoring
> emotional intelligence, a set of traits—some might call it character—
> that also matter immensely for our personal destiny. Emotional life is
> a domain that, as surely as math or reading, can be handled with
> greater or lesser skill, and requires its unique set of competencies.[26]

As mothers, we must be sure that we aren't blindsided by the culture and that, in addition to nurturing the moral and spiritual aspects of our daughters' selves, we pay attention to how we—and our daughters' other "teachers"—nurture their emotional intelligence, as well as our own. It becomes clear that the degree to which we have developed our own emotional intelligence has a great deal to do with how we parent.

Looking at the "domains" that constitute "emotional intelligence" brings to mind many of the themes we've already touched upon in this book. The concept of emotional intelligence encourages us to address other, nonacademic aspects of our child's education which may, in the long run, be just as important to her future as anything else she has learned. Importantly, these are skills that can be taught and enhanced, which belies the idea of intelligence as a fixed trait. We offer them, in Goleman's terms, as another way of looking at what we need to pay attention to as we serve as our daughters' guides on the journey:[27]

**Knowing one's emotions.** This is self-awareness and is, according to Goleman, the "keystone" of emotional intelligence. Knowing what we feel when we feel it is a large part of self-understanding, and one of the tasks our children will take on in adolescence. As Goleman puts it, "People with greater certainty about their feelings are better pilots of their lives, having a greater sense of how they really feel about personal decisions from whom to marry to what job to take."

As mothers, we need to give our daughters room to express and identify their emotions. Being able to differentiate between thoughts and emotions that are responses to an immediate situation is an important life skill, particularly in adolescence. Encourage your daughter to think about the consequences of acting on impulse, on the one hand, and on examined thoughts on the other. As Goleman points out, being able to identify emotions frees our children to make better choices overall, but especially in those areas that, in adolescence, are subject to societal and peer pressure, such as drugs and sex.

*Mangaging emotions.* Given what science has taught us about girls' and women's propensity for "rumination," this is particularly important. In addition to helping your daughter focus on "identifying emotions," encourage her to "manage" them. Too often, by ignoring or denying emotions, girls internalize them. As a strategy, Goleman discusses "self-talk"—the ability to open up an inner dialogue that "reframes" a situation and opens up the various and possible ways of reacting to it. Thinking about a problem or a painful experience in different terms often permits us to cope with it more easily and to resolve it more fruitfully. Interestingly, drawing on research, Goleman suggests that disordered eating may be directly linked both to the inability to identify emotions and the inability to "manage" them. Seen from this point of view, disordered eating habits become a way of self-soothing, an unhealthy substitute for managing emotion.

Mother-daughter conversations about distinguishing the different feelings a situation may arouse in us are one way of teaching our girls about this aspect of emotional intelligence.

*Motivating oneself.* According to Goleman, an important part of self-motivation is emotional self-control. In his book, he recounts a fascinating study that sums up key aspects of motivation and control: "Just imagine that you are four years old, and someone makes the following proposal: If you'll wait until after he runs an errand, you can have two marshmallows as a treat. If you can't wait until then, you can have only one—but you can have it right now."[28] This test, performed by psychologist Walter Mischel, measured "the eternal battle between impulse and restraint, id and ego, desire and self-control, gratification and delay." Needless to say, the more impulsive four-year-olds grabbed one marshmallow immediately; others waited for the experimenter's return and got two. In followup studies done when these children were adolescents, Mischel found that the children who were able to wait for the experimenter to come back were "more socially competent; personally effective; self-assertive; and better able to cope with the frustrations of life. They were less likely to go to pieces, freeze, or regress under stress, or become rattled and disorganized when pressured; they embraced challenges and pursued them even in the face of difficulties . . ."[29]

In a society that tends to sing the praises of instant gratification, it's important that we encourage our girls to take the long view; we need to foster their understanding that certain goals will take time and effort to achieve. Once again, our attitudes toward "failure"—or, seen from another point of view, our insistence that the trajectory always be upward—will play an important role in how our daughters see their own success and failure. According to David Goleman, an important part of motivation is optimism or hopefulness. He cites a study done at the University of Kansas, which studied the responses of students hoping to achieve a grade of B in a course but who received a D on the first exam; the study found that students with high hopes were more motivated to set high goals for themselves and to work hard to reach that goal. In contrast, students with moderate hopes were less determined than their hope-filled peers; pessimistic students were simply demoralized.

Patience and staying the course are virtues we need to support in our daughters. Helping them understand that the occasional setback often marks the pathway to success is another.

*Recognizing emotions in others.* This is what we call "empathy." Encourage your daughter to break out of the self-referential shell that is sometimes part and parcel of adolescence. When a family fight breaks out—when she picks on her younger sibling, or begins to squabble with you, for example—use the opportunity to emphasize the importance of both resolving conflicts and recognizing what others are feeling and thinking. Talk to her about what it would be like to be on the receiving end of some of the things she's said; bolster her emotional intelligence by having her examine other possible solutions or responses to the problem at hand.

*Handling relationships.* Understanding this as a skill that can be learned and improved on is a tremendous asset not just in adolescence but in later life. What is life, after all, save a web of relationships—with family, friends and acquaintances, neighbors, coworkers and bosses? Using the skills of emotional intelligence—both those pertaining to the self and to others—yields an adolescent who is more confident in her ability to communicate, more able to say what she means, and more attuned to the communications of others. Honing these skills—becoming a better listener, understanding what the other person is really saying and why he or she is saying it—will not only bolster your daughter's ability to negotiate the cliques and crowds of adolescence but will help her manage both her friendships and romantic relationships with greater ease.

### Stay involved in her education.

We use the word "education" here in the broadest sense; buck the trend and don't abdicate your responsibility by assuming that others will do the work for you. *Do* inform yourself about the curriculum—even after middle school—and do make a point of finding out about your child's teachers, even during the high school years. Knowing what she is working on and learning opens up your role in her educational life—and broadens your role beyond that of "the person who looks at my grades." Try to define "education" as broadly as you might "success"—remember that there are many experiences that broaden the mind and the spirit. In *See Jane Win: The Rimm Report on How 1,000 Girls Became Successful Women*, the authors report that the "three most common reasons the women of our study chose for recommending their careers to others were that the careers were 'challenging,' 'makes a contribution,' and 'creative.' " Interestingly, "financially satisfying" was not chosen by a large number of women. The authors advise parents to "teach your daughter to value the three Cs"—challenge, contribution, and creativity. If they are afraid to try new experiences, problem-solve with them on how to be daring and courageous."[30]

We talked to Dr. Diana Chapman Walsh, President of Wellesley College and the mother of a daughter who is now in her late twenties. When we asked her how the experiences of girls today are different from those of their mothers, she told us, "The pressure on girls today is enormous. Not only do they expect more of themselves but more and more is expected of them at earlier and earlier ages. It's easy to forget that growing up is a developmental process and even at the age of eighteen, when they are ready to enter college, they are still actively growing and questioning, just beginning to frame the answers to the question 'What is meaningful in the world?' "

### Remember the spiritual self.

When you think about it, it isn't at all surprising that one of the most moving and inspiring books published in the twentieth century was one written by an adolescent girl in a time of terrible trouble—Anne Frank. Her room in the secret "annex"—now preserved as a museum—is, in important respects, not very different from those of adolescent girls everywhere. On the walls are still the pictures—cut out of magazines—of movie stars and other people the young Anne admired; like adolescent girls everywhere, she worried not just about the meaning of life but about her changing body, her periods, and whether she would ever find true love. Her father excised the details of her fractious relationship to her mother from the *Diary* when it was first published, apparently because he felt that since both his wife and daughter had perished, Anne's version of events should not be shared. As adolescent girls puzzle out who they are, they also—in one way or another—take on the questions of meaning in the universe. Many of them will discover faith, while others will lose it; some of them, in the process, will discover their true calling.

In her book *Kitchen Table Wisdom*, Rachel Naomi Remen, M.D., tells the story of how her childhood was animated by two seemingly separate worlds: that of her grandfather, an orthodox rabbi and reader of Jewish mystical texts who engaged her "in the search for what is Real," and the world of medicine, the world of her uncles and cousins who "were men of science, distant, cultured, intellectual, and successful." These worlds were connected but in opposition, since her father, uncles, and cousins—as she puts it—"rewarded me for having the right answers" while "my grandfather had rewarded me for having the right questions." While saying that indeed she wants to be a doctor, she dreams instead of becoming a rabbi. She writes that she chose medicine because of a novel she read when she was twelve, a historical novel about the life of Saint Luke called *The Road to Bithynia*. Her discussion of her epiphany captures the special way in which an adolescent suddenly understands the larger world:

> I had not known that Luke was a physician. *The Road to Bithynia* originally appealed to me because the Gospel According to Luke was my favorite part of the Christmas story. The book was written by a physician, Frank Slaughter, who told Luke's story with all the power and credulity of his own personal knowledge of the practice of medicine. I read the novel four times, stunned to find that all physicians were not like my uncles, that it might be possible to be a physician in a way that my grandfather would have understood. That being a physician could become a means to better know and serve life and the source of life.[31]

In fact, research confirms the importance of the spiritual self to the health and hardiness of adolescent girls. We interviewed Dr. Lisa Miller, Assistant Professor of Philosophy and Education at Teachers College, Columbia University, who has done extensive research into the effect of spirituality on adolescent girls, and she told us that, "what we've found is that one of the most protective factors against those forms of morbidity that are most prevalent among girls—such as depression—is a personal sense of spirituality and a personal sense of connection to the Divine. We've replicated the results in a number of studies and it's clear that, while personal spirituality is protective in all adolescents, it is more protective in girls than in boys against depression." This fact, she thinks, may explain part of the marked gender differences in rates of depression since "our culture is just beginning to grow and improve the cultivation of the spiritual life of adolescents. Certainly, there have been a lot of active and highly successful religious institutions but, equally, there are a lot of kids who aren't involved in religious institutions, and who have no language for, no sense of reality about spiritual life." The data suggests, she goes on to say, "that girls who have a unified sense of spirituality and the body, girls for whom all the hallmarks of feminine bodily maturation—sexuality, fecundity, the onset of menstruation—are bound up with their spiritual life are much more resilient against depression." It is, she says, "so damaging for girls to think that their physical maturation—the proof of their womanhood—is, in fact, separated from a pristine, spiritual life—or that their sexuality is divorced or separate from their spiritual life. In fact, they are closely bound together. Many of these 'epidemics'—such as depression—may well be healed when the split between the body and the soul is healed."[32]

Finally, Dr. Miller reminds us that "there is empirical evidence supporting what some spiritual teachers have said for some time: that adolescence is a window of spiritual awakening." As mothers, we need to balance all the cultural messages about the female body and beauty—and all the other messages connected to the surface of things—by encouraging our daughters to take stock and cultivate their inner selves or "souls." If your daughter is not involved with a specific religious institution or youth group, do encourage her to explore the various answers different faiths have offered to the question of what it means to be human—and how precisely that connects to the human vision of the Divine.

And do celebrate the spiritual aspect not only of your daughter's self but of your own. Focusing on the spiritual aspects of our selves yields a very different perspective on the questions posed by midlife.

### Appreciate the ways in which you and your daughter are different.

Sometimes, the very closeness of the mother-daughter dyad threatens to become less a life embrace than a stranglehold. The ways in which our daughters are different from us may sometimes cause tension or frustration. The go-getter, can-do mother bemoans her daughter's tendency to procrastinate, while another, always immaculately groomed, cringes at the sight of her daughter's uncombed hair and grubby tee shirts. Try to put the differences in perspective *before* you react to them. Are they really important to you?

Sometimes, our enormous emotional investment in our children makes it hard for us to see our daughters as they really are. The intensity with which we want them to be happy and successful may blind us to the fact that solutions we've arrived to meet life's challenges aren't the only ones out there. In their book *Friends for Life: Enriching the Bond Between Mothers and Their Adult Daughters*, Susan Jonas and Marilyn Nissenson summarize not just their experiences as mothers but those of the 113 women they interviewed by writing: "In our attempts to be intimate we sometimes assume that our feelings and thoughts are the same as our daughters' feelings and thoughts. It's the 'I understand exactly what you mean' syndrome. . . . As a mother you may have the best intentions in the world but if you have neglected to hear a daughter out, then any opinions or feelings you express have the potential to do harm."[33] Even though they are addressing the mother-daughter relationship in the years of young adulthood, the point is well taken.

### Remember the Persian carpet.

The image we used in "Troubled Waters"—that of the Oriental rug in which the weaver's mistakes are woven into the design as a reminder that nothing of this earth is truly "perfect"—is one we should all to try to hang on to. Is striving for "perfection" the lesson we want to teach our daughters? Or do we want, instead, to encourage them to see themselves as clearly as they can, and to accept both their strengths and their weaknesses with grace?

It's worth noting, in this context, that—as a society—we are not doing very much to model the latter. If our daughters learn to see the body as a "project" through media messages, then, equally, they learn it at home. According to the American Society of Plastic Surgeons, between 1992 and 2000 the number of cosmetic surgeries performed in the United States increased by 198 percent; in a single year, from 1999 to 2000, plastic surgeries increased 9 percent. More disturbingly, in 1998, more than twenty-four thousand plastic surgeries were performed on teenagers under the age of eighteen, representing 2 percent of all plastic surgeries; by the year 2000, the number had risen to sixty-five thousand representing 4 percent of the total. While the preponderance of these were nose reshapings, breast augmentation and liposuction together represented seven thousand cases. In the year 2000, more than 6 million cosmetic surgical and nonsurgical procedures were performed on American women.[34]

Because parental consent is required under the age of eighteen, we wondered about the parents of these sixty-five thousand adolescents, and turned to Dr. Loren Eskenazi, a plastic surgeon and a feminist, who told us that when she interviews girls under the age of eighteen, "I am trying to sort out the extent of the daughter's autonomy from the mother. What usually happens is they've already rehearsed what they are going to say—and usually one or the other is the primary speaker. But just because the daughter is doing the talking doesn't necessarily mean that she's autonomous. I've had mothers who have actually drawn on photographs to show exactly what they want, and mothers who have said nothing at all. For my part, I have to be attentive to a mother who is trying to 'fix' her daughter. Separating what each of them perceives as the 'need' for change is also critical. I need to know what level of discomfort the daughter has with the aspect of her body she wants to change. I need to know that her expectations are realistic. And I need to know that she wants this for herself—and that she has wanted to change this aspect of herself for at least a year or longer."[35]

Transformation always takes place inside first. Keep that in mind, and remind yourself and your daughter of the Persian carpet.

In *Gift from the Sea*—another necessity for every woman's bookshelf—Anne Morrow Lindbergh plumbs the connection between the passage into midlife with adolescence:

> For is it not possible that middle age can be looked upon as a period of second flowering, second growth, even a second kind of adolescence? It is true that society in general does not accept this interpretation of the second half of life. And therefore this period of expanding is often tragically misunderstood. The signs that presage growth, so similar, it seems to me, as those in early adolescence: discontent, restlessness, doubt, despair, longing, are interpreted falsely as signs of decay; one accepts them, quite rightly, as growing pains. One takes them seriously, listens to them, follows where they lead. One is afraid. Naturally. Who is not afraid of pure space—that breath-taking empty space of an open door? But despite fear, one goes to the room beyond.[36]

The "breath-taking empty space of an open door" captures perfectly the mixture of heady idealism, boundless energy, and deep uncertainty that characterizes adolescence for nearly everyone. In middle age, though, instead of seeing the "signs that presage growth" and that "pure space" for what they are, Lindbergh says, we do anything we can "rather than face them." If we could face them, she writes, we might see these signs of growth as "angels of annunciation," of "a new stage in living," when "one might be free for growth of mind, heart, and talent; free at last for spiritual growth. . . ."

The ways in which the two separate but connected journeys of mother and daughter reflect on each other yields another insight into how, as mothers, we can learn from the connection. Teaching our daughters about life permits us to focus on what our own journeys thus far have taught us—allowing us to look anew at the mountain that is life and to reflect on the purpose of the climb.

## CHAPTER SEVEN

# Sailing Toward the Future

In the last year, I've felt more trusting of Ashley's ability to manage her own life. I've seen her make big decisions for herself and see that she is quite mature and so I can relax a bit more. Of course, when she's driving, I still think she's going too fast or is too far off the road or too far in the middle. It's very hard to give up control. This trust in her decisions feels like respect for her as an individual, a young adult choosing her own life path. It also feels like more space between us—I'm more free to live my own life. What's surprising is how much she still needs me in an emotionally dependent kind of way. Ashley is in a very serious relationship with her best friend from high school. They've known each other since fifth grade. So another shift this year is that I accept part of my time with her is with the two of them. I happen to love this boy and think he's the greatest so that makes it easy. But this gives me a clue about her entering into a lifelong relationship/marriage and how that is a shift for us. So I envision that relationship (or perhaps another) being her primary one, rather than hers to me.

Rachel, fifty-two, psychologist, and mother to Ashley, age nineteen

LATE AT NIGHT, sitting alone in the kitchen, I try to imagine what Kate and Rachel will be like fifteen or even twenty years from now. I try to summon up images of the men they will decide to ally themselves with, the life choices they will make. Will Kate's deep love and interest in the animal world translate into a profession—as a veterinarian or a zoologist, perhaps—or will she discover other passions? Will her sketchbook, now always at the ready, be a fixture in her life? Or will her extraordinary imagination—captured now by science fiction and fantasy novels—be the starting place for other explorations? At thirteen, Rachel is ebullient, mercurial, and quick to voice her opinions; will she stay that way, or will experience temper and tone her down? Do I see her in the corporate boardroom or as a reporter, traveling the world? Or as a scientist? Will she find something about which she will feel truly passionate, or will she be content to live on the surface?

Of course, it's impossible to know. Both of my daughters are still on the threshold of self-discovery, a process that begins during the years of adolescence but continues on through most of a lifetime. Who they will be—in the most important sense—won't be settled for years to come. Sitting at my own kitchen table, I realize that my own mother, sitting at the kitchen table in our old house in Fort Wayne, Indiana, couldn't possibly have imagined all the things that did and didn't happen to me thus far in my life—which probably is just as well. I know that I, her eldest daughter, have been a source of both pride and bewilderment, and sometimes, when I am ready to embark on my latest venture, I hear her quite literally hold her breath—if just for a second. For the most part, my choices in life have not been her choices, to be sure; her passions and her commitments have always been different from my own. No one—including my mother—could have predicted either my successes or my failures from the vantage point of the old kitchen table—not when I was sixteen, twenty-six, or even, for that matter, thirty-six.

People are always either bemused or amazed when they learn that even now, as I am about to turn fifty, I still speak to my parents, Joy and Sandy, every day. I know most people think it's somehow out of character—I am, after all, an independent person who doesn't pay a whole lot of attention to what other people think. And I can tell, by the looks on their faces, my daily phone calls seem to hint that a part of me still isn't somehow "grown-up," "secure," or "independent" enough or that there are important character flaws that I've otherwise managed to hide from the world. In turn, I was amused when someone told me the story of a young woman, in her early twenties, whose New York therapist told her that "part of her problem" is that she still talks to her mother back home almost every night. She hasn't, in his view, "individuated" enough. What would he say about me, I wonder? Is this a problem I need to fix? I don't think so.

Our culture emphasizes the importance of independence—not just during adolescence but into adulthood. Over and over, we confuse "independence" with "separation" and "rebellion"—as if the model of the original thirteen states is all we have—but is that kind of "independence" really what we are after, either for ourselves or for our daughters? Isn't the much harder part combining independence with relatedness, holding on to the boundaries of self while forging meaningful connections? Doesn't true independence involve exposing the meaning of our choices by being able to engage in dialogue, even when there is disagreement? My parents' opinions, even when I don't agree with them, are always important to me; they help refine my thinking and my choices. When they do disagree with me, their objections help me keep the limitations and risks of my choices in mind. Their support—though hardly unqualified—has been an enormous help to me as I've managed the business of living and choosing. They have always let me go my own way even when they were totally sure that the way I had chosen wasn't the right one.

And there is a lesson I have learned from my parents, one that we each must face as the mothers of adolescent daughters: the art of letting go. This is not to be confused with leaving our daughters to their own devices or being content to let them be "a tribe apart" but something infinitely more subtle. Shepherding our daughters through adolescence requires that we give them love, support, safe haven, *and*, when the time is right, permission to leave us behind; it also requires that we give ourselves permission, in turn, to move on to another stage of life. Like everything else, learning to let go is a process, which we must learn during the course of the journey. Just as we once eased into letting our children crawl out of our sight for a brief moment and, later, steeled ourselves as they walked through the doors of the kindergarten classroom alone, so, too, the years of adolescence are a time when we practice letting them go out into the world to make their own choices, a single step at a time. With bated breath, we watch year by year, judging the competence of their stride until, finally, we are convinced they can do it on their own. And with a quick intake of breath, we watch them walk through a doorway of their own choosing.

How hard this is to do in real life is captured by an ancient myth, which reminds us that the dilemmas posed by the changing demands of motherhood—and the different stages of a woman's life—are as old as the human race. The ancient Greeks told the story of Demeter and her daughter, Kore or Persephone, in many variations and we offer you its simplest telling. Demeter, the earth-mother goddess of the grain, had one daughter, Persephone, whom she loved more than anything on the earth. Under her mother's watchful eye, the child grew more beautiful day by day, until she became a young woman. The girl's beauty did not go unnoticed and the god of the underworld, Pluto, fell in love her. He knew, though, that Demeter would never give her daughter up or permit her to marry. So one day, while Persephone was picking flowers with her friends, Pluto opened up the earth and snatched her. He took her to the underworld where he married her and made her his queen. Frantic, Demeter searched the earth for her daughter but no one would tell her where she was. The intensity of her grief caused the earth to dry up and wither, and all of humankind suffered. Finally, Zeus, chief among the gods, intervened and decreed that Perse-phone be returned to her mother, provided that she had eaten nothing in the underworld. But Persephone had been tempted by the sweet seeds of a pomegranate and so Zeus ruled that she would live half the year on earth with her mother and half the year with her husband, god of the underworld. Each year, when Persephone left her mother, the earth died off; with her return each spring, the world would flower.

On one level, this is a myth about the seasons but it is also a story about the "seasons" of a woman's life. Persephone or Kore (which means "maiden") is poised to become a woman, and to take her mother's place in the cycle. But Demeter (whose name contains the root for "mother," or "meter") can't let go of either her motherhood or her daughter, which sets the story in motion. The "loss" of her daughter—which is precisely what Demeter has tried to avoid—is finally sealed when Persephone chooses to taste the pomegranate, symbolizing the life choices each woman makes independent of her mother and that help determine her life path. The cycle of change in life, the myth tells us, is inexorable and can never be staved off. Stages of life are left; identities discarded and exchanged; the daughters of mothers become, in turn, mothers of daughters themselves. As our daughters emerge into womanhood, our womanhood is recast and redefined, a sea change that involves what author Judith Viorst has called a "necessary loss."

But on another level entirely, the myth reminds us that from this necessary loss comes the promise of new growth, new generations of women. Letting go changes the nature of the ultimate reunion of mother and daughter; they meet face to face as women, newly independent of each other but still connected, and their embrace confirms the life cycle. The myth tells us that the cycle of rebirth—of spring, of new and succeeding generations—can only take place when the mother acknowledges that the hard work of protecting and sheltering is done, and that she is finally able to let go. Each spring, the world bursts into flower when Demeter's daughter returns to her on a new and different footing.

It is a lesson we all need, in time, to learn.

## CHAPTER EIGHT

# Other Lessons: A Postscript

It's really a wonder that I haven't dropped all my ideals, because they seem so absurd and impossible to carry out. Yet I keep them, because in spite of everything I still believe that people are really good at heart. I simply can't build up my hopes on a foundation consisting of confusion, misery, and death.

—Anne Frank, *Anne Frank: The Diary of a Young Girl*

In the aftermath of September 11 and subsequent events, Americans have struggled to deal with what some have called the "new normal"—which, of course, isn't "normal" at all. No use of "normal"—which the dictionary defines as "conformity with an established norm"—can rationally include the reality of hijacked airplanes flying into skyscrapers and office complexes filled with people going about their ordinary lives, or envelopes dusted with life-threatening materials. The world in which our children are coming of age seems, to our eyes, radically changed and we wondered aloud what we needed to do to help them understand and cope with those changes.

In search of answers, we talked to Stephanie Brandt, M.D., a psychiatrist in New York City who is both a specialist in issues pertaining to adolescent girls and the mother of two adolescent daughters. Once again, she reminded us that adolescence is a "mentally flexible age," and that, without denying either the gravity of the situation or the depth and seriousness of people's reactions and symptoms, nonetheless "the tragedies have also heightened adolescents' awareness of important issues." She stressed that "moral development is a primary task of adolescence" and noted that "the situation has heightened the emotional and intellectual struggle surrounding moral dilemmas, raising many questions— from the situation of women in Afghanistan to the necessity or use of war and the death penalty to that of the responsibility of the individual to the community." These are, she notes, important questions for adolescents to face. She emphasizes that parents need to judge how ready their daughters are to listen and absorb; as she puts it, "Information is power as long as you don't overwhelm your children with information. Remember that adolescents are still children who need your protection. As a parent you have to know what your child is ready to hear, how capable she is of engaging in productive, helpful, abstract thinking."

Even in our own households, our daughters' responses were individual, reflecting not just their maturity but their personalities. On September 11, I was at the Denver airport, waiting to catch a plane to New York, which, once the country's commercial fleet was grounded, never left. Four days later, I ended up driving home to San Francisco. Of my two daughters, it was the older, fifteen-year-old Kate who was more affected, in part because she has visited New York with me many times and, indeed, a year ago, had flown alone from New York to California. She is also empathetic and introspective by nature and, not surprisingly, the horrific images and stories affected her profoundly. At just under thirteen, Rachel was buffered both by her age, by the distance that separated her from those events, and by the pace of life that went on normally, for children at least, in northern California. I, on the other hand, felt myself take a deep breath driving over the Golden Gate in those weeks and, when I was able to fly to New York, took an even deeper one as I took in the changed cityscape and the ways in which "normal" life had been altered.

Peg's daughter, Alexandra, lives across the Hudson River from New York City, which she visits almost every weekend. She has friends whose parents or relatives worked in or near the Twin Towers and, although all were safe, their stories were tremendously disquieting. Even though she suffered no personal loss, she felt terrific empathy and sadness for those who had; she wanted to visit the impromptu shrines that sprung up all over New York, and signed memorial books at firehouses and left mementos. She read some of the thousands of homemade sheets of paper—taped to walls, phone booths, and street lamps—describing the missing in words and photographs, asking for help and information. At thirteen-and-a-half, she has struggled actively with moral issues raised by the combination of humanitarian efforts and warfare.

It is too early for any one of us to know how life in all parts of America has changed and how we and our children have been affected. For many of our older adolescent children, September 11 will—emotionally, psychologically, and intellectually—represent a watershed moment in their lives as the assassination of President John F. Kennedy and other events did for some of their parents. For some of our adolescent daughters and sons, their ideas about the world, about safety and risk, about social responsibility, about bravery and cowardice—at the very moment that they are just beginning to formulate those thoughts—have been radically altered. As one mother of a fourteen-year-old son puts it, "Sam has always been a worrier, and the events since September 11 are affecting him deeply. This manifests itself as an increased interest in news and world events. He is baffled by the hostility toward America and Americans he has just recently discovered. Like many adults, he can't stop reading articles, frightening himself, then reading more. He asks a lot of questions, and is frustrated by my lack of answers. Although his increased interest in world events, and in reading and watching the news, seems to be a step along the road to maturity, his apparent belief that I have all the answers—including some prescient knowledge of what's going to happen in the end—reminds me that he is still a child in many ways." The mother of a ten-year-old girl reports that her daughter doesn't seem to be enormously affected, not on the surface at least. "But," she says quietly, "she did ask me why the people did it—and while I did my best to explain it, I felt I hadn't really answered her question, probably because I can't entirely answer it myself."

Karen Zager, Ph.D., coauthor with Alice Rubenstein, Ed.D., of *The Inside Story on Teen Girls* and a psychologist in private practice in New York, emphasizes the range of responses to the events. The largest group of girls, she tells us, are not deeply affected; the events have not disturbed their personal sphere or their functioning. There are also those who are affected on a philosophical level; these girls are "already socially conscious, have a heightened social awareness, and are those who, before September 11, did a range of volunteer work, such as feeding the homeless or working at the local animal shelter." While these girls are not personally devastated by the events, they may be very upset or concerned. "Nonetheless," Dr. Zager says, "these girls are okay because they have an outlet through the volunteer work that they do. They do not feel as helpless or powerless as other people do." The third group, though, is the most worrisome; these are the girls who, according to Dr. Zager, are already fragile, have underlying problems, and may come from dysfunctional families. They may be having a traumatic reaction—showing signs of extreme anxiety or depression, eating or sleeping too much or too little. If we see our daughters falling into this latter group, it is vital that we seek professional help.

Now it's more important than ever that all of us engage our daughters in meaningful dialogue as both domestic and world events unfold. Respecting the boundaries of "I-Thou" parenting—making sure that we manage our own fears and anxieties—is a task each of us must take on. Knowing our daughters by listening—by understanding where they find themselves emotionally, psychologically, and intellectually—takes on special meaning when we gauge the degree of forthrightness with which we discuss the issues at hand. As Dr.

Stephanie Brandt tells us, "How we talk is less related to age than it is to psychological development. At roughly age thirteen, girls lose the ability to see themselves as little people in a family and begin to see themselves as people in a larger community, in a larger world. Once that happens—and it doesn't happen all at once but in fits and starts—it's not helpful for parents to treat their daughters like ten-year-olds because they no longer can go back to seeing themselves or the world as they did as children. If you treat them like babies, they will stop talking to you. And when adolescents stop talking to you, they act out more—which is what we all worry about."

Times such as these test us as parents because the fear is, to some degree, realistic. Dr. Zager reminds us that, in one sense, what we need to do isn't altogether different from what we have done all along as mothers: "Parents have to walk a fine line . . . being reasonably cautious—doing those things that are within your power to do—without being carried away by fear, especially about those things we can't control. This isn't altogether different from what we do as our children grow up—allowing them first to go off to kindergarten and then, later, to go to parties where there might be drugs or alcohol or permitting them to get into a car with a teenaged driver." Parents can be positive and proactive, she counsels. "Inform yourself and discuss the politics and economics of the countries involved, and explore what has bred such hatred. You can also talk about bravery and heroism, and how communities have come together. Volunteer as a family or become more involved in spiritual activities you can do together."

There are important life lessons and strengths we and our children can garner from the events that now perplex and frighten us. As Anne Frank wrote, in a tiny room darkened by curtains amidst another maelstrom: "I can feel the suffering of millions and yet, if I look up into the heavens, I think it will all come right, that this cruelty too will end, and that peace and tranquillity will return again."

# ENDNOTES

## Chapter One

[1]Thomas Hine, *The Rise and Fall of the American Teenager* (New York: Avon Books, 1999), 8.

[2]Spending statistic taken from Teenage Research Unlimited, Inc.'s website at www.teenresearch.com.

[3]Harvard Eating Disorders Center, as cited in *The Body Wise Eating Disorders Information Packet for Middle School Personnel* (Washington, D.C.: Office of Women's Health/U.S. Department of Human Resources, 1999).

[4]Office of Women's Health at www.4woman.gov.

[5]Statistics on the prevalence of eating disorders vary from source to source, partly because physicians are not required to report eating disorders to any government or other agency. On its website, last updated in August of 1998, the American Academy of Child and Adolescent Psychiatry put the number as "high as 10 in 100." A survey done by the National Association of Anorexia Nervosa and Associated Disorders in 1990 showed that 11 percent of high school students (male and female) suffered from eating disorders; they noted, however, that the survey did not include children in early adolescence, so the percentage could be higher. The Harvard Eating Disorders Center has lower statistics for the incidence of anorexia and bulimia, but notes that "15% of young women have substantially disordered eating attitudes and behaviors." According to Anorexia Nervosa and Related Eating Disorders, Inc., more than half of teenaged girls are, or think they should be, on diets. They are trying to lose all or part of the 40 pounds normally gained between the ages of 8 and 14.

[6]Carnegie Council on Adolescent Development, *Great Transitions: Preparing Adolescents for a New Century* (New York: Carnegie Council on Adolescent Development, 1996), 27.

[7]Study conducted by the Kaiser Family Foundation and Children Now: *Talking with Kids about Tough Issues: A National Survey of Parents and Kids*

(Menlo Park, CA: Kaiser Family Foundation/Children Now, March 1, 1999).

[8]The National Center on Addiction and Substance Abuse at Columbia University (CASA), *The 1998 CASA National Survey of Teens, Teachers, and Principals*, 9. The National Center on Addiction and Substance Abuse at Columbia University (CASA), *Back to School: 1999 National Survey of American Attitudes on Substance Abuse, Teens and Their Parents*, 14.

[9]*The New York Times*, 3 July 2000, p. 1.

[10]National Center for Education Statistics, *Youth Indicators* (1996), 34.

[11]www.childstat.gov, Table POP5A.

[12]While father-headed single families have been increasing, the preponderance of children of divorced parents live with their mothers; 10 percent live with a single mother and a partner. Source: www.childstat.gov, Table POP5A.

[13]The National Marriage Project, "The State of Our Unions, 2000" (New Brunswick, New Jersey: The National Marriage Project, 2000), 32.

[14]This statistic varies from source to source. In the introduction to *Coping with Divorce, Single Parenting, and Remarriage* (Mahwah, NJ: Laurence Erlbaum Associates, 1999), editor E. Mavis Hetherington uses 1 in 10 for "at least two divorces of their residential parents" (p. viii).

[15]For one view on the long-term emotional effects of divorce on children, see Judith S. Wallerstein, Julia M. Lewis, and Sandra Blakeslee, *The Unexpected Legacy of Divorce: A 25 Year Landmark Study* (New York: Hyperion Books, 2000).

[16]Bureau of Labor Statistics, Washington, D.C., 1999 (on the website, www.bls.gov).

[17]Yupin Bae, Susan Choy, Claire Geddes, Jennifer Sable, and Thomas Snyder, *Trends in Educational Equity of Girls and Women NCES 2000-030*. U.S. Department of Education, National Center for Education Statistic (Washington, D.C.: U.S. Government Printing Office, 2000). Close to 70 percent of mothers in two-parent households and almost 60 percent of mothers in single-parent households were "highly" involved in school from grades K through 5. By grades 6 through 8, only 51 percent of mothers in two-family households were "highly" involved; among single mothers, it dropped to below 45 percent. Similarly, in *Great Transitions*, the Carnegie Council reports that the time American children spend with their parents has decreased significantly in the last few decades. They also cite a 1988 survey of eighth graders that found that 27 percent spent two or more hours alone after school. See also Jeffrey Capizzano, Kathryn Trout, and Gina Adams, *Childcare Patterns*

*of School-Age Children with Employed Mothers*, Occasional Paper no. 41 (Washington, D.C.: The Urban Institute, September 2000).

[18]Peggy Orenstein, *Flux: Women on Sex, Work, Love, Kids, and Life in a Half-Changed World.* (New York: Doubleday, 2000).

[19]Interview with Dr. Claudia Edwards.

[20]Beth A. Abramovitz, M. S., and Leann L. Birch, Ph.D., "Five-year-old girls' ideas about dieting are predicted by their mothers' dieting," *Journal of the American Dietetic Association* 100, no. 10 (October 2000).

[21]Association of American University Women, *Hostile Hallways: The AAUW Survey on Sexual Harassment in America's Schools* (Washington, D.C.: AAUW, 1993).

[22]Nicki Crick, Ph.D., and Maureen Bigbee, M.S., M.S.W., "Relational and Overt Forms of Peer Victimization," *Journal of Consulting and Clinical Psychology*, 66, no. 2.

[23]Kaiser Family Foundation and *YM* magazine, *National Survey of Teens: Teens Talk about Dating, Intimacy, and their Sexual Experiences* (Menlo Park, CA.: Kaiser Family Foundation/*YM* magazine, 1998), 9.

[24]Judith Viorst, *Necessary Losses* (New York: Fireside Books, 1986).

## Chapter Two

[1]Barton Schmitt, M.D., cited on the Child's Hospital of Iowa website: (Children's Virtual Hospital) http://www.vh.org/Patients/IHB/Peds/Psych/Rebellion.html

[2]*COSMO Girl!*, August 2000, 162.

[3]*YM* magazine, May 2000, p.36.

[4]*Girls' Life*, April/May 1999, 52.

[5]Patricia Hersh, *A Tribe Apart: A Journey into the Heart of American Adolescence* (New York: Ballantine Books, 1998), 22.

[6]Jeffrey Capizzano, Kathryn Trout, and Gina Adams, *Childcare Patterns of School-Age Children with Employed Mothers*, Occasional Paper no. 41 (Washington, D.C.: The Urban Institute, September 2000), and telephone interview with Jeffrey Capizzano.

[7]National Research Council and Institute of Medicine, Board on Children, Youth, and Families Forum on Adolescence, "Risks and Opportunities: Synthesis of Studies on Adolescence," ed. Michele D. Kipke (Washington, D.C.: National Academy Press, 1999), 11.

[8]The Council of Economic Advisors, *Teens and Their Parents in the 21st Century* (Washington, D.C: May, 2000), 18–23.

[9] Mary Pipher, *Reviving Ophelia: Saving the Selves of Adolescent Girls* (New York: Ballantine Books, 1994), 103.

[10] Hope Edelman, *Motherless Daughters: The Legacy of Loss* (New York: Dell Publishing, 1994), xxvii.

[11] William S. Pollack, *Real Boys: Rescuing Our Sons from the Myths of Boyhood* (New York: Henry Holt, 1999).

[12] Carol Gilligan, *In a Different Voice: Psychological Theory and Women's Development* (Cambridge, MA: Harvard University Press, 1982).

[13] Lyn Mikel Brown and Carol Gilligan, *Meeting at the Crossroads: Women's Psychology and Girls' Development* (New York: Ballantine Books, 1993), 217.

[14] Peggy Orenstein, *SchoolGirls: Young Women, Self-Esteem, and the Confidence Gap* (New York: Anchor Books, 1994), 69.

[15] Terri Apter, *Altered Loves: Mothers and Daughters During Adolescence* (New York: Ballantine Books, 1991), 72.

[16] Interview with Dr. Mary Eberly. See also Mary B. Eberly, Raymond Montemmayor, and Daniel Flannery, "Variation in Adolescent Helpfulness in a Family Context," *Journal of Early Adolescence*, 13, no. 3 (August 1993), 228–45. Mary B. Eberly and Raymond Montemayor, "Adolescent Affection and Helpfulness Toward Parents: A Two-Year Follow-up," *Journal of Early Adolescence* 19, no. 2 (May 1999), 226–48. Mary B. Eberly and Raymond Montemayor, "Doing Good Deeds: An Examination of Adolescent Prosocial Behavior in the Context of Parent-Adolescent Relationships," *Journal of Adolescent Research* 13, no. 4 (October 1998): 403–32.

[17] Joseph P. Allen, Kathleen Boykin McElhaney, and Kathy L. Bell, "Autonomy in Discussions vs. Autonomy in Decision-making as Predictors of Developing Close Friendship Competence," paper presented at the Biennial Meetings of the Society for Research on Adolescence, March 21, 2000, Chicago, Illinois.

[18] Dr. Robin Tepper, "Parental Regulation and Adolescent Discretionary Time-Use Decisions: Findings from the NLSY97," in *Social Awakenings: Adolescents' Behavior as Adulthood Approaches*, ed. R. T. Michael (New York: Russell Sage Foundation, 2001), 83.

[19] National Research Council and Institute of Medicine, Board on Children, Youth, and Families Forum on Adolescence, "Risks and Opportunities: Synthesis of Studies on Adolescence," ed. Michele D. Kipke (Washington, D.C.: National Academy Press, 1999), 15.

[20] *The New York Times*, 3 October 2000, p. 1.

[21] Rick S. Zimmerman, Ph.D., and Katherine A. Atwood, M.Sc.D. "Predictors of first sexual intercourse in the 9th through 12th grade: How do

they change over time?" Unpublished paper presented at the 128th Annual Meeting of the American Public Health Association in November 2000.

[22]Interview with Lisa Diamond, Ph.D.

[23]Interview with Peter Scales, Ph.D.

[24]Deborah Turgelun-Todd, Ph.D., *Clinical Psychiatry News* 5, no. 28 (2000): 41.

[25]Laura Duberstein Lindberg, Scott Boggess, Laura Porter and Sean Williams, *Teen Risk-Taking: A Statistical Portrait* (Washington, D.C.: The Urban Institute, 2000).

[26]Interview conducted with Peter Scales, Ph.D.

[27]Lynn Ponton, *The Romance of Risk: Why Teenagers Do the Things They Do* (New York: Basic Books, 1997), 273.

[28]Interview with Peter Scales, Ph.D.

[29]Interview with Peggy Orenstein.

[30]Henry J. Kaiser Family Foundation, *Kids and Media at the New Millennium* (Menlo Park, CA, 1999), 5.

[31]Henry J. Kaiser Family Foundation, *Kids and Media at the New Millennium* (Menlo Park, CA, 1999).

[32]The UCLA Internet Report, *Surveying the Digital Future* (Los Angeles: UCLA Center for Communication Policies, 2000).

[33]Interview with Dr. Ilene Berson.

[34]Dale Kinkel, Kirstie Cope, Wendy Jo Maynard Farinola, Erica Biely, Emma Rollin, and Edward Donnerstien, *Sex on TV: Content and Context*, University of California, Santa Barbara, Henry J. Kaiser Family Foundation, February 1999. It's worth noting that only 4 percent of shows involving sexual content incorpoated any message about the risks or responsibilities pertaining to sexual behavior.

[35]Cited in *Teens, Sex, and the Media: 200 Issue Briefs* (Studio City, CA: Mediacope Press).

[36]The Alan Guttmacher Institute, "Facts in Brief: Teen Sex and Pregnancy," September 1999.

[37]Nathalie Bartle, Ed.D., with Susan Lieberman, Ph.D. *Venus in Blue Jeans: Why Mothers and Daughters Need to Talk About Sex* (Boston and New York: Houghton Mifflin Company, 1998), 82.

[38]The Kaiser Family Foundation, MTV, and *Teen People. What Teens Know and Don't (But Should) About Sexually Transmitted Diseases* (Menlo Park, CA, March 1999).

[39]Alan Guttmacher Institute, "Facts in Brief: Teen Sex and Pregnancy," September 1999 (www.agi-usa.org).

[40]American Academy of Pediatrics, "Policy Statement," *Pediatrics* 104, no. 4 (October 1999).

[41]Paul M. Thompson, Jay N. Gledd, Roger Woods et al., "Growth Patterns in Developing Brain Detected by Doing Continuum Mechanical Tensor Maps," *Nature* 404 (March 9, 2000).

[42]Apter, *Altered Loves*, 75.

[43]Martin Buber, *I and Thou*. Translated by Walter Kaufmann (New York: Touchstone, 1996), 62 ff.

## Chapter Three

[1]Gail B. Slap, M.D., and Martha M. Jablow, *Teenage Health Care: The First Comprehensive Family Guide for the Preteen to Young Adult Years* (New York: Pocket Books, 1994), 21.

[2]Slap and Jablow, *Teenage Health Care*, 21.

[3]Marcia E. Herman-Giddens, Eric J. Slora, Richard C. Wasserman, Carlos J. Bourdony, Manju V. Bhapkar, Gary G. Koch, and Cynthia M. Hasemeir, "Secondary Sexual Characteristics and Menses in Young Girls Seen in Office Practice," *Pediatrics*, no. 4 (April 1997): 505–12.

[4]Herman-Giddens et al., "Secondary Sexual Characteristics and Menses in Young Girls Seen in Office Practice," 505–12. Paul B. Kaplowitz, M.D., Sharon E. Oberfield, M.D., and the Drug and Therapeutics and Executive Committees of the Lawson Wilkins Pediatric Endocrine Society, "Reexamination of the Age Limit for Defining When Puberty is Precocious in the United States: Implications for Evaluation and Treatment," *Pediatrics*, 104, no. 4 (October 1999): 936–41.

[5]For a popular summary, see Lisa Belkin, "The Making of an Eight-Year-Old Woman," *The New York Times Magazine*, December 24, 2000, 38–43.

[6]Early onset of puberty has been connected with both behavioral disorders and depression; see Jeanne Brooks-Gunn and Edward O. Reiter, "The Role of Pubertal Processes," in *At the Threshold: The Developing Adolescent*, S. Shirley Feldman and Glenn R. Elliott, eds. (Cambridge, MA: Harvard University Press, 1990), 40–42. Also see J. Graber, P. M. Lewisohn, J. R. Seeley, and J. Brooks-Gunn, "Is Psychopathology Associated with the Timing of Pubertal Development?" *Journal of the American Academy of Child and Adolescent Psychiatry*, 36 (1997): 1768–76.

[7]Beth A. Abramowitz, M.S., and Leann Birch, Ph.D., "Five-year-old Girls' Ideas about Dieting Are Predicted by their Mothers' Dieting," *Journal of the American Dietetic Association*, 100, no. 10 (October 2000).

[8]Nancy E. Sherwood, Ph.D., and Dianne Neumark-Sztainer, Ph.D., P.Ph., RD, "Internalization of the Sociocultural Ideal: Weight-related Attitudes and Dieting Behaviors among Young Adolescents," *American Journal of Health Promotion* 15, no. 4 (2001): 228–31. In this study of Girl Scouts, with the mean age just over 10, 29 percent reported dieting to lose weight—a disturbing percentage since the Girl Scouts actively promote self-esteem. Another study of the Girl Scouts showed that lasting changes to modifying body image attitudes and dieting behaviors through a program was difficult: Dianne Newmark-Sztainer, Ph.D., MPH, RD, Nancy E. Sherwood, Ph.D., Tanya Coller, MPH, RD, and Peter J. Hannan, M. Stat., "Primary Prevention of Disordered Eating Among Preadolescent Girls: Feasibility and Short-Term Effect of a Community-Based Intervention," *Journal of the American Dietetic Association*, 100, no. 12 (December 2000): 1466–73.

[9]Naomi Wolf, *The Beauty Myth: How Images of Beauty Are Used Against Women* (New York: Anchor Books, 1991), 157.

[10]Michael Cohen, Ph.D., Jennifer Scott, Ph.D., Pat Tobin, Connie Kim, and Sara Giciardo, *Girls Speak Out: Teens Before their Time* (New York: The Girl Scout Research Institute, 2000), 30.

[11]*The New York Times*, 2 April 2001, C1–C6.

[12]Joan Jacobs Brumberg, *The Body Project: An Intimate History of American Girls* (New York: Vintage Books, 1995), xviii.

[13]Brumberg, *The Body Project*, 212.

[14]Jacqueline E. Darroch, David Landry, and Susheela Singh, "Changing Emphases in Sexuality Education in U.S. Public Secondary Schools, 1988–1999," *Family Planning Perspectives* 32, no. 5 (September/October 2000): 205–211.

[15]Barbara Zax, Ph.D., and Stephan Poulter, Ph.D., *Mending the Broken Bough: Restoring the Promise of the Mother-Daughter Relationship* (New York: Berkeley Books, 1998), 2–3.

[16]Ann Crittenden, *The Price of Motherhood: Why the Most Important Job in the World Is Still the Least Valued* (New York: Henry Holt and Company, 2001).

[17]Robert Coles, *The Moral Intelligence of Children: How to Raise a Moral Child* (New York: Plume Books, 1998), 7.

[18]Elizabeth Debold et al., "Cultivating Hardiness Zones for Adolescent Girls: A Reconceptualization of Resilience in Relationships with Caring Adults," in *Beyond Appearance*, edited by Norine G. Johnson, Michael C. Roberts, and Judith Worell (Washington, D.C.: American Psychological Association, 1999), 191.

[19]Leslie A. Gavin and Wyndol Furman, "Adolescent Girls' Relationships with Mothers and Best Friends," *Child Development* (1996): 381.

[20]Gavin and Furman, 385.

[21]Gavin and Furman, 385.

[22]For a summary of the research see Elizabeth Debold et al., "Cultivating Hardiness Zones for Adolescent Girls: A Reconceptualization of Resilience in Relationships with Caring Adults," in *Beyond Appearance: A New Look at Adolescent Girls*, Norine G. Johnson, Michael C. Roberts, and Judith Worell, eds. (Washington, D.C.: American Psychological Association, 1999), 192.

[23]Interview with Dr. Jacquelynne Eccles.

[24]Laurence Steinberg, "Autonomy, Conflict, and Harmony," in *At the Threshold: The Developing Adolescent*, S. Shirley Feldman and Glenn R. Elliott, eds. (Cambridge, MA: Harvard University Press, 1990), 273.

[25]Kathleen M. Brown, Ph.D., Robert P. McMahon, Ph.D., Frank M. Biro, M.D., Patricia Crawford, D.Ph., R.D., George B. Schreiber, D.Sc., Shari L. Similo, M.S., Myron Waclawiw, Ph.D., and Ruth Striegel-More, Ph.D., "Changes in Self-esteem in Black and White Girls Between the Ages of 9 and 14 years: The NHLBI Growth and Health Study," *Journal of Adolescent Health* 23 (1998): 7–19.

[26]Jacquelynne Eccles, Bonnie Barber, Deborah Jozefowicz, et al., "Self-Evaluations of Competence, Task Values, and Self Esteem," in *Beyond Appearance: A New Look at Adolescent Girls*. Norine G. Johnson, Michael C. Roberts, and Judith Worell, eds. (Washington, D.C.: American Psychological Association, 1999), 74.

[27]Jacquelynne Eccles, et al., 59.

[28]Spencer, S., and Steele, C.M., "Under Suspicion of Inability: Stereotype Vulnerability and Women's Math Performance," in *Beyond Appearance: A New Look at Adolescent Girls*, Norine G. Johnson, Michael C. Roberts, and Judith Worell, eds. (Washington, D.C.: American Psychological Association, 1999), 61.

[29]Eccles, et al., 60, citing various studies.

[30]Eccles, et al., 56, citing various studies.

[31]Valanne L. Hendersen and Carol S. Dweck, "Motivation and Achievement," in *At the Threshold: The Developing Adolescent*, S. Shirley Feldman and Glenn R. Elliott, eds. (Cambridge, MA: Harvard University Press, 1990), 321–322.

[32]Eccles, et al., "Self Evaluations of Competence, Task Values, and Self-Esteem," in *Beyond Appearance*, 60.

[33] Susan Nolen-Hoeksma and Joan S. Girgus, "Worried Girls: Rumination and the Transition to Adolescence" (paper presented at the 106th Annual Convention of the American Psychological Association, San Francisco, August 1998). Susan Nolen-Hoeksma and Girgus, J. S., "The Emergence of Gender Difference in Depression During Adolescence," *Psychological Bulletin* 115 (1994): 424–43.

[34] Jacquelynne Eccles, Bonnie Barber, Deborah Jozefowicz, Oksana Melnchuk, and Mina Vida, "Self-Evaluations of Competence, Task Values, and Self-Esteem," in *Beyond Appearance: A New Look at Adolescent Girls*, Norine G. Johnson, Michael C. Roberts, and Judith Worell, eds. (Washington, D.C.: American Psychological Association, 1999), 77.

[35] Annie Dillard, *An American Childhood* (New York: Harper & Row, Publishers, 1988), 35.

[36] A. Rae Simpson, Ph.D., *Raising Teens: A Synthesis of Research and a Foundation for Action* (Boston: Center for Health Communications, Harvard School of Public Health, 2001), 6.

[37] Christine Winquist Nord, DeeAnn Brinhall, and Jerry West, "Fathers' Involvement in Their Children's Schools" (NCES 98-091) (Washington, D.C.: U.S. Department of Education, National Center for Education Statistics, 1997), 7.

[38] Schonert-Reichl, K. and Mullen, J., "Correlates of Help-Seeking in Adolescence," *Journal of Youth and Adolescence* 25 (1996): 705–31.

[39] Terri Apter, *Altered Loves: Mothers and Daughters During Adolescence* (New York: Ballantine Books, 1991), 81–87.

[40] Elizabeth Debold, Lyn Mickel Brown, Susan Weseen, and Geraldine Kearse Brookins, "Cultivating Hardiness Zones for Adolescent Girls: A reconceptualization of resilience in relationships with caring adults," in *Beyond Appearance: A New Look at Adolescent Girls*, Norine G. Johnson, Michael C. Roberts, and Judith Worell, eds. (Washington, D.C.: American Psychological Association, 1999), 195.

## Chapter Four

[1] Susan Harter, "Self and Identity Development," in *At the Threshold: The Developing Adolescent*, S. Shirley Feldman and Glenn R. Elliott, eds. (Cambridge, MA: Harvard University Press, 1990), 353.

[2] Jacquelynne S. Eccles, "When School is Out," in *The Future of Children* 9, no. 2 (Los Altos, CA: The David and Lucile Packard Foundation, Fall

1999). See also Doris R. Entwisle, "Schools and the Adolescent, in *At the Threshold*, 197–224.

[3]Interview with Dr. Peter Scales.

[4]Terri Apter, *The Myth of Maturity: What Teenagers Need from Parents to Become Adults* (New York and London: W. W. Norton and Company, 2001).

[5]Apter, *The Myth of Maturity*, 22.

[6]See A. Rae Simpson, *Raising Teens: A Synthesis of Research and a Foundation for Action* (Boston: Center for Health Communications, Harvard School of Public Health, 2001), and Robert William Blum et al., *Reducing the Risk*.

[7]Todd E. Feinberg, *Altered Egos: How the Brain Creates the Self* (Oxford and New York: Oxford University Press, 2001), 30–31.

[8]Feinberg, *Altered Egos*, 31.

[9]Feinberg, *Altered Egos*, 31.

[10]Feinberg, *Altered Egos*, 31.

[11]Feinberg, *Altered Egos*, 31.

[12]Susan Harter, "Self and Identity Development," in *At the Threshold: The Developing Adolescent*, S. Shirley Feldman and Glenn R. Elliott, eds. (Cambridge, MA: Harvard University Press, 1990), 357.

[13]Tonja R. Nansel, Ph.D., Mary Overpeck, Dr.PH, Ramni S. Pilla, Ph.D., June Ruan, M.A., Bruce Simons-Morton, Ed.D., MPH, and Peter Scheidt, MD, MPH, "Bullying Behaviors Among U.S. Youth: Prevalence and Association with Psychosocial Adjustment," *Journal of the American Medical Association* 285, no. 16 (April 25, 2001): 2094–2100.

[14]B. Bradford Brown, "Peer Groups and Peer Cultures," in *At the Threshold: The Developing Adolescent*, S. Shirley Feldman and Glenn R. Elliott, eds. (Cambridge, MA: Harvard University Press, 1990), 177.

[15]Brown, "Peer Groups and Peer Cultures," 185.

[16]Ritch C. Savin-Williams and Thomas J. Berendt, "Friendship and Peer Relations," in *At the Threshold: The Developing Adolescent*, S. Shirley Feldman and Glenn R. Elliott, eds. (Cambridge, MA: Harvard University Press, 1990), 277.

[17]Lyn Mikel Brown, Niobe Way, and Julia L. Duff, "The Others in My I: Adolescent Girls' Friendships and Peer Relations," in *Beyond Appearance: A New Look at Adolescent Girls*, Norine G. Johnson, Michael C. Roberts, and Judith Worell, eds. (Washington, D.C.: American Psychological Association, 1999), 216.

[18]Savin-Williams and Berndt, "Friendship and Peer Relations," in *At the*

*Threshold: The Developing Adolescent*, S. Shirley Feldman and Glenn R. Elliott, eds. (Cambridge, MA: Harvard University Press, 1990), 296–97.

[19]Brown, "Peer Groups and Peer Cultures," 174.

[20]Savin-Williams and Berndt, "Friendship and Peer Relations," 307.

[21]Elizabeth Debold, Marie Wilson, and Idelasse Malave, *Mother-Daughter Revolution: From Good Girls to Great Women* (New York: Bantam Books, 1994), 231–2.

[22]Laurence Steinberg with Wendy Steinberg, *Crossing Paths: How Your Child's Adolescence Triggers Your Own Crisis* (New York: Simon & Schuster, 1994), 67.

[23]Patricia A. Adler and Peter Adler, *Peer Power: Preadolescent Culture and Identity* (New Brunswick, New Jersey, and London: Rutgers University Press, 1998), 209.

[24]Reed W. Larson, Gerald L. Clore, and Gretchen A. Wood, "The Emotions of Romantic Relationships," in *The Development of Romantic Relationships in Adolescence*, Wyndol Furman, B. Bradford Brown, and Candace Fiering, eds. (Cambridge, MA: Cambridge University Press, 1999), 25.

[25]Deborah Tollman, "Feminity as a Barrier to Positive Sexual Health for Adolescent Girls," *Journal of the American Medical Women's Association*, 54 (1999): 133–8.

[26]Carol Lynn Martin and Richard A. Fabes, "The Stability and Consequences of Young Children's Same-Sex Peer Interactions," *Developmental Psychology* 37, no. 3 (2001): 431–46.

[27]Adler and Adler, *Peer Power*, 550.

[28]Herant Katchadourian, "Sexuality," in *At the Threshold: The Developing Adolescent*, S. Shirley Feldman and Glenn R. Elliott, eds. (Cambridge, MA: Harvard University Press, 1990), 347.

[29]Sharon Thompson, *Going All the Way: Teenage Girls' Tales of Sex, Romance, and Pregnancy* (New York: Hill and Wang, 1995), 5.

[30]Lynn Ponton, *The Sex Lives of Teenagers: Revealing the Secret World of Adolescent Boys and Girls* (New York: Dutton, 2000), 25.

[31]Peggy Orenstein, *Schoolgirls: Young Women, Self-Esteem, and the Confidence Gap* (New York: Anchor Books, 1995), 56.

[32]Tollman, "Feminity as a Barrier to Positive Sexual Health for Adolescent Girls," 133.

[33]Adler and Adler, *Peer Power*, 179–80.

[34]William Pollack, *Real Boys: Rescuing Our Sons from the Myths of Boyhood* (New York: Henry Holt and Company, 1999), 150.

[35]Pollack, *Real Boys*, 150.

[36]Thompson, *Going All the Way*, 42.

[37]Terri Apter, *Altered Loves: Mothers and Daughters During Adolescence* (New York: Ballantine Books, 1990), 157.

[38]Herant Katchadourian, "Sexuality," in *At the Threshold*, 333.

[39]R. W. Larson, G. L. Clore, and G. A. Wood, "The Emotions of Romantic Relationships, in *The Development of Romantic Relationships in Adolescence*, 25.

[40]Willard W. Hartrup, "Foreword" in *The Development of Romantic Relationships in Adolescence*, xv.

[41]R. W. Larson, G. L. Clore, and G. A. Wood, "The Emotions of Romantic Relationships," in the *Development of Romantic Relationships in Adolescence*, 30.

[42]B. Bradford Brown, Candice Fiering, and Wyndol Furman, "Missing the Love Boat," in *The Development of Romantic Relationships in Adolescence*, 9.

[43]R. W. Larson, G. L. Glore, and G. A. Wood, "The Emotions of Romantic Relationships," in *The Development of Romantic Relationships in Adolescence*, 39.

[44]The following observations are drawn from B. Bradford Brown, "You're Going Out with Who?" pp. 291–329 in *The Development of Romantic Relationships in Adolescence*.

[45]Brown, "You're Going Out with Who?" 311.

[46]Brown, "You're Going Out with Who?" 312.

[47]Brown, "You're Going Out with Who?" 297.

[48]Brown, "You're Going Out with Who?" 316–17.

[49]Brown, "You're Going Out with Who?" 321.

[50]Mary Pipher, *Reviving Ophelia: Saving the Selves of Adolescent Girls* (New York: Ballantine Books, 1996), 254–55.

[51]Douglas Kirby, Ph.D., *Emerging Answers: Research Findings on Programs to Reduce Teen Pregnancy* (Washington, D.C.: National Campaign to Prevent Teen Pregnancy, 2001), 8. Available online at www. teen pregnancy. org.

[52]Debra W. Haffner, M.P.H., "What's Wrong with Abstinence-Only Sexuality Education Programs?" SIECUS Report Articles 25, no. 4 (http//:www.siecus.org/policy.Sreoirr/srep0003.html).

[53]Lisa Remez, "Oral Sex Among Adolescents: Is It Sex or Is It Abstinence?" *Family Planning Perspectives* 32, no. 6, (November/December, 2000): 300.

[54]Lynn Ponton, *The Sex Lives of Teenagers: Revealing the Secret World of Adolescent Boys and Girls* (New York: Dutton, 2000), 261.

[55]Interview with Dr. Pepper Schwartz.

[56]Phyllis Moen, Mary Ann Erikson, and Donna Dempster McClain, "Their Mother's Daughters? The Intergeneration Transmission of Gender Attitudes in a World of Changing Roles," *Journal of Marriage and the Family* 59 (May 1997): 291.

[57]Jay G. Silverman, Ph.D., Anita Raj, Ph.D., Lorelei A. Mucci, Ph.D., and Jeanne E. Hathaway, M.D., MOH, "Dating Violence against Adolescent Girls and Associated Substance Use, Unhealthy Weight Control, Sexual Risk Behavior, Pregnancy, and Suicidality," *Journal of the American Medical Association* 286, no. 5, (August 1, 2000): 574.

[58]Centers for Disease Control facts on dating violence: (www.cdc.gov/ncipc/factsheets/datviol.html).

[59]Ann F. Caron, *Don't Stop Loving Me: A Reassuring Guide for Mothers of Adolescent Daughters* (New York: Harper Perennial, 1991), 63.

[60]Peter L. Benson, Anu R. Sharma, and Eugene C. Roehllkepartain, *Growing Up Adopted: A Portrait of Adolescents and their Families* (Minneapolis, MN: The Search Institute, 1994).

[61]Benson et al., *Growing Up Adopted*, 62.

[62]Caitlin Ryan and Donna Futterman, *Lesbian and Gay Youth: Care and Counseling* (New York: Columbia University Press, 1998), 4.

[63]Ryan and Futterman, *Lesbian and Gay Youth*, 10.

[64]Ryan and Futterman, *Lesbian and Gay Youth*, 16.

[65]Ryan and Futterman, *Lesbian and Gay Youth*, 16.

[66]Ritch C. Savin-Williams, *Mom, Dad. I'm Gay: How Families Negotiate Coming Out* (Washington, D.C.: American Psychological Association, 2001).

[67]Savin-Williams, *Mom, Dad. I'm Gay*, 96.

[68]Joan B. Kelly, Ph.D., "Children's Adjustment in Conflicted Marriage and Divorce: A Decade Review of Research," *Journal of the American Academy of Child and Adolescent Psychiatry* 39, no. 8, (August 2000): 964.

[69]Kelly, "Children's Adjustment in Conflicted Marriage and Divorce," 968.

[70]Judith S. Wallerstein, Julia M. Lewis, and Sandra Blakeslee, *The Unexpected Legacy of Divorce: A 25 Year Landmark Study* (New York: Hyperion, 2000), 69–70.

[71]Shelli Avenevoli, Frances M. Sessa, and Laurence Steinberg, "Family Structure, Parenting Practices, and Adolescent Adjustment: An Ecological Examination," in *Coping with Divorce, Single Parenting, and Remarriage*, ed. E. Mavis Hetherington (Mahwah, New Jersey: Laurence Erlbaum Associates, 1999), 85.

[72]Susan Silverberg Koerner, Stephanie L. Jacobs, and Meghan Raymond, "When Mothers Turn to Their Adolescent Daughters: Predicting Daughters' Vulnerability to Negative Adjustment Outcomes," *Family Relations* 49, no. 3, (2000): 301–09.

[73]E. Mavis Hetherington, "Should We Stay Together?" in *Coping with Divorce, Single Parenting, and Remarriage*, 112–114.

[74]Hetherington, "Should We Stay Together?" 113.

[75]Hetherington, "Should We Stay Together?" 112.

[76]James H. Bray, "From Marriage to Remarriage and Beyond: Findings from the Developmental Issues in Step Families Research Project," in *Coping with Divorce, Single Parenting, and Remarriage*, 258.

[77]Bray, "From Marriage to Remarriage and Beyond," 258.


## Chapter Five

[1]U.S. Department of Health and Human Services, *Mental Health: A Report of the Surgeon General* (Rockville, MD: U.S. Department of Health and Human Services, 1999), 129.

[2]U.S. Department of Health and Human Services, *Mental Health: A Report of the Surgeon General*, 124.

[3]For a summary of the research, see Lisa Sheeber, Ph.D., Betsy Davis, Ph.D., and Hyman Hops, Ph.D., "Gender Specific Vulnerability to Depression in Children of Depressed Mothers," in *Children of Depressed Parents: Alternative Pathways to Risk for Psychopathology*, eds. S. H. Goodman and I. H. Gotlib (Washington, D.C.: American Psychological Corporation, in press). See also Xioja Ge, Rand D. Conger, Frederick O. Lorenz, Michael Shanahan, and Glen H. Elder, "Mutual Influences in Parent and Adolescent Psychological Distress," *Developmental Psychology* 3, no. 3 (May 1995): 406–19. It's noteworthy that, in a study of adult women (Susan Nolen-Hoeksema, Carla Grayson, and Judith Larson, "Explaining the Gender Difference in Depressive Symptoms," *Journal of Personality and Social Psychology* 77, no. 5 (November 1991: 1061–72), the authors conclude, "The results of this study suggest that women carry a thread of vulnerabilities to depressive symptoms compared to men: more chronic strain, a greater tendency to ruminate when distressed, and a lower sense of mastery over their lives."

[4]Betsy Davis, Lisa Sheeber, Hyman Hops, and Elizabeth Tildesley, "Adolescent Responses to Depressive Parental Behaviors in Problem-Solving Interactions: Implication for Depressive Symptoms," *Journal of*

*Abnormal Child Psychology* 28, no. 5 (2000): 451–65. Lisa Sheeber, Nicholas Allen, Betsy Davis, and Erik Sorenson, "Regulation of Negative Affect During Mother-Child Problem-Solving Interactions: Adolescent Depressive Status and Family Processes," *Journal of Abnormal Child Psychology* 28, no. 5 (2000): 467–79.

[5]Interview conducted via e-mail with Dr. Betsy Davis and Dr. Lisa Sheeber of the Oregon Research Institute.

[6]National Institute for Mental Health, "Depression in Children and Adolescents: A Fact Sheet for Physicians" (http://www.nimh.nih.gov/publicat/depchildresfact.cfm).

[7]U.S. Department of Health and Human Services, *Mental Health: A Report of the Surgeon General* (Rockville, MD: U.S. Department of Health and Human Services, 1999), 151–152.

[8]U.S. Department of Health and Human Services, *Mental Health: A Report of the Surgeon General*, 152.

[9]National Institute for Mental Health, "Depression in Children and Adolescents: A Fact Sheet for Physicians."

[10]*Mental Health: A Report of the Surgeon General*, 153.

[11]Constance Hammen, Ph.D., and Patricia Brennan, "Depressed Adolescents of Depressed and Nondepressed Mothers: Tests of an Interpersonal Impairment Hypothesis," *Journal of Consulting and Clinical Psychology* 69, no. 2, (April 2001): 284–94.

[12]Substance Abuse and Mental Health Services Administration (SAMSHA), "Mental Health Problems for Children and Adolescents" fact sheet (www.SAMSHA.gov/statistics/statustics.html).

[13]National Institute of Mental Health, "Depression in Children and Adolescents: A Fact Sheet for Physicians" (http://www.nimh.nih.gov/publicat/depchildresfact.cfm), citing B. Birmaher, N. D. Ryan, D. E. Williamson et al., "Childhood and Adolescent Depression: A Review of the Past 10 Years, Part 1," *Journal of the American Academy of Child and Adolescent Psychiatry* 35, no. 11 (1996): 1427–39.

[14]Michael Windle and Rebecca C. Windle, "Depressive Symptoms and Cigarette Smoking Among Middle Adolescents: Prospective Associations and Intropersonal and Interpersonal Influences," *Journal of Consulting and Clinical Psychology* 69, no. 2 (2001): 215–26.

[15]U.S. Department of Health and Human Services, *Mental Health: A Report of the Surgeon General* (Rockville, MD: U.S. Department of Health and Human Services, 1999), 140.

[16]New York University, *Child Study Center Letter* 4, no. 3 (January/February 2000): 2.

[17]According to the Child and Adolescent Bipolar Foundation (*www.bpkids. org*), it is unknown how many children and adolescents are affected by bipolar disorder; they note that incidence is between 1 percent and 2 percent of adults worldwide. However, they also note, "It is suspected that a significant number of children diagnosed in the United States with attention-deficit disorder with hyperactivity (ADHD) have early-onset bipolar disorder instead of, or along with, ADHD." They also cite the American Academy of Child and Adolescent Psychiatry that up to one-third of children and adolescents diagnosed with depression may actually be experiencing the early onset of bipolar disorder.

[18]Statistics on the incidence of eating disorders among college-age women vary. The Harvard Eating Disorders Center cites a study that found that 3 percent were bulimic, 61 percent were classified as having some intermediate form of disordered eating behaviors, as opposed to 33 percent who reported normal eating habits. (Study cited: L. B. Mintz and N. E. Betz, "Prevalence and correlates of eating disordered behaviors among undergraduate women," *Journal of Counseling Psychology* 35 no. 4 (1988): 463–71.

[19]Again, estimates vary—partly because, according to ANRED (Anorexia Nervosa and Related Eating Disorders, Inc.), health professionals are not required to report eating disorders to a health agency and because those afflicted with eating disorders tend to be secretive (www.anred.com/stats/html).

[20]National Institute of Mental Health, "Eating Disorders: Facts about Eating Disorders and the Search for Solutions," NEW, Publication No. 01–4901 (2001) notes "that the mortality rate among people with anorexia is about 12 times higher than the annual death rate among females 15–24 in the general population," citing P. F. Sullivan, "Morality in Anorexia Nervosa," *American Journal of Psychiatry* 152, no. 7 (1995): 1073–74. Recovery statistic from Harvard Eating Disorders Center (*www.hedc.org/pressrm/faqs.htm*), citing P. K. Keel, J. E. Mitchell, K. B. Miller, et al., "Long-term outcome of bulima nervosa," *Archives of General Psychiatry* 56, no. 1 (1999): 63–69.

[21]Interview with Dr. Anne Becker.

[22]Caroline Walker Bynum, *Holy Feast and Holy Fast: The Religious Significance of Food to Medieval Women* (Berkeley and Los Angeles: University of California Press, 1988), 191.

[23]Kim Chernin, *The Hungry Self: Women, Eating, and Identity* (New York: Harper & Row, 1986), 43.

[24]Naomi Wolf, *The Beauty Myth: How Images of Beauty Are Used Against Women* (New York: Anchor Books, 1992), 208.

[25]Joan Jacobs Brumberg, *The Body Project: An Intimate History of Teenage Girls* (New York: Vintage Books, 1998), 195.

[26]Wolf, *The Beauty Myth*, 202.

[27]The "causes" of eating disorders are unknown. In "Eating Disorders: Facts about Eating Disorders and the Search for Solutions," The National Institute of Mental Health notes that several studies suggest "a high heritability of anorexia and bulimia"; as possible avenues of research, they point to the "neurobiology of social behavior relevant to eating disorders and the neuroscience of feeding behavior," as well as "the role of gonadal steroids." The Harvard Center on Eating Disorders, in its fact sheet, states, "Although no one variable has been found to 'cause' an eating disorder, research has discerned that certain personality characteristics, genetic disposition, environment, and biochemistry all play significant roles in the development of eating disorders."

[28]The Harvard Eating Disorders Center, "Understanding Eating Disorders: Helping Your Child" (www.hedc.org/undrstnd/helpc.htm).

[29]The National Center on Addiction and Substance Abuse at Columbia University (CASA), *National Survey of American Attitudes on Substance Abuse VII Teens* (New York: February 2001).

[30]Robert William Blum, M.D., Ph.D., and Peggy Mann Rinehart, *Reducing the Risk: Connections that Make a Difference in the Lives of Youth*, Add Health, Bethesda, Maryland (1997).

[31]Partnership for a Drug-Free America, "How Can I Talk to My Child About Drugs—Grades 7–9" (*www.drugfreeamerica.com*).

[32]Center for Disease Control dating violence statistics (www.cdc.gov/ncipc/factsheets/datviol.html).

[33]Jill Murray, *But I Love Him: Protecting Your Teen Daughter from Controlling, Abusive Dating Relationships* (New York: Regan Books, 2000), 50.

[34]Murray, *But I Love Him*, 160.

[35]Barbara Zax, Ph.D., and Stephan Poulter, Ph.D., *Mending the Broken Bough: Restoring the Promise of the Mother-Daughter Relationship* (New York: Berkeley Books, 1998), 72–97.

## Chapter Six

[1]Harold Kushner, *When All You've Ever Wanted Isn't Enough: The Search for a Life that Matters* (New York: Pocket Books, 1986), 50–51.

[2]Alvin Rosenfeld, M.D., and Nicole Wise, *The Over-Scheduled Child: Avoiding the Hyper-Parenting Trap* (New York: St. Martin's Griffin, 2001), xvi.

[3]Rosenfeld and Wise, *The Over-Scheduled Child*, xxciii.

[4]Elizabeth Debold, Marie Wilson, and Idelesse Malave, *Mother-Daughter Revolution: From Good Girls to Great Women* (New York: Bantam Books, 1994), 146.

[5]Terri Apter, *Secret Paths: Women in the New Midlife* (New York: W. W. Norton & Company, 1995), 26.

[6]Apter, *Secret Paths*, 31.

[7]Apter, *Secret Paths*, 36.

[8]Joan Borysenko, Ph.D., *A Woman's Book of Life: The Biology, Psychology, and Spirituality of the Feminine Life Cycle* (New York: Riverhead Books, 1996), 143.

[9]Borysenko, *A Woman's Book of Life*, 153.

[10]Apter, *Secret Paths*, 279.

[11]Nancy Friday, *My Mother My Self: The Daughter's Search for Identity* (New York: Delacorte Press, 1977), 383–4.

[12]Marian Wright Edelman, *Lanterns: A Memoir of Mentors* (Boston: Beacon Press, 1999), 166.

[13]Valanne L. Henderson and Carol S. Dweck, "Motivation and Achievement," in *At the Threshold*, 311.

[14]Henderson and Dweck, "Motivation and Achievement," 324.

[15]See Claudia M. Mueller and Carol S. Dweck, "Praise for Intelligence Can Undermine Children's Motivation and Performance," *Journal of Personality and Social Psychology* 75, no. 1 (1998): 33–52. The six studies conducted by the authors illuminate the connection between praising children ten- to twelve-year-olds for performance or effort and concepts of intelligence as either fixed or malleable.

[16]Silvia B. Rimm, Ph.D., with Sara Rimm-Kaufman, Ph.D., and Ilonna Rimm, M.D., Ph.D., *See Jane Win: The Rimm Report on How 1,000 Girls Became Successful Women* (New York: Crown Publishers, 1999), 16.

[17]Laurence Steinberg, "Autonomy, Conflict, and Harmony in the Family Relationship," in *At the Threshold*, 266.

[18]Peggy Orenstein, *Flux*, 111.

[19]Rosenfeld and Wise, *The Over-Scheduled Child*, 150.

[20]Rosenfeld and Wise, *The Over-Scheduled Child*, 152.

[21]Robert Coles, *The Moral Intelligence of Children*, 5.

[22]Coles, *The Moral Intelligence of Children*, 34–41.

[23]Donald L. McCabe's study, "Student Cheating in American High Schools" (May 2001), not yet published in print form, can be viewed on The Center for Academic Integrity's website: www.academicintegrity.org.

[24]E-mail interview with Donald L. McCabe.

[25]Goleman, *Emotional Intelligence*, 34.

[26]Goleman, *Emotional Intelligence*, 36.

[27]Goleman, *Emotional Intelligence*, 43–44.

[28]Goleman, *Emotional Intelligence*, 80–81.

[29]Goleman, *Emotional Intelligence*, 81–82.

[30]Rimm, et al., *See Jane Win*, 16–17.

[31]Rachel Naomi Remen, M.D., *Kitchen Table Wisdom: Stories That Heal* (New York: Riverhead Books, 1996), xxii.

[32]Interview with Dr. Lisa Miller.

[33]Susan Jonas and Marilyn Nissenson, *Friends for Life: Enriching the Bond Between Mothers and Their Adult Daughters* (New York: Harvest Books, 1997), 304.

[34]Source of statistics: The American Society of Plastic Surgeons (www.plasticsurgery.org).

[35]Interview with Dr. Loren Eskenazi.

[36]Anne Morrow Lindberg, *Gift from the Sea* (New York: Pantheon Books, 1977), 86–87.

## General Sources of Information

American Academy of Child and
Adolescent Psychiatry
3615 Wisconsin Avenue, NW
Washington, DC 20016-3007
202-966-7300 or 800-333-7636
www.aacap.org

American Psychiatric Association
1400 K Street, NW
Washington, DC 20005
202-682-6000
www.psych.org

American Psychological Association
Public Communications
750 First Street, NE
Washington, DC 20002
202-336-5500
www.apa.org

Center for Disease Control and
  Prevention (CDC)
Public Inquiries
1600 Clifton Road
Atlanta, GA 30333
800-311-3435
www.cdc.gov

Center for Mental Health Services
Child, Adolescent, and Family Branch
5600 Fishers Lane
Rockville, MD 20857

301-443-1333
www.mentalhealth.org

Federation of Families for Children's
  Mental Health
1021 Prince Street
Alexandria, VA 22314-2971
703-684-7710
www.ffcmh.org

GIRL POWER!
U.S. Department of Health and
  Human Services
www.health.org/gpower/index.htm

National Alliance for the Mentally Ill
Children and Adolescents Network
Colonial Place Three
2107 Wilson Blvd., Suite 300
Arlington, VA 22201-3042
800-950-6264
www.nami.org

National Institute of Mental Health
  (NIMH)
Office of Communications and Public
  Liaison
6001 Executive Blvd., Room 8184
MSC 9663
Betheseda, MD 20892-9663
301-443-4513
www.nimh.nih.gov

National Maternal and Child Health
  Clearinghouse
2070 Chain Bridge Road, Suite 450
Vienna, VA 22182-2536
888-434-4624
www.nmchc.org

National Mental Health Association
1021 Prince Street
Alexandria, VA 22314-2971
703-684-7722 or 800-969-6642
www.nmha.org

National Parent Information Network
www.npin.org

New York University Child Study
  Center
550 First Avenue
New York, NY 10016
212-263-6622
www.AboutOurKids.org

Office on Women's Health
Department of Health and Human
  Services
200 Independence Avenue, SW, Room
  730B
Washington, DC 20201
203-690-7650
www.4woman.gov

U.S. Department of Education
400 Maryland Avenue, SW
Washington, DC 20202-0498
800-872-53276
www.ed.gov

U.S. Department of Health and
  Human Services
200 Independence Avenue, SW
Washington, DC 20201
www.hhs.gov

## Depression

Child and Adolescent Bipolar
  Foundation
1187 Willmette Avenue, PMB#331
Willmette, IL 60091
847-256-8525
www.bpkids.org

Depression Education Program
National Institute of Mental Health
6001 Executive Boulevard, Room 8184
MSC 9663
Betheseda, MD 20852-9663
301-443-4513 or 800-421-4211
www.nimh.nih.gov/publict/depression-
  menu.cfm

Depression and Relative Affective
  Disorders Association (DRADA)
Meyer 3-181, 600 North Wolfe Street
Baltimore, MD 21287-7381
401-955-4647
www.med.jhu.edu/drada

National Depressive and Manic
  Depressive Association
730 North Franklin Street, Suite 501
Chicago, IL 60610-3526
800-826-3632
www.ndmda.org

National Foundation for Depressive
   Illnesses, Inc.
P.O. Box 2257
New York, NY 10116
212-266-4260 or 800-239-1265
www.depression.org

## Anxiety Disorders

Anxiety Disorders Association of
   America
11900 Parklawn Drive, Suite 100
Rockville, MD 20852
301-231-9350
www.adaa.org

Anxiety Disorders Education Program
National Institute of Mental Health
60001 Executive Boulevard, Room 8184
MSV 9663

Betheseda, MD 20852-9663
301-443-9438 or 888-826-9438
www.nimh.nih.gov/anxiety

Obsessive Compulsive Foundation
337 Notch Hill Road, Suites 3 and 4
North Branford, CT 06571
203-315-2190
www.ocfoundation.org

## Eating Disorders

American Anorexia Bulimia
   Association, Inc.
418 East 17th Street
New York, NY 10021
212-575-6200
www.aabainc.org

American Dietetic Association (ADA)
216 West Jackson Boulevard
Chicago, IL 60606
312-899-0040
www.eatright.org

Anorexia Nervosa and Related Eating
   Disorders, Inc. (ANRED)
P.O. Box 5102
Eugene, OR 97401
503-344-1144
www.anred.com

Eating Disorders Awareness and
   Prevention, Inc.
603 Stewart Street, Suite 803
Seattle, WA 98101
800-931-2237
www.edap.org

Harvard Eating Disorders Center
356 Boylston Street
Boston, MA 02116
888-236-1188, x.100
www.hedc.org

National Association of Anorexia
   Nervosa and Associate Disorders
P.O. Box 7
Highland Park, IL 60035
847-831-3436
www.anad.org

## Drugs, Tobacco, and Alcohol

American Council on Drug Education
164 W. 74th Street
New York, NY 10023
899-488-3784
www.acde.org

Center for Substance Abuse Protection
5600 Fisher Lane, Rockwall III
Rockville, MD 20857
301-443-0365
www.nnadal@samsha.gov

Drug and Alcohol Treatment Referral
  Hotline
800-662-4357

The National Center on Addiction and
  Substance Abuse at Columbia
  University
633 Third Avenue
New York, NY 10017-6706
212-841-5200
www.casacolumbia.org

National Center for Tobacco-Free Kids
1707 L Street, NW, Suite 800
Washington, DC 20005
800-284-5437
www.tobaccofreekids.org

National Clearinghouse for Alcohol
  and Drug Information
P.O. Box 2345
Rockville, MD 20847-2345
301-468-2600
www.health.org

National Council on Alcoholism and
  Drug Dependence, Inc.
20 Exchange Place, Suite 2902
New York, NY 10005
212-269-7797
www.ncadd.org

National Institute of Alcohol Abuse
  and Alcoholism
6000 Executive Boulevard, Willco
  Building
Betheseda, MD 20892-7003
301-443-5080
www.niaaa.nih.gov

Office of National Drug Control
  Policy
P.O. Box 6000
Rockville, MD 20849-6000
800-666-3332
www.whitehousedrugpolicy.gov
www.theantidrug.com

Parenting Is Prevention Project
www.parentingisprevention.org

Partnership for a Drug-Free America
405 Lexington Avenue, 16th floor
New York, NY 10174
212-922-1560
www.drugfreeamerica.com

SAMSHA's National Clearinghouse for
  Alcohol and Drug Information
P.O. Box 2345
Rockville, MD 20847-2345
800-729-6686
www.health.org

## Dating Violence and Rape

Violence Against Women Office
810 7th Street, NW
Washington, DC 20531
202-307-6026
www.ojp.usdoj.gov/vawo

National Center for Injury Prevention
   and Control
Division of Violence Prevention
Centers for Disease Control and
   Prevention
Mailstop K60
4770 Buford Highway
Atlanta, GA 30341-3724
770-488-4362
www.cdc.gov

National Crime Prevention Council
1000 Connecticut Avenue, NW, 13th
   floor
Washington, DC 20036
202-466-6272
www.ncpc.org

National Domestic Violence Hotline
800-799-7233 or 800-333-7233

National Violence Resource Center
www.nsvrc.org

RAINN (Rape, Abuse, Incest, National
   Network)
635-B Pennsylvania Avenue, SE
Washington, DC 20003
1-800-656-4673 (rape crisis counselor
   number, 24/7)

Rape Treatment Center
Santa Monica, UCLA Medical Center
1250 16th Street
Santa Monica, CA 90404
310-319-4000
www.911rape.org

## Sex Education, STDs, and Sexuality

CDC National Prevention
   Information Network
www.cdncpin.org

Mother's Voices
165 West 46th Street, Suite 701
New York, NY 10036
212-730-2777
www.mvoices.org

National Campaign to Prevent Teen
   Pregnancy
1776 Massachusetts Avenue, NW,
   Suite 200
Washington, DC 20036
202-478-8500
www.teenpregnancy.org

Parents, Family, Friends of Lesbians
   and Gays
1726 M Street, NW, Suite 400
Washington, DC 20036
202-467-8180
www.plag.org

Planned Parenthood Federation of
   America, Inc.
810 Seventh Avenue
New York, NY 10019
800-669-0156
www.ppfa.org

Sexuality Information and Education
   Council of the U.S. (SIECUS)
130 West 42nd Street, Suite 350
New York, NY 10036
212-819-9770
www.siecus.org

Talking to Kids About Tough Issues
www.talkingwithkids.org

# SELECT BIBLIOGRAPHY

Abramovitz, Beth, M.S. and Leann L. Birch, Ph.D. "Five-year-old girls' ideas about dieting are predicted by their mothers' dieting," *Journal of the American Dietetic Association* 100, no. 10 (October 2000).

Adler, Patricia A. and Peter Adler. *Peer Power: Preadolescent Culture and Identity*. New Brunswick, New Jersey and London: Rutgers University Press, 1998.

The Alan Guttmacher Institute, "Facts in Brief: Teen Sex and Pregnancy," September 1999.

Allen, Joseph P., Kathleen Boykin McElhaney, and Kathy L. Bell. "Autonomy in Discussions vs. Autonomy in Decision-making as Predictors of Developing Close Friendship Competence," paper presented at the Biennial Meetings of the Society for Research on Adolescence, Chicago, Illinois, March 21, 2000.

American Academy of Pediatrics. "Policy Statement," *Pediatrics* 104, no. 4 (October 1999).

Apter, Terri. *Altered Loves: Mothers and Daughters During Adolescence*. New York: Ballantine Books, 1991.

———. *The Myth of Maturity: What Teenagers Need from Parents to Become Adults*. New York and London: W. W. Norton and Company, 2001.

———. *Secret Paths: Women in the Midlife*. New York: W. W. Norton and Company, 1995.

Association of American University Women. *Hostile Hallways: The AAUW Survey on Sexual Harassment in America's Schools*. Washington, D.C.: AAUW, 1993.

Bae, Yupin, Susan Choy, Claire Geddes, Jennifer Sable, and Thomas Snyder. *Trends in Educational Equity of Girls and Women NCES 2000-030*. Department of Education, National Center for Education Statistics. Washington, D.C.: U.S. Government Printing Office, 2000.

Bartle, Natalie, Ed.D., with Susan Lieberman, Ph.D. *Venus in Blue Jeans: Why Mothers and Daughters Need to Talk About Sex*. Boston and New York: Houghton Mifflin Company, 1998.

Belkin, Lisa. "The Making of an Eight-Year-Old Woman," *The New York Times Magazine*, 38–43, December 24, 2000.

Bell, L.A. "Something's wrong here and it's not me: Challenging the dilemmas that block girls' success." *Journal for the Education of the Gifted* 12 (1989): 118–30.

Benson, Peter L., Anu R. Sharma, and Eugene C. Roehllkepartain. *Growing Up Adopted: A Portrait of Adolescents and Their Families*. Minneapolis, Minn.: The Search Institute, 1994.

Blum, Robert William, M.D., Ph.D. and Peggy Mann Rinehart. *Reducing the Risk: Connections That Make a Difference in the Lives of Youth*. Division of General Pediatrics & Adolescent Health, University of Minnesota Adolescent Health Program, 1997.

Borysenko, Joan, Ph.D. *A Woman's Book of Life: The Biology, Psychology, and Spirituality of the Feminine Life Cycle*. New York: Riverhead Books, 1996.

Brown, Kathleen M., Ph.D., Robert P. McMahon, Ph.D., Frank M. Biro, M.D., Patricia Crawford, Dr., P. H., R. D., George B. Schreiber, D.Sc., Shari L. Similo, M. S., Myron Waclawiw, Ph.D., and Ruth Striegel-More, Ph.D. "Changes in Self-esteem in Black and White Girls Between the Ages of 9 and 14 Years: The NHLBI Growth and Health Study," *Journal of Adolescent Health* 23 (1998): 7–19.

Brown, Lyn Mikel. *Raising Their Voices: The Politics of Girls' Anger*. Cambridge, Mass.: Harvard University Press, 1998.

Brown, Lyn Mikel and Carol Gilligan. *Meeting at the Crossroads: Women's Psychology and Girls' Development*. New York: Ballantine Books, 1993.

Brumberg, Joan Jacobs. *The Body Project: An Intimate History of Teenage Girls*. New York: Vintage Books, 1998.

Buber, Martin. *I and Thou*, translated by Walter Kaufmann. New York: Touchstone/Simon & Shuster, 1996.

Bynum, Caroline Walker. *Holy Fast and Holy Feast: The Religious Significance of Food to Medieval Women*. Berkeley and Los Angeles: University of California Press, 1988.

Capizzano, Jeffrey, Kathryn Trout, and Gina Adams. *Childcare Patterns of School-Age Children with Employed Mothers*, Occasional Paper no. 41, Washington, D.C.: The Urban Institute, September 2000.

Carnegie Council on Adolescent Development. *Great Transitions: Preparing Adolescents for a New Century*. New York: Carnegie Council on Adolescent Development, 1996.

Caron, Ann F. *Don't Stop Loving Me: A Reassuring Guide for Mothers of Adolescent Daughters*. New York: Harper Perennial, 1991.

Chernin, Kim. *The Hungry Self: Women, Eating, and Identity*. New York: Harper & Row, 1986.

Cohen, Michael, Ph.D., Jennifer Scott, Ph.D., Pat Tobin, Connie Kim, and Sara Giciardo, *Girls Speak Out: Teens Before Their Time*. New York: The Girl Scout Research Institute, 2000.

Coles, Robert. *The Moral Intelligence of Children: How to Raise a Moral Child*. New York: Plume Books, 1999.

———. *The Spiritual Life of Children*. Boston: Houghton Mifflin, 1990.

The Council of Economic Advisors. *Teens and Their Parents in the 21st Century*. Washington, D.C.: gov't pub: May 2000.

Crick, Nicki, Ph.D. and Maureen Bigbee, M.S., M.S.W. "Relational and Overt Forms of Peer Victimization," *Journal of Consulting and Clinical Psychology* 66, no. 2 (1998): 337–347.

Crittenden, Anne. *The Price of Motherhood: Why the Most Important Job in the World Is Still the Least Valued*. New York: Henry Holt and Company, 2001.

Darroch, Jacqueline E., David Landry, and Susheela Singh. "Changing Emphases in Sexuality Education in U.S. Public Secondary Schools, 1988–1999," *Family Planning Perspectives* 32, no. 5 (September/October 2000), 204–211.

Davis, Betsy, Lisa Sheeber, Hyman Hops, and Elizabeth Tildesley. "Adolescent Responses to Depressive Parental Behaviors in Problem-Solving Interactions: Implication for Depressive Symptoms," *Journal of Abnormal Child Psychology* 28, no. 5 (2000): 451–65.

Debold, Elizabeth, Marie Wilson, and Idelasse Malave. *Mother-Daughter Revolution: From Good Girls to Great Women*. New York: Bantam Books, 1994.

Dillard, Annie. *An American Childhood*. New York: Harper & Row, Publishers, 1988.

Eberly, Mary B., and Raymond Montemayor. "Adolescent Affection and Helpfulness Toward Parents: A Two-Year Follow-up," *Journal of Early Adolescence* 19, no. 2 (May 1999): 226–48.

———. "Doing Good Deeds: An Examination of Adolescent Prosocial Behavior in the Context of Parent-Adolescent Relationships," *Journal of Adolescent Research* 13, No. 4, (October 1998): 403–32.

Eberly, Mary B., Raymond Montemayor, and Daniel Flannery. "Variation in Adolescent Helpfulness in a Family Context," *Journal of Early Adolescence* 13, no. 3, (August 1993): 228–45.

Edelman, Hope. *Motherless Daughters: The Legacy of Loss*. New York: Dell Publishing, 1994.

Edelman, Marian Wright. *Lanterns: A Memoir of Mentors*. Boston: Beacon Press, 1999.

Erikson, Erik H. *Identity: Youth and Crisis*. New York: W. W. Norton and Company, 1968.

Feinberg, Todd. *Altered Egos: How the Brain Creates the Self.* Oxford and New York: Oxford University Press, 2001.

Feldman, S. Shirley and Glen R. Elliott, eds. *At the Threshold: The Developing Adolescent.* Cambridge, Mass.: Harvard University Press, 1990.

Frank, Anne. *Anne Frank: The Diary of a Young Girl.* Translated by B. M. Mooyaart-Doubleday. New York: Pocket Books, 1969.

Friday, Nancy. *My Mother My Self: The Daughter's Search for Identity.* New York: Delacorte Press, 1977.

Furman, Wyndol, B. Bradford Brown, and Candice Fiering, eds. *The Development of Romantic Relationships in Adolescence.* Cambridge U.K. and New York: Cambridge University Press, 1999.

Gavin, Leslie A. and Wyndol Furman. "Adolescent Girls' Relationships with Mothers and Best Friends," *Child Development* 67 (1996): 381.

Ge, Xioja, Rand D. Conger, Frederick O. Lorenz, Michael Shanahan, and Glen H. Elder. "Mutual Influences in Parent and Adolescent Psychological Distress," *Developmental Psychology* 3, no. 3 (May 1995): 406–19.

Gilligan, Carol. *In a Different Voice: Psychological Theory and Women's Development.* Cambridge, Mass.: Harvard University Press, 1982.

Gilligan, Carol, Annie G. Rogers, and Deborah L. Tolman, eds. *Women, Girls, & Psychotherapy: Reframing Resistance.* New York and London: Harrington Park Press, 1991.

Graber, J., P. M. Lewisohn, J. R. Seeley, and J. Brooks-Gunn. "Is Psychopathology Associated with the Timing of Pubertal Development?" *Journal of the American Academy of Child and Adolescent Psychiatry* 36 (1997): 1768–76.

Hammen, Constance, Ph.D., and Patricia Brennan. "Depressed Adolescents of Depressed and Nondepressed Mothers: Tests of an Interpersonal Impairment Hypothesis," in *Journal of Consulting and Clinical Psychology* 69, no. 2 (April 2001): 284–94.

Henry J. Kaiser Family Foundation. *Kids and Media at the New Millennium.* Menlo Park, CA: November 1999.

Henry J. Kaiser Family Foundation and Children Now. *Talking with Kids about Tough Issues: A National Survey of Parents and Kids.* Menlo Park, CA: Kaiser Family Foundation/Children Now, March 1, 1999.

Henry J. Kaiser Family Foundation and YM Magazine. *National Survey of Teens: Teens Talk about Dating, Intimacy, and Their Sexual Experiences.* Menlo Park, CA: Kaiser Family Foundation/YM magazine, May 1998.

Henry J. Kaiser Family Foundation, MTV, and *Teen People. What Teens*

*Know and Don't (But Should) About Sexually Transmitted Diseases*. Menlo Park, CA: March 1999.

Herman-Giddens, Marcia E., Eric J. Slora, Richard C. Wasserman, Carlos J. Bourdony, Manju V. Bhapkar, Gary G. Koch, and Cynthia M. Hasemeir. "Secondary Sexual Characteristics and Menses in Young Girls Seen in Office Practice," *Pediatrics* 99, no. 4 (April 1997): 505–12.

Hersh, Patricia. *A Tribe Apart: A Journey into the Heart of American Adolescence*. New York: Ballantine Books, 1998.

Hetherington, E. Mavis, editor. *Coping with Divorce, Single Parenting, and Remarriage*. Mahwah, New Jersey: Laurence Erlbaum Associates, 1999.

Hine, Thomas. *The Rise and Fall of the American Teenager*. New York: Avon Books, 1990.

Johnson, Norine G., Michael C. Roberts, and Judith Worell, eds. *Beyond Appearance: A New Look at Adolescent Girls*. Washington, D.C.: American Psychological Association, 1999.

Jonas, Susan, and Marilyn Nissenson. *Friends for Life; Enriching the Bond Between Mothers and Their Adult Daughters*. San Diego and New York: Harcourt Brace & Company, 1997.

Kaplowitz, Paul B., M.D., Sharon E. Oberfield, M.D., and the Drug and Therapeutics and Executive Committees of the Lawson Wilkins Pediatric Endocrine Society. "Reexamination of the Age Limit for Defining When Puberty Is Precocious in the United States: Implications for Evaluation and Treatment," *Pediatrics* 104, no. 4 (October 1999): 936–41.

Kelly, Joan B., Ph.D. "Children's Adjustment in Conflicted Marriage and Divorce: A Decade Review of Research," *Journal of the American Academy of Child and Adolescent Psychiatry* 39, no. 8 (August 2000).

Kinkel, Dale, Kirstie Cope, Wendy Jo Maynard Farinola, Erica Biely, Emma Rollin, and Edward Donnerstien. *Sex on TV: Content and Context*. University of California, Santa Barbara, The Henry Kaiser Family Foundation, February 1999.

Kirby, Douglas, Ph.D. *Emerging Answers: Research Findings on Programs to Reduce Teen Pregnancy*. Washington, D.C.: National Campaign to Prevent Teen Pregnancy, 2001.

Lindberg, Laura Duberstein, Scott Boggess, Laura Porter, and Sean Williams. *Teen Risk-Taking: A Statistical Portrait*. Washington, D.C.: The Urban Institute, 2000.

Lindbergh, Anne Morrow. *Gift from the Sea*. New York: Pantheon Books, 1997.

Martin, Carol Lynn and Richard A. Fabes. "The Stability and Consequences of Young Children's Same-Sex Peer Interactions," *Developmental Psychology* 37, no. 3 (2001): 431–46.

Moen, Phyllis, Mary Ann Erikson, and Donna Dempster McClain. "Their Mother's Daughters? The Intergeneration Transmission of Gender Attitudes in a World of Changing Roles," *Journal of Marriage and the Family* 59 (May 1997): 281–93.

Mueller, Claudia M. and Carol S. Dweck. "Praise for Intelligence Can Undermine Children's Motivation and Performance," *Journal of Personality and Social Psychology* 75, no. 1 (July 1998): 33–52.

Murray, Jill. *But I Love Him: Protecting Your Teen Daughter from Controlling, Abusive Dating Relationships.* New York: Regan Books, 2000.

Nansel, Tonja R., Ph.D., Mary Overpeck, Dr. P H, Ramni S. Pilla, Ph.D., June Ruan, M.A., Bruce Simons-Morton, Ed.D., MPH, and Peter Scheidt, M.D., MPH. "Bullying Behaviors Among U.S. Youth: Prevalence and Association with Psychosocial Adjustment," *Journal of the American Medical Association* 285, no. 16 (2001): 2094–2100.

The National Center on Addiction and Substance Abuse at Columbia University (CASA). *National Survey of American Attitudes on Substance Abuse VI Teens.* New York: February 2001.

———. *The 1998 CASA National Survey of Teens, Teachers, and Principals.* New York: September 1998.

———. *Back to School: 1999 National Survey of American Attitudes on Substance Abuse, Teens and Their Parents.* New York: August 1999.

National Center for Education Statistics. *Youth Indicators.* 1996.

The National Marriage Project, "The State of Our Unions, 2000," New Brunswick, New Jersey: The National Marriage Project, 2000.

National Research Council and Institute of Medicine, Board on Children, Youth, and Families Forum on Adolescence. "Risks and Opportunities: Synthesis of Studies on Adolescence," ed. Michele D. Kipke. Washington, D.C.: National Academy Press, 1999.

Newmark-Sztainer, Dianne, Ph.D., MPH, RD., Nancy E. Sherwood, Ph.D., Tanya Coller, MPH, RD, and Peter J. Hannan, M. Stat., "Primary Prevention of Disordered Eating Among Preadolescent Girls: Feasibility and Short-Term Effect of a Community-Based Intervention," *Journal of the American Dietetic Association* 100, no. 12 (December 2000): 1466–73.

*The New York Times*, July 3, 2000, vol. CXLIX.

Nolen-Hoeksma, S. and J. S. Girgus, "The Emergence of Gender Difference in Depression During Adolescence," *Psychological Bulletin*, 115, 1994, 424–443.

Nolen-Hoeksema, Susan, Carla Grayson, and Judith Larson. "Explaining the Gender Difference in Depressive Symptoms," *Journal of Personality and Social Psychology* 77, no. 5 (November 1999): 1061–72.

Nolen-Hoeksma, Susan and Joan S. Girgus. "Worried Girls: Rumination and the Transition to Adolescence," Paper presented at the 106th Annual Convention of the American Psychological Association, San Francisico, August 1998.

Nord, Christine Winquist, DeeAnn Brinhall, and Jerry West, "Fathers' Involvement in Their Childrens' Schools," NCES 98-091, U.S. Department of Education, National Center for Education Statistics, Washington, D.C., 1997.

Orenstein, Peggy. *Flux: Women on Sex, Work, Love, Kids, and Life in a Half-Changed World*. New York: Doubleday, 2000.

———. *Schoolgirls: Young Women, Self-Esteem, and the Confidence Gap*. New York: Anchor Books, 1994.

Pipher, Mary. *Reviving Ophelia: Saving the Selves of Adolescent Girls*. New York: Ballantine Books, 1994.

Pollack, William. *Real Boys: Rescuing Our Sons from the Myths of Boyhood*. New York: Henry Holt, 1999.

Ponton, Lynn. *The Romance of Risk: Why Teenagers Do the Things They Do*. New York: Basic Books, 1997.

———. *The Sex Lives of Teenagers: Revealing the Secret World of Adolescent Boys and Girls*. New York: Dutton, 2000.

Remen, Rachel Naomi, M.D. *Kitchen Table Wisdom: Stories That Heal*. New York: Riverhead Books, 1996.

Remez, Lisa. "Oral Sex Among Adolescents: Is It Sex or Abstinence?" *Family Planning Perspectives* 32, no. 6 (November/December 2000): 298–304.

Ryan, Caitlin and Donna Futterman. *Lesbian and Gay Youth: Care and Counseling*. New York: Columbia University Press, 1998.

Savin-Williams, Ritch C. *Mom, Dad. I'm Gay: How Families Negotiate Coming Out*. Washington, D.C.: American Psychological Association, 2001.

Schwartz, Pepper, Ph.D. *Ten Talks Parents Must Have With Their Children About Sex and Character*. New York: Hyperion, 2000.

Sheeber, Lisa, Nicholas Allen, Betsy Davis, and Erik Sorenson. "Regulation of Negative Affect During Mother-Child Problem-Solving Interactions: Adolescent Depressive Status and Family Processes," *Journal of Abnormal Child Psychology* 28, no. 5 (2000): 467–79.

Sherwood, Nancy E., Ph.D., and Dianne Neumark-Sztainer, Ph.D., MPH., RD. "Internalization of the Sociocultural Ideal: Weight-related Attitudes and Dieting Behaviors Among Young Adolescents, *American Journal of Health Promotion* 15, no. 4 (2001): 228–231.

Silverberg Koerner, Susan, Stephanie L. Jacobs, and Meghan Raymond. "When Mothers Turn to Their Adolescent Daughters: Predicting Daughters' Vulnerability to Negative Adjustment Outcomes," *Family Relations* 49, no. 3 (2000): 301–309.

Silverman, Jay G., Ph.D., Anita Raj, Ph.D., Lorelei A. Mucci, Ph.D., and Jeanne E. Hathaway, M.D., MOH. "Dating Violence Against Adolescent Girls and Associated Substance Use, Unhealthy Weight Control, Sexual Risk Behavior, Pregnancy, and Suicidality," *Journal of the American Medical Association* 286, no. 5 (August 1, 2000).

Simpson, A. Rae. Phd.D. *Raising Teens: A Synthesis of Research and a Foundation for Action.* Boston: Center for Health Communications, Harvard School of Public Health, 2001.

Slap, Gail B., M.D., and Martha M. Jablow. *Teenage Health Care.* New York: Pocket Books, 1994.

Steinberg, Laurence with Wendy Steinberg, *Crossing Paths: How Your Child's Adolescence Triggers Your Own Crisis.* New York: Simon & Schuster, 1994.

Stepp, Laura Sessions. *Our Last Best Shot: Guiding Our Children Through Early Adolescence.* New York: Riverhead Books, 2000.

Taylor, Jill McLean, Carol Gilligan, and Amy M. Sullivan. *Between Voice and Silence: Women and Girls, Race and Relationship.* Cambridge, Mass.: Harvard University Press, 1995.

Tepper, Robin, "Parental Regulation and Adolescent Discretionary Time-Use Decisions: Findings from the NLSY97," in *Social Awakenings: Adolescents' Behavior As Adulthood Approaches,* ed. R. T. Michael. New York: Russell Sage Foundation, 2001.

Thompson, Paul M., Jay N. Gledd, and Roger Wood. "Growth Patterns in Developing Brain Detected by Doing Continuum Mechanical Tensor Maps," *Nature* 404 (March 9, 2000).

Thompson, Sharon. *Going All the Way: Teenage Girls' Tales of Sex, Romance, and Pregnancy.* New York: Hill and Wang, 1995.

Tollman, Deborah. "Feminity As a Barrier to Positive Sexual Health for Adolescent Girls," *JAMWA* 54 (1999): 133–38.

The UCLA Internet Report, *Surveying the Digital Future.* Los Angeles: UCLA Center for Communication Policies, October 2000.

U.S. Department of Health and Human Services. *Mental Health: A Report of the Surgeon General.* Rockville, MD: U.S. Department of Health and Human Services, Substance Abuse and Mental Health Services Administration, Center for Mental Health Services, National Institutes of Health, National Institute of Mental Health, 1999.

Wallerstein, Judith S., Julia M. Lewis, and Sandra Blakeslee. *The Unex-*

*pected Legacy of Divorce: A 25 Year Landmark Study*. New York: Hyperion Books, 2000.

Windle, Michael and Rebecca C. Windle. "Depressive Symptoms and Cigarette Smoking Among Middle Adolescents: Prospective Associations and Intrapersonal and Interpersonal Influences," *Journal of Consulting and Clinical Psychology* 69, no. 2 (2000): 215–26.

Wolf, Naomi. *The Beauty Myth: How Images of Beauty Are Used Against Women*. New York: Anchor Books, 1992.

Zax, Barbara, Ph.D. and Stephan Poulter, Ph.D. *Mending the Broken Bough: Restoring the Promise of the Mother-Daughter Relationship*. New York: Berkley Books, 1998.

*Child Study Center Letter,* New York University, vol. 4, no. 3, January/February 2000.

# Index